GIRLS CAN MOVE
MOUNTAINS

Rewriting the Rules of
Female Entrepreneurship

SOLANGES VIVENS, D.H.L.

GIRLS CAN MOVE MOUNTAINS: REWRITING THE RULES OF FEMALE ENTREPRENEURSHIP

1405 SW 6th Avenue • Ocala, Florida 34471 • Phone 352-622-1825 • Fax 352-622-1875
Website: www.atlantic-pub.com • Email: sales@atlantic-pub.com
SAN Number: 268-1250

Library of Congress Control Number: 2019055584

Printed in the United States

PROJECT MANAGER: Meaghan Summers
INTERIOR LAYOUT AND JACKET DESIGN: Nicole Sturk
PHOTOGRAPHY: Daniella Monestime

Table of Contents

SOLANGE

Noun:

1. Widely known to be the coolest member of the human race. A person of extraordinary abilities.

2. A superior being conceived as the product of human evolution.

Synonyms:

Awe-inspiring, magnificent, wonderful, amazing, stunning impressive, spectacular, grand, clever, striking, charming, exquisite, luxurious, amazing, kind, cute, intellectual, sincere, adorable, lovable, delightful, winsome, and crazy.

Note from the Author

My story begins in Haiti, when a chance encounter on a dark, isolated road between a working-class man and a wealthy woman with a flat tire led to a relationship that impacted my family's hopes of building a better life. After I came to America as a teenager, I worked my way to the top of my field from my modest beginning as a factory laborer to an entrepreneurial titan and policy maker in the healthcare industry—in nursing home management, nursing education, and home healthcare. Through determination and courage in the face of poverty, language barriers, racism, immigration hurdles, and sexism, I built a happy family and a business empire in the politically fraught climate of Washington, D.C.

Some of the lessons I learned along the way came from wise people and mentors while others came through the hard work of dealing with adversity and finding a way to prevail. I developed guiding principles and skills that enabled me to succeed and push past times when my prospects felt hopeless. I am happy to share these "Rules to Live By" at the beginning of each chapter in this book. Later, at the end of the chapter, I will leave you with a reflection and some meditations or exercises—all inspired by the turtle, an ancient symbol of feminine wisdom and strength.

It is my hope that the wisdom of the turtle will help you delve more deeply into your own progress and gain more faith in your own potential for success and happiness.

Cheers,
Solanges Vivens

RULES TO LIVE BY

It will help you better understand how the first three rules play out in life if you take a moment to reflect on them before you delve into my story. Keep them in mind as you read about how my journey toward success began in a Haitian town, in a big family—filled with love but little money—and how this journey was all changed by an act of kindness.

Rule #1: Believe in Luck

Before I was even born, luck played a central role in the direction my life would take. A chance encounter on a dark road between my father and a wealthy woman completely changed my fate; the woman, Lucienne, then followed her gut instinct and searched for my father to repay him for his kindness, which completely altered the course my life would take. You will see later in the book that, in many circumstances, both in my business life and in my personal relationships, when I had little or no control over the outcome, I let go and let God—or His people—guide my path.

Rule #2: Be Kind

My father's kindness to Lucienne multiplied exponentially when she returned it by seeking my father out and helping him secure a better job. Lucienne benefitted in return: she got the godchild she always wanted, and her love for me spread abundance to the rest of my family. Throughout my life, I have been blessed both by giving and receiving kindness. You will see how stepping up when someone in my profession needed a helping hand led me to my husband. The same act of kindness also helped me gain independence (see chapter six, "Sweet & Sour," for the driver's license anecdote). We should be kind because it feels good, not because we expect something in return.

Rule #3: Be Persistent and Tenacious Despite Challenges

Lucienne persisted in finding my father when other people would have been put off by our neighborhood. Throughout my life, that kind of tenacity is something I strove for, whether I was going to school despite a debilitating illness (see chapter two, "Lucky") or forging a career path in a field with few to no black Haitian immigrants (see chapter eight, "The Fishing Expedition").

My own migration to the Unites States, and my assimilation into society, required a level of resolve I did not know I had, whether I was learning to speak English, or working in a foul-smelling factory (see chapter four, "Joining the Workforce"). I knew I was headed in the right direction, and I did not alter my course when things got tough. I have always looked for that kind of certainty and focus in the people I admire most such as my husband who was relentless in his pursuit of me (see chapter six, "Sweet & Sour").

I say keep your focus, surround yourself with tenacious champions, and never give up.

1
────

Unexpected Encounters

Port-au-Prince, 1945. It was well past midnight, and Lucienne found herself alone on a dark, isolated road. The crickets were loud, and the young woman shivered with a combination of fright and chill from the damp air. She could also hear the owls, and their faint hooting seemed to mourn the fact that she had not a clue as to how to change an unexpected flat tire. Lucienne had a bit of a fiery spirit, though. She ignored the voices of the creepy crawlers of the night as she put on a cloak of bravery and determination to change the tire herself. She knew this to be a task easily completed by those who had the knowledge. Maybe she could figure it out, even though she had never been in a situation that required her handy skills. The senator's hired help usually took care of such tasks.

Seconds turned into minutes, and minutes into an hour, with no success. Tired and frustrated, Lucienne berated herself for her decision to stay out a little later than usual. Perhaps it was the late hour or the secluded location of her vehicle, but the few cars that did drive down the road zoomed past her, not one stopping to come to her aid. As she bent down once again next to the tire of the Citroën, she saw the headlights of the fast-approaching truck rapidly turn the corner.

It's going to hit me, she thought.

She jumped up quickly and pressed her body against the car.

The dump truck narrowly missed hitting her.

Ambroise noticed the sudden motion in his rearview mirror and came to an abrupt stop. He then made a U-turn at the next intersection and returned to the Citroën pulled over on the side of the road. As he exited the truck, he saw the fear in the woman's eyes. He understood that she felt vulnerable. After all, he was black, and she was mulatto. He was poor, and she was dressed in the finest clothing. He drove a truck that delivered human waste to a landfill, and she was the daughter of a senator—a fact he would come to learn later. He never expected to find a woman of her stature stranded on the side of the road. How disastrous it would have been if he had struck her with his truck when he had come around the corner.

"Don't be afraid," he said. "Do you need help?"

The woman replied in a soft, shaky voice, "I can't do it!"

She wore a beautifully tailor-made floral dress with a full skirt of damask fabric, a light-colored elbow length cardigan with a delicate trim, and the prettiest shoes he had ever seen on a woman. She looked completely out of place on this road all alone.

Ambroise was able to detect a bit of her frustration, so he diverted her fears quickly and told her to please have a seat in the car. When she was safely in the car and out of harm's way, he began to change the tire.

Within minutes, the man had replaced the flat tire, which he put in the trunk of the Citroën; he gave Lucienne a thumbs up. Before he turned to leave, she rolled down the window halfway, still a little frightened. Her voice shaking, she said, "Sir, I need to pay you."

"Lady, you may go now," the truck driver told her softly. He had a gentle smile.

"I was stranded, and you saved me," Lucienne said. "So many before you passed me by and did not stop." She was about to start crying. "I want to do something for you!"

"Go home, now, and get some rest," he said. "You look tired and weary. There are still some hours left before daybreak."

She insisted on returning his kindness, but, once again, he refused.

"Can you at least tell me your name and where you live?" she shouted as he walked away.

He looked over his shoulder. "Ambroise … Ambroise Vivens."

"But where do you live?"

By then, he was already in the truck, rushing because he was late for his delivery. "Magloire Ambroise Avenue," he shouted back.

He drove off.

"Ambroise Vivens. Magloire Ambroise Avenue."

She repeated his name and address over and over, all the way home, so that she would not forget it. The fact that his name was also in the name of the street he lived on made it just a little easier. As soon as she entered her home, now safe and sound, she ran to her bedroom to retrieve her notebook from her writing desk. She scribbled down the information so that she would not forget the man who had come to her rescue.

If it had not been for Ambroise, where would she be now?

Lucienne awoke at the break of dawn and joined her family for breakfast. It was customary for the senator, his wife, and his children to partake in the morning meal together and talk about the day ahead. As soon as she sat down in the breakfast room, Lucienne told the others about the dramatic details of the previous night—about her fear for her safety, and about the many cars that had passed her without stopping to help.

"They probably thought you were a *lougawou*," her mother said, "a creature of the night in human form. Ambroise was probably as afraid of you as you were of him."

At the very mention of Ambroise's name, her eyes welled with tears, and Lucienne clutched the small string of pearls around her neck. She expressed how grateful she was that he had come to her aid. Her father, the senator, was so touched that he, too, agreed that they must find this man and thank him properly for his kindness and chivalry. After all, his daughter could have been kidnapped—or worse. She could have been killed on that road. He and the family said a silent prayer, thanking God for her safety.

*   *   *

Lucienne was on a mission to find Ambroise, her rescuer. Relentlessly, she drove down Magloire Ambroise Avenue, where many of the houses did not have numbers. She spoke to some of the men who played cards or dominos. She spoke to women selling their goods by the side of the road. She spoke to children playing in their front yards. When no one was able to point her in the right direction and tell her where to find Ambroise, she decided to continue her search by foot, walking through the narrow alleyways between the houses. She had never experienced walking through a neighborhood where the houses were so closely clustered together, separated only by very small gaps with gullies that carried, on both sides, dirty and smelly water from each of the houses. She looked on in disbelief and shock, trying to understand the serenity she read on the faces of the locals who seemed to be content, despite the dire circumstances of their everyday lives.

As much as she was trying to be invisible, Lucienne stood out. People gave her curious looks, probably wondering what this young "white" woman was doing in this black neighborhood.

Finally, she spotted Ambroise.

He sat at a table, playing checkers on a wooden *damier*, facing a fierce-looking opponent as several other spectators stood over them, watching the game.

Damier—as it is called in Haiti—is a game of concentration, so Haitian men do not like to be disturbed while playing. Lucienne was very aware that she should not call out Ambroise's name to get his attention. She tried to stand still, but she was anxious to talk to him, now that she had found him. She moved closer and closer, until he lifted his head with a loud laugh, celebrating a brilliant move. She caught his eyes, and he froze.

The attention turned toward Lucienne, and she knew everyone wondered why she was there. What did she want with Ambroise?

Ambroise was a married man with four children and a fifth one on the way. He did not care so much about his own reputation, as he was a known womanizer—a incorrigible *kòk*. No. He felt, once again, compelled to protect *her*. He thought of her safety, as she was a stranger in these parts. *Do I even acknowledge her?* he wondered. *Do I finish the game, or do I just get up and go home?* Ambroise continued to play, pretending that he had not noticed her. Before long, however, a young boy approached his chair and whispered in his ear, "Mademoiselle Lucienne would like to talk to you."

Finally, Ambroise put down the pieces reluctantly, as he was ahead in the game that he so enjoyed. It was his pastime and method of relaxation when he was not working. He spoke loudly enough for all to hear. "Hey, you are the lady I helped with the flat tire last night." He got up and walked towards her. "What are you doing here? What do you want?" he asked, puzzled.

She smiled. "Thank you for saving my life."

The crowd soon grew larger, everyone within earshot. *Ambroise, a hero? Ambroise, the savior of a white woman?*

"I need to talk to you," Lucienne continued without hesitation. "Can we do so privately?"

"I'll take you to my wife," Ambroise said.

He excused himself and walked away with Lucienne, heading towards his house, which was several alleys away. Women were cooking on charcoal fires on the porches of some of the houses with detached wood frames and galvanized roofs; they used wooden spoons to stir the contents of their iron clay pots, and the meals smelled heavenly. Small children ran naked, laughing as they played in the dirt. Dogs slept in the gullies, trying to stay cool on this tropical island where the temperature could rise well above 100°F.

Six small steps led to Ambroise's tiny house, and the narrow landing immediately adjoined the living room.

Ambroise introduced Lucienne to his wife Francesca. "This is the lady I told you about last night. The one with the flat tire."

Francesca's legs and ankles were swollen, her belly taut with her unborn daughter and the corn on the cob she had just eaten as a snack. At night, she would later say, she slept propped up on a stack of pillows. Lucienne thought how unfortunate it was that Ambroise worked a night shift, as a sewage truck driver, when he had a very pregnant wife and four children at home.

"I can't believe she found you," Francesca said. "Hello, Lucienne. It's a pleasure to meet you." As was customary in Haiti, Francesca welcomed her to her home by adding, "May I offer you some coffee?"

Lucienne soon fell in love with the couple and their boy and three little girls—humble people just barely surviving the hardship of a lower-class family. She visited for over an hour, during which they became well-acquainted as the conversation touched on many different topics. Lucienne told them about her father, the senator, about her brother, and even about her desire to one day be married with children of her own. She enjoyed seeing the Vivens children play and interact with their parents; it brought back joyful memories of her youth.

As it was getting late, Lucienne asked if they would allow her to visit again.

*   *   *

At dinner with her family that night, Lucienne could not stop talking about Ambroise and his wife. She was fond of them and, with four children and another one on the way, it did not seem easy for them to make ends meet. She wanted to change that. The senator frowned, as he did not want his only daughter to be seen in that neighborhood; she was not to become a frequent visitor on Magloire Ambroise Avenue.

Against her father's advice, however, Lucienne continued to visit Francesca, who had become a true friend. On her visits, she brought food for the family and, at times, she also gave them money. On many weekend afternoons, while

Ambroise played checkers with his friends, Lucienne would drive with speed and focus; she went straight to the Vivens house, since now she knew her way through the alleys that were once so unfamiliar to her.

One day, Lucienne expressed her sadness at never having been asked to be a godmother to a child. Haiti was officially a Catholic country, and it was considered one of the greatest honors to carry a baby to the altar for baptism and take a vow to protect and parent the child if something should ever happen to the birth parents. That night, Francesca discussed with Ambroise the idea of asking Lucienne to be the godmother of their unborn child. They were both afraid of a rejection: they were so poor that Lucienne might turn down the offer, even though she had expressed a desire to be a godmother. They decided not to ask her until after the baby was born.

Lucienne convinced her father to meet the family. The senator agreed with one stipulation—that they would come to him. So, Lucienne arranged for Ambroise and Francesca to visit the senator on a Sunday morning, at their estate located in an upper-class area of Port-au-Prince, in a neighborhood called Lalue.

The estate was grand, with multiple stories and a wraparound porch, and areas of seating specifically arranged for conversation. The walls were painted pink, blue and white—the typical colors of Haitian homes—but while the colors were indicative of a tropical island, the architecture was clearly European. The furniture throughout was French provincial and highly influenced by the colonizers of the 1700s who had wanted to recreate the palaces of their native land. Beautiful paintings hung on the walls, the most prominent being a portrait of the senator holding a hat and a cane. It was the largest painting that Francesca and Ambroise had ever seen. In fact, Francesca and Ambroise were in awe at everything in the beautiful chateau. They never imagined being privileged enough to enter as guests of the senator. *How divinely ordered,* Ambroise thought, *that two families so completely different from one another could come together through a simple act of kindness and develop a lifetime friendship.*

"My father will be down soon," Lucienne announced.

Lucienne, Francesca, and Ambroise sat over coffee on the outdoor porch, for a casual conversation about marriage and children.

They also talked about Ambroise's night job, and Lucienne said, "The senator is looking for a driver. I was able to convince him to talk to you, Ambroise, before he hired anyone. Are you interested in having a daytime job instead of working the graveyard shift?"

"You mean for Ambroise to be the senator's driver?" Francesca asked, in awe at the prospect of a new position for her husband.

Lucienne laughed at Francesca's eagerness. She imagined what it would mean to these young parents to get a job so well-regarded on the island. If everything went well, Ambroise would no longer work nights hauling human waste. He could be home in the evenings with his family, help his young children with homework, and share a bed every night with his wife. Lucienne was happy to help this young, amiable couple; furthermore, she hoped to become the new baby's godmother—something she so desperately wanted.

"Yes," she said, with a great smile on her face. "That's what I mean."

Francesca let out a small squeak and, holding her very big belly, did not give Ambroise the chance to reply first. "Oh, yes!"

Ambroise walked to the railing. He needed to control his nerves and, to do that, he needed a little privacy. From where he stood, he could see the senator's backyard. Not too far from an outhouse, the servants' quarters—one for the housemaids and one for the male servants—were covered with a sheet metal roof and painted in sandy brown. In an enclosed kitchen outdoors, the cooks prepared succulent meals. The garden was immaculate, and the fragrance of the flowers filled the air.

He still could not comprehend how a simple gesture of kindness—one he would have done for anyone—could have resulted in this kind of opportunity. After a few minutes, Ambroise rejoined the two ladies' conversation, which no longer had anything to do with the job offer.

Ambroise was a man of few words who was still overwhelmed by a sense of shock and gratitude. He simply said, "I will accept."

"You will?" Francesca beamed with joy. "You will accept the senator's offer?"

"Yes," he replied, both nervous and excited. He turned to face Lucienne and said, "Thank you."

The senator suddenly appeared, walking through the door from the living room. As he greeted them, both Francesca and Ambroise stood up and extended their hands to the Senator. Francesca intensely watched her husband as he answered the senator's questions.

The interview went well, and Ambroise was hired as the senator's chauffeur.

The ride home in the taptap (a public bus) was animated. Francesca talked about all the saints she had prayed to at church and the number of candles she had lit from the day she had found out about her pregnancy. Ambroise spoke about all he was going to be able to do for his family now that he had a position that was prestigious and paid better. Still, he worried that the job required that he wear black shoes, black socks, black pants, and a white shirt. As a nighttime truck driver, he had never followed a dress code; he only had one Sunday suit and no available funds to purchase anything new. Thankfully, Ambroise was able to get money from his father and borrow from some friends in order to come up with enough for one outfit. He would manage with just one until he was paid.

It is true: Haitians are poor. But we are proud islanders.

Ambroise looked impeccable on his first day and every day thereafter. Every evening, Francesca washed and starched her husband's only white shirt; every day, she woke up at the crack of dawn to iron his uniform. She did this for the whole month, until they saved enough money to purchase more white shirts and an extra pair of trousers.

Occasionally, Ambroise saw Lucienne while picking up or dropping off the senator at the house and, at every encounter, Lucienne asked how Francesca was faring. One day, Ambroise proudly announced the birth of a baby girl. Lucienne congratulated him and, not having access to her car, she urged Ambroise to take her to the mother and the baby. On the way to the house, Lucienne insisted on making a couple of stops, so that she could buy as much as she could for the visit.

What a surprise it was for Francesca, when Ambroise walked in with Lucienne carrying bags of goodies not only for Francesca, but for the baby girl as well.

Finally, after coffee and small talk, Francesca asked, "Would you like to see the baby?"

Lucienne nodded and followed her inside the bedroom where the baby was quiet, but wide awake. With Francesca's permission, she reached down and lifted the baby carefully, holding the small girl as though she was her own. She looked at the baby's pretty face and kissed her forehead and her cheeks, all the while caressing the baby's hands with her thumb.

Witnessing all this affection, Francesca asked, "Would you like to be her godmother?"

"Yes, I would love to," Lucienne said joyfully and without hesitation. "Thank you."

Throughout her lifetime, Lucienne would never marry nor have any children of her own. As the godmother, she was given the privilege of naming the child together with the birth parents.

They chose to name her Solange.

Sol, in French, is short for the word *soleil*, meaning the sun—warm, loving, inviting. *Ange* means angel. Thus, "Solange" means "angel of the sun."

MAKE IT WORK FOR YOU!

Rule #1: Believe in Luck

Reflection: Roll with the Tide

A sea turtle goes on amazing journeys. She may travel as far as 10,000 miles with little more than a gland in her head to guide her towards her final destination. There are a variety of obstacles that stand in her way, from marine predators to stormy seas to the tide's pull, that could thwart her journey. Instinctively, she trusts that she will reach the end of her journey exactly where she belongs, even if it is not where she intended to go when she began. There is a beautiful lesson to be learned in allowing yourself to go in the direction you are led, even if it does not make sense at the time.

- Reflect on what was going on in the world and in your immediate family when you were born. How did forces outside your control impact the person you are today? How can that make you a better person in the future?

- When has luck made a difference in your path? Have you ever missed a lucky opportunity due to doubt? How can you invite good fortune into your future?

Rule #2: Be Kind

Reflection: We Are All in the Same Ocean

Turtle hatchlings enter the world with a daunting task ahead of them. The minute they exit the shell, they are subject to land predators waiting to snatch them up and gobble them down, and that is just on solid land. Once they are in the open ocean, prey is all around them. It is easier to survive in terrible circumstances when others step in to be kind, whether it is the adult turtle that goes out of her way for a lost hatchling or the fish at the "turtle cleaning stations" that clean away algae deposits on migrating turtle shells. We are all a part of the same ocean. It is important to be kind.

- Is there someone you know whose kindness made a difference, either in your own life or in someone else's? What change did that kindness bring?

- Do not be afraid to help a random stranger. Whether it is giving directions to someone who is lost or returning a dropped wallet to its owner. Little acts of kindness are blessings. The next time you do something kind, pay attention to how your body feels. Pretty good, huh?

Rule #3: Be Persistent and Tenacious Despite Challenges

Reflection: If You Fall into a Pit, Dig Your Way Out

The moment a hatchling turtle begins its journey toward the sea, it approaches the shoreline steadfast, paying no mind to the obstacles standing between it and the shore. The turtles move toward the shoreline with focus. They do not give up. If they fall into a pit, they dig their way out. If a hatchling is removed from a beach and placed in a box, it does not just sit there, it clambers to get out and move on with its journey.

- Have you ever felt like there was something you could not accomplish, because the obstacle seemed insurmountable but, when you focused on the task, found it was easy to persevere? Find a mantra for yourself—one you can repeat when it seems like it is just too much. Whenever you reach the point of giving up, take a deep breath and say your mantra out loud.

- What are the obstacles you are currently facing in life? Make a list of them. As you read this book, build a second list of strategies that worked for me when I was facing an obstacle. Can any of those help you reach your goals?

RULES TO LIVE BY

Haiti is part of who I am. In chapter two, I give you a little background on the history of my family and my country, because, to some degree, we are all impacted by the history that came before us. These next rules built an early foundation in my outlook on life. It is important to know where you are from so that you do not allow others' perceptions of you—or of your roots—to limit where you will wind up.

Rule #4: Honor your Roots

As you will read, I come from an island with a complex history. Haiti is in my blood; it is a core element of my identity. My understanding of Haiti is much richer than the typical worldview, which often seems to be limited to the country's economic status, the natural disasters it has been impacted by, and the years of political strife. Beyond the sound bites on the evening news, there is another Haiti—one built by a strong determination to throw off the shackles of colonization and slavery. My Haiti has a rich language born from our African roots, and my heritage have formed my decisions. My culture keeps me grounded in the very important lessons of history, and sharing that culture keeps me connected to what is important.

In my family, we take care of each other. My sister helped bring me to the United States (see chapter three, "Leaving"), and, as soon as I could, I made sure I helped others in my family reach their own goals (see chapter five, "Nursing School"). Growing up, there were not any nursing homes in Haiti, because families took care of their own. I remembered the importance of elder care when I was building my career and tried to treat my residents as if they were part of my family. I can remember watching my mother care for her mother as she aged, and when my own mother became elderly, I made sure she had everything she needed. In some cultures, caring for family, let alone strangers, is not the norm; the bond between parent and child is tight in my country.

Rule#5: Show Initiative and Rise Above Expectations/ Limitations

I learned early to be resourceful and make a lot out of very little. When no disposable diapers were available to change my baby sister, there were cloth and pins (see chapter two, "Lucky"). I also learned to take initiative: if my grandmother was busy and the babies were fussing, I stepped up and pitched in to help. Throughout my life, people I have looked up to have been go-getters, like my father who started with very little, and I have always tried to follow their example.

Like the turtle, do not be afraid to stick your neck out. Do things when you see they need to be done, and rise above any expectations or limits placed on you by others. In school, I found that the children who sat in the back row became back-row learners; they did not have high expectations set for their progress, and so they did not strive to achieve much (see chapter two, "Lucky"). I always tried to position myself in the front row, even when I got the feeling I did not belong.

There will always be people who do not like you or just do not know your capabilities. I have been refused seats in a restaurant based solely on my skin color (see chapter three, "Leaving"), been dismissed because of my accent (see chapter five, "Nursing School"), and I just refuse to accept that other people's limits have any merit. You have to learn to believe in yourself, because other people are not always going to have faith in you. It can be lonely when you are the only person who knows what you are capable of, but, eventually, others will catch on soon enough.

Keep dreaming big. See what is possible in your mind's eye, and then believe in it.

2

Lucky

Located in the Caribbean Sea, Haiti (Ayiti) shares a border with the Dominican Republic; together, they form the tropical island of Hispaniola, said to have been "discovered" by Christopher Columbus in 1492. First ruled by the Spaniards, Hispaniola was later ruled by Britain, France, and Spain (again) because of her lush mountains and the abundance of cocoa, cotton, sugarcane, coffee, and other natural resources—some rare—produced cheaply through free labor provided by enslaved Africans brought to the island. By the middle of the 17th century, Haiti became fully colonized by the French, and, by 1780, Haiti was one of the wealthiest colonies in the western world.

But a war was brewing. The slaves would soon rebel against the French colonists who abused them. This served as the main catalyst for the Haitian revolution. Other factors led to the fight for freedom, including the clash between the Catholic rites practiced by the French and the Voodoo religion practiced by the African slaves. A lack of communication also fostered resentment: the French spoke French while the Africans used Creole, which was not a dialect understood by the French. During the war, each group used their own language to plan strategies and communicate in secrecy.

The class structure that developed during colonial times persisted in Haiti after its independence in 1804. In 1945, the minority light-skinned mulattoes—who were Catholic, French-speaking Haitians, like Lucienne's family—were at odds with the majority dark-skinned, Voodoo-practicing Creole speakers, like Francesca's family. At the intersection was Ambroise's family, whose ancestors were born of a Frenchman and an African Creole woman. Ambroise was technically a mulatto, like Lucienne, but the dark-skinned complexion of his family had worked against any possibility of class privilege.

In 1815, immediately after the French revolution, one of three brothers from Bordeaux, France, arrived in Haiti to assist in the rebuilding of the country. He was an engineer, and Haiti was in desperate need of his expertise to build roads and bridges. This white Frenchman produced several children as a result of his union with a black Creole woman, and those children were Ambroise's ancestors.

Francesca's lineage traced back to a village from a rural province in Haiti called Leogane. She had two sisters, and they each had a middle-school education. Her father had died at a young age, and the girls were raised by their mother, a professional laundress who hand-washed her clients' clothes and pressed them with a hot coal iron for a few gourdes. In those days, depending on the market, one American dollar was the equivalent of ten Haitian gourdes.

Francesca and Ambroise met during the festivities held on the occasion of a first communion, the second sacrament in the Catholic religion. As it was customary, a group of young adults had gathered in a house to shower the blessed child with religious songs and partake in the reception. Ambroise spotted a young, brown-skinned, beautiful, slender woman with long silky hair, a lovely smile and a great singing voice. Ambroise was mystified and very attracted to her. He boldly followed her to her home, where he requested her mother's permission to court her daughter. Before long, he was the man of the house. Francesca's mother had the son she never had, and her sisters had gained a brother. They relocated with Ambroise to a bigger house and, together, Ambroise and Francesca started a family. All their children were delivered by a midwife in their home—a midwife whom Ambroise picked up on his trusty bicycle, which, at the time, was his only mode of transportation.

Ambroise was 16 years older than Francesca and already the father of two daughters. As the Don Juan of his neighborhood, he had managed to get two sisters who lived in the same house pregnant at the same time. His two daughters were born months apart. They grew up with their mothers in the same household and eventually became very close to Ambroise and Francesca's children.

Haiti, long liberated from French oppression, was now occupied by the United States of America, with Antoine Louis Leocardie Elie Lescot as president between 1941 and 1946. Under Lescot, the island was in constant turmoil; Haiti suffered its worst economy, and the island was nearly bankrupt. A member of the country's light-skinned elite, Lescot ruled with intimidation, and, by force, he used the political climate of World War II to sustain his power and his ties to the United States, which had a major influence on the affairs of the island. He created his own distinct army called the "chefs de section," mainly a group of rural police chiefs.

By early 1946, a fierce student demonstration erupted near the national palace, the Palais National. Large crowds gathered in the streets of Port-au-Prince and ransacked the homes of government authorities. A civil war broke out for days between the mulatto-dominated government and the black military guards because of the mistreatment by the mulattoes. Tear gas seeped inside the houses of civilians, and innocent citizens huddled behind closed doors, fearing for their lives and praying for protection against the violence on the streets.

On one of those fearful but otherwise beautifully sunny days in May, Francesca's water broke. Ambroise risked his life, confronting the unruly mob on his bicycle, in search of the midwife. Outside, tear gas permeated the air and fumigated the crowded streets; inside, Francesca was in labor.

This baby was not about to wait until the streets were safe.

The night before, Ambroise had observed a moon pregnant with promise, and an unusual bright star shone in the night sky. These were all auspicious signs. He was sure that this child would be different: she would bring warmth and bliss to others. She would make him lucky.

In the end, the young mother gave birth to a healthy eight-pound baby girl who later, at baptism, received the name Solange.

I became the angel of the sun.

Not only did I bring joy to the family but also comfort during a period of civil unrest and great fear among a population on this island that seemed to exist in the bosom of suffrage.

Lucienne now had the godchild that she was waiting for; she was the proud godmother of a baby girl that she could see, feel, and touch. Her visits to the Vivens' house continued, as did her financial support of my care. My parents, Ambroise and Francesca, nurtured their relationship with Lucienne. Their friendship was good, not only for the baby, but for the entire family, as Lucienne visited with bags of bread, cheese, milk, coffee, sugar, and anything else that she believed the family needed. She collected clothes from her friends and family, and my mother, who was a seamstress, used the fabric from the donated clothes to make pretty dresses for all four of her daughters.

The senator, Lucienne's father, accepted the fact that I, Solange, in a way, belonged to his daughter, and he welcomed this cute little chocolate baby as a member of their family.

At the age of five, I started kindergarten ("jardin d'enfants") in a small school within walking distance of my parent's home. I quickly became the darling of Madame Emmanuel, the owner of the pre-school. Just like Lucienne, Madame—as we called her—fell in love with me and showered me with pretty clothes and ribbons and barrettes for my hair. I was chosen for all the school plays. I was loved but, surprisingly, not spoiled. My parents believed that I was a true angel: their lucky child, their gift from God. My father would often refer to me as his lucky charm, since their socio-economic life had changed for the better with my birth.

I had an infectious smile, a great disposition, and was a nonstop talker from the moment that I learned to speak. That was my way of controlling, directing, and taking charge of my world, even as a child.

I was the favored flower girl at weddings.

My parents, who had lived in a common-law relationship for many years, got married in an elaborate ceremony. Family and friends from across the island attended the wedding. Lucienne and the senator did not, however, as it was not proper protocol for him to come to these parts of town. The separation based on class was very much practiced in Haiti. There were the rich, the middle class, the poor, and then the very poor. It is because of this classism that the senator and Lucienne could not show their support in public; their presence at the wedding would have exacerbated the existing class tension.

Although Lucienne could not attend the wedding, she used that opportunity to dress her goddaughter, one of the flower girls, as a petite bride. My dress, white and long, covered my pretty lace socks, which could only be seen when I lifted the dress as I walked, for fear of falling. A lovely white straw hat lay on top my long, black, shoulder-length curls. Lace gloves and gold earrings accessorized my outfit.

My mother was more than fine with her baby girl stealing the show. She was proud and happy to have her relationship with Ambroise blessed by the parish priest and their union accepted by the church. Her heart filled with love for her youngest daughter. She beamed with happiness at how cute I looked that day. My father and mother believed that I had special powers—that I was born lucky.

So did Ana, my maternal grandmother, who took pleasure in sharing stories about me. "This little girl," she told people, "is going places. Oh, Lord! She is going places in her life!"

She told people about the one time my father took me on his bicycle to a soccer game at the National Stadium. I was six years old, and soccer was—and still is—the number one sport in Haiti. The halftime attraction was a grand raffle using the admission ticket number for the drawing. To his surprise, my dad heard his number announced over the stadium's loudspeaker. He could not believe he had the winning ticket! He had attended games at this stadium both in his youth and as an adult and had never won a prize. He told everyone—and believed it himself—that he only won because he had taken me, Solange, to the game. "It was her win, not mine," Ambroise said. "She was the lucky one."

The next day, he was even more surprised when the prize was delivered to the house: a phonograph, which was manually cranked to play records the size of a large pizza. Everyone in the house was impressed with this machine. In those days, having a phonograph at your house, particularly in the area where we lived, signified that someone had "arrived" financially. Ambroise, who already had a Napoleon complex at 5'0", now walked around the neighborhood like a "chef de section," a chief of the community.

To those around him, he was a smart man. One of six children—three brothers and three sisters—Ambroise had attended high school and was considered in those days, especially in the environment in which he lived, to be a well-educated man. And, truth be told, he was a smart man. Despite experiencing many ordeals in life, Ambroise managed to provide for his overgrown household. We all still lived in the same house: Ambroise and Francesca, their five children, my grandmother, and my mother's two sisters. My father had to figure out, on his own, a way to improve our family's lifestyle.

When my grandmother, Ana, sold a piece of land that she owned in Leogane, the town where she was born, she granted the funds to Francesca. Ambroise, who had also inherited some money after the death of his father, used the combined funds to build a bigger home for his family in a more affluent section of Port-au-Prince. He moved to the new house with his wife and children, leaving the old house for his mother-in-law and her other two daughters.

*   *   *

From the beginning of their common-law life, my parents gave birth to a child every two years. In those days, there was no birth control. Making love was a great form of relaxation and entertainment that led to pregnancy. It was the luck of the draw whether a woman got pregnant or not after a sexual event.

My parents' firstborn was a boy (Gerald) followed every two years by a girl. Everyone was so used to Francesca being pregnant every two years, so they were baffled by a gap of three, four, then five years. This large lapse was a rarity for them.

It was during this fifth year that finally Francesca became pregnant once more.

Family and friends were questioning Mother Nature: had she been playing a trick on them, or had this mystery child, Solange, been manipulating and controlling her environment in utero?

Everyone thought that I—their lucky child, their blessing—was going to be my parents' last birth, so imagine everyone's surprise when, five years after my birth, Francesca was once again pregnant. She was not yet done enjoying Ambroise, and, thus, continued to do her share of populating the world, giving birth not only to their sixth child (Mirlene) but also to their seventh (Antonine), eighth (Jean Claude), and ninth (Ambroise Jr.).

Altogether, they had three sons and six daughters, in addition to Ambroise's out-of-wedlock son who by now had joined their household. Yet, their socio-economic situation continued to improve, and Francesca was able to hire a housekeeper to help her manage the house, the large yard, and the many children. She also hired two *restavèks*, teenagers who attended night school and worked as servants during the day in exchange for room and board. Having met her husband when she was a young adult, Francesca had never held a job outside of the home. She was dedicated in her role as a wife and a mother. She was the perfect executive when it came to managing her household.

It has been said that I am a true middle child, the fifth out of Francesca and Ambroise's nine children with four older siblings and four younger siblings—the pillar holding this family together. There was constant rivalry with Edith, the sister who immediately preceded me, and extreme affection—and even a kind of motherly love—for Mirlene, the sister who followed me.

In the 1940s, there were no Pampers. Babies wore thick cloth diapers secured by very large silver-colored safety pins. I often watched my mother change Mirlene's diapers, so, one day, alone with my baby sister, I decided to take matters into my own hands and change the diaper on my own. My grandmother, who was home babysitting us, was outside washing clothes, and I was ready to put into practice what I had watched my mother do whenever the baby cried.

I climbed on a chair, and then from the chair to the table to gain the necessary height to pull down a diaper from the nicely folded bundle on the shelf. I then climbed back down to attend to my crying baby sister. In those days, babies were not placed to sleep on a bed, but rather on a special floor mat made of banana leaves. A thick cloth pad was laid down for comfort, and the baby was covered with a sheet. This setup was within an easy reach for me.

When I carried the wet diaper outside to my grandmother so that she could wash it, the old woman jumped from behind the galvanized basin filled with sudsy, soapy water, and ran inside, expecting to find the baby howling with pain, even bleeding from safety-pin punctures. To her astonishment, the baby was quiet and the diaper placed efficiently.

I became known as the babysitter extraordinaire, and this story was told repeatedly by my grandmother. "Believe me," she would say, "this child is going places. She is so bossy, she may never be able to keep a man in her life or get married. But, oh, God, is she going places!"

I was both curious and assertive as a toddler and grew even more so as I got older—a characteristic that became very helpful to me as a leader in my later years. As I sought in-depth knowledge, I loved school and believed education to be the key to success.

The school system in Haiti used a grade average from about a dozen courses to determine a student's standing in the class. Students sat in the classroom based on their averages. The student with the highest average was considered number one and sat on the first bench, on the first row, next to the second highest average, then the third and the fourth, and so on, down to the students with the lowest averages on the last bench. Each bench held four or five students, with the smartest kids in front and the rest falling in line behind them. The seating arrangement allowed the brighter children to continue getting high marks, while the "slackers" were left behind. At an early age, I learned that, in life, we control what we can and work around the given. My goal was to sit on the first two benches—always. I studied with some of my classmates and also studied on my own to make sure that I mastered the material.

I was very competitive and commanded respect from my peers. I was well liked by them and by my teachers. I never missed school, for fear that my classmates would learn something that I did not. I competed not only against my classmates but against myself. Even back then, being ahead of the pack was in the forefront of my mind. Fearless, I was never afraid to stick my neck out in any situation. But, like a turtle, I tried my best to only take calculated risks.

I never told my mother when I did not feel well, for fear that she would keep me home from school for the day. She only realized that I was sick when I fell asleep in the middle of the day or failed to be the first one up to get ready for school.

My elementary school, École Sainte-Bernadette, was located across from the ocean where the fishermen sold their fresh catch of the day. Every Friday, I crossed the street, being very careful not to get hit by a car or a taptap—a small van for hire—on the busy streets of Carrefour. I purchased fresh fish for my maternal grandmother Ana, whom I affectionately called my "Grand Ana," and then walked to her house to deliver what she had given me the money to buy. We ate the fish together after she cooked it, and we drank black coffee until I was picked up by my father on his way home from work.

In the Caribbean, in those days, there were no nursing homes. Children were expected to care for their elders, thus my grandmother lived with one of her daughters and remained an active member of the family until her death at the age of 92. I have fond memories of the time I spent with my Grand Ana. She was very instrumental in helping me become the person I grew up to be.

I also liked spending time with my godmother. When I grew old enough to travel about town alone, I made a trip almost every Sunday to visit with my godmother at the senator's house where she and her brother, who was now married, lived with his family. I grew up in a loving relationship with Lucienne. I enjoyed wearing the beautiful clothes she provided for me, eating good food, and reading thrilling story books.

Lucienne's brother had a child soon after I was born. She was also Lucienne's goddaughter; the two of us were lovingly referred to as "Lucienne's daughters."

My godmother drove me home at the end of our visits and, on the way, she stopped at a store to buy me gum and candy, cheese and cakes, and an assortment of other goodies to take home with me. At times, she even gave me money. My siblings and even my mother patiently awaited my return, knowing full well that I would not come home empty-handed. In the early days, this ritual at times was a necessity, especially before Ambroise started his own business. From a very young age, I took the serious role of supporting my family on my shoulders.

Ambroise might have been a man of very small stature, but he was very street smart. He eventually emerged as a small king in the place where he lived. My parents grew to be successful, because they repeatedly managed to find the positive in every negative event that penetrated the walls of their household. They managed to instill in all their children an unfailing optimism, no matter what the circumstances, as each day is a new opportunity that brings its own challenges and its own victories.

My father was a man who saw his glass half full, never half empty. He had been climbing the ladder of success since I was born, he told his friends. With his mind set on upward mobility, he had grown a taptap business. He had first purchased a single taptap that he was leasing out to drivers while he was fully employed as a chauffeur to the senator. When the senator lost his Senate seat on Election Day, Ambroise became a full-time businessman: he purchased a second taptap and started to pick up passengers himself along the street, dropping them off at a designated area. He was soon able to hire several drivers. He bought himself a used car, a "Picard," and ditched his bicycle. He created a middle-class family out of a low-class family, and he became a big fish in the small pond of his neighborhood.

My mother was a seamstress who took pride in dressing up her girls. She taught us to always hold our heads high and be proud of who we are. "People only talk about important people," she would tell us. "If they talk about you, it's because you are important"

Because he had managed to change his method of locomotion—from walking to owning a bicycle to owning a car—and because he had a little bit of money in his pocket, my father became a sought-after man by the many women around him, even though they were aware that he was married with several children. He became a Haitian Don Juan who continued populating the island with children, not only inside but also outside of his marriage.

Ambroise and Francesca were sitting on their front porch one day, when a woman came to inform the husband that "his son" had been left unattended by the mother for many hours; the baby, she said, could be heard crying inside the house.

At that time, Francesca was very pregnant with her third child. "What son are you talking about?" she asked in shock. Francesca was always aware of her common-law husband's promiscuity, but having a child in the confines of this established relationship was a different matter.

Ambroise did not acknowledge her question. He knew of the child, so got up and started to walk away. Francesca followed her husband to another home.

When they entered the room, they found an absolutely beautiful baby boy crying on a floor mat. He was no more than a couple of months old. Francesca followed her motherly instincts and grabbed the baby off the floor. She held him close to her chest, as she understood the child's need for closeness and affection. She took the baby boy home until the mother could be found, and only then did Ambroise answer all her questions. The baby's diaper was changed, and he was fed.

The mother never came to claim the boy. Francesca was a saint. She not only forgave her husband's bad behavior but rescued his son as well, raising him, Reginald, as her own.

As though Ambroise had not done enough damage to his marriage and to his wife, he managed to also impregnate one of Francesca's housekeepers who lived in their home. He was truly a rolling stone: wherever he laid with a woman, he impregnated her. Altogether, Ambroise had thirteen known children. The rumors around the island regarding his infidelity were so rampant, however, that even Ambroise had no idea how many children he really had fathered.

Because of his behavior and the way he used his money and his relationships with women, he became very protective of his daughters. My mother, who was 16 years younger than him, could have been considered his seventh daughter in their household. He was as firm, domineering, and controlling of every move she made as he was with each of his daughters. We all grew up scared of him but respectful. He was a good father in general, a careful provider, but he was overprotective. On our way to school—and on the rare occasions when we were allowed to attend a play or a movie—we were to travel in a group, despite the fact that we were of different ages and each had our own circles of friends. The young men in the neighborhood sarcastically called us "The Cadets" and, whenever we left the house, it was not unusual for us to hear, "The Cadets are out!" coming loudly—and mockingly—from a group of boys standing at a street corner.

We were never allowed to sleep at a friend's house or go to school field trips to the beach. Sometimes, my father agreed to let us go only to change his mind the next day, after we had already made all the plans. There was one disappointment after another. But, in the end, "The Cadets" remained very close to each other, even well into our senior years.

MAKE IT WORK FOR YOU!

Rule #4: Honor your Roots

Reflection: Your Roots Grow Deep

Turtles remember where they hatched. Scientists believe that, inside female sea turtles, there is an internal magnetic compass that is imprinted with the location of their birthplace. When it is time to lay their eggs, most of them swim thousands of miles back to the exact beach where they hatched to build their nests and lay the next generation of eggs.

- Make a list of some attributes, both positive and negative, about the culture, family, or community you grew up in. How have these shaped you? How have they limited you? Pick the ones you want to keep in mind as you journey toward success, and feel free to discard the ones that limit you.

- What would you like to pass along to the next generation that follows you? Whether or not you plan to have children of your own, what kind of legacy would you like to leave for the future?

Rule #5: Show Initiative and Rise Above Expectations/ Limitations

Reflection: Survivors Keep Going!

Fossil records from 210 million years ago indicate that sea turtles managed to outlive dinosaurs. Their migrations continue despite predators, human destruction of their nesting sites, pollution, famine, and other factors such as climate change. They focus on a direction and keep going through the worst the world has to offer, and it has worked for them for millions of years. They have been in tough spots and have faced the danger of extinction, but the strong turtles pull through and survive.

- Think of a time when you did something positive and unexpected on your own initiative. What reaction were you met with? How did it change how you view your potential?

- What limitations do you face in your journey to success? How many are based on preconceptions of others or cultural norms? Make a list of things you think may be holding you back. Then, go back through the list and cross off any that are due to other people's perceptions of what you can accomplish. Those are largely illusionary.

RULES TO LIVE BY

In this chapter, you will read about some major life changes I went through when, as a teenager, I came to the United States from Haiti. It was a lot to experience in a short amount of time, but the lessons I learned were some of the most important on my journey. Maintaining composure and focus will keep you on track. Be willing to make sacrifices along the way.

Rule # 6: Keep Your Feelings in Check

It is okay to cry. It is sometimes necessary to let out emotion so that you can focus on the task ahead. Crying allows you to purge overwhelming feelings and self-doubt, so that you can move forward. When I first arrived in the United States and could not understand the language, I would often cry out of frustration (see chapter three, "Leaving"). When I was done, it was like I had a clean slate and could focus on learning to speak English, or whatever other obstacle I was facing at the time. Later, when I learned I would have to take a job as a nanny to earn my visa, I cried out of disappointment, but, in the wake of my tears, I found the strength to accept a job I felt was beneath me (see chapter four, "Joining the Workforce"). Crying is a natural way to clean out your emotional reservoir, so you can refill it with positive vibes.

But watch out for situations that drain you and cause you to react in a way that is not constructive or healthy. If you find that you are having trouble regulating emotions on your own, it is important to seek help from a professional, but some simple strategies may also help you keep cool under fire. There was a time when a medical condition made me lash out at my husband (see chapter 11, "How Did We Do It?"). He kept calm in his response and helped me see there was more to my tantrums than I realized at the time. If you find yourself crying repeatedly over the same issues or reacting out of anger, it is time to figure out what is not working for you; stop crying and lashing out and find composure.

My sister, Edith, and I spent years tearing each other apart fighting and crying before I realized the fighting was not doing either of us any good (see chapter two, "Lucky"). Do not allow other people to rob you of your joy. I never let other people affect the way I feel or act. When you do not control your emotions, you give others more power over you; deny them that power. You will see further in my story how, time and time again, I felt anger but chose to project an air of calm confidence. There is a certain satisfaction in seeing other people's reactions when you do not respond to their provocations. Your reactions should not be dictated by other people's stimulations. Learning to remain steady in the face of adversity can be the difference between success and failure.

Rule #7: Remain Focused

I learned early on that it is important to remain focused. In chapter three, you will read about my schoolgirl days in Haiti. When I was terribly ill, I still maintained focus on my studies, because I knew education was a key to success.

Do not allow challenges to sidetrack you. Later in the book, you will read about my difficulties with immigration, like the mountain of legal forms I had to complete, despite not knowing the language fluently. I got through it all by remaining focused, even in the aftermath of a devastating sexual assault. The violent incident was traumatizing, but I had no choice but to put the experience to the side to reach my goal of bringing my sister to the United States. It was not an easy situation to be in, but I got through.

There are plenty of distractions in life—some of them terrible—and it is up to you to make a conscious decision not to allow yourself to lose sight of your goals. There will be plenty of people to support you on your journey, but keep your eyes on the prize at all costs.

Rule #8: Be Willing to Make Sacrifices

I might not have gone as far in life were it not for the sacrifices others made on my behalf. My parents, for example, knew that sending me to the United States was in my best interests because of the political situation in Haiti. I was young, and they wanted to keep me close to ensure I was taken care of properly and had everything I needed. They knew that the situation in Haiti was so dangerous that my life was in peril; I would be safer if I left. As a result of that sacrifice, I was able to build a successful career and, in turn, help my family improve their quality of life.

Good parents will do anything for their children. When I was sick, my father figured out a cure for my illness, because he was desperate to make sure I did not suffer. This goes beyond parenting: whenever something is at stake, we find strength to sacrifice what we need to get through. You will read later about some of the sacrifices I had to make to advance my career, including limiting quality time with my family and choosing to specialize my work in a field that was outside of what I had initially planned for myself. It is never easy to make sacrifices, but the benefits of doing so outweigh the disadvantages.

3

Leaving

It cannot be stated strongly enough how difficult it was for my family to raise nine children on the island of Haiti, especially during the teenage years of their first five offspring. The five-year gap between my birth, and the four others that followed it, created a huge problem for Francesca and Ambroise, who had to simultaneously deal with adolescent behaviors and infant temper tantrums.

As the older group of children, we had our own issues with sibling rivalry and competition for attention, and a serious drive for independence. Physical fights, mainly between me and my sister Edith, grew even more violent. Edith believed our mother and father loved me more than they did her, and her jealousy manifested itself in many ways. She instigated fights, yet she expected our parents to settle the disputes in her favor. She suffered with eczema, asthma, and other illnesses, such as anxiety, that were brought about by her own insecurities. When we both became adults, I realized the unfortunate position my sister Edith was in and did everything in my power to mend the relationship. Regrettably, no matter what I did, it would never be enough to soothe the feelings she had been harboring for decades. I made it a point to get along with everyone in the family, including my sister Edith, and I strove not to allow anyone or anything to spoil the joy I get around my relatives, especially my sisters.

As a teenager, I became ill with recurring bouts of very high fevers, sore throats, and general malaise that progressed to stiffness in the joints. At times, I became so stiff that I could not sit; instead, I lay on the back seat of the car on my way to the public clinic, where I was given injections for the pain and a cream to relieve the stiffness. The trips to the clinic brought me temporary relief, but the fevers and stiffness returned once the effect of the medication wore off. My feet and hands swelled up. I was sick off and on from the ages of thirteen to fifteen. I looked abnormally thin and weak. The illness also stunted my growth in the middle of my teenage years. To my horror, I often had to miss a lot of school. Needless to say, the meager social life that Ambroise allowed me was rendered even more meager by the illness.

For three years, my parents dealt with a sick child, but none of the doctors could find a diagnosis; at a loss, these health professionals worried about my health and wellbeing, trying to find a way to get relief for this teenager whose physical development was stunted by illness. Ambroise believed that the neighbors were practicing Voodoo in an attempt to steal his daughter's luck, knowing full well how he had broadcasted about me being the lucky charm.

Out of desperation, my father cooked a pot of cornmeal mixed with a very large amount of sea salt, filled a sock with this mixture and wrapped it around my ankles to decrease the edema that had developed there. Ambroise was not a formally educated physician, but he was an excellent bush doctor. It was not until I became a nursing student that I realized, during an anatomy and physiology class, how smart my father was. For a class assignment, I came across the word "osmosis" and learned that water goes where salt is. I stopped reading and repeated, over and over: "Water goes where salt is." *Ambroise,* I thought, fascinated. *Oh, my God! That is what you were doing, putting the heavily salted cornmeal on my feet when I was sick. You were getting the water out of my ankles.* How in the world did he know that the salted cornmeal would decrease the edema? I knew the answer to that question: although some Haitians might not have the level of education required to know about osmosis, they have a tea, an oil, or an herbal treatment for every illness. Ambroise was no exception, and he would have done anything to save his child.

Francesca's godfather, The Doctor, was a general practitioner on the island. He, too, cared for me and was baffled by this mysterious illness. I wonder today if even The Doctor knew anything about osmosis. Since telephone technology had not yet made its way to Haiti, news usually traveled by foot. One day, my mother's godfather, The Doctor, sent someone to our house, asking Francesca to bring me to him for an examination. I was taken to the appointment by both my mother and father. To their surprise, they were introduced to a white man, a physician friend of The Doctor, who was on a short visit to the island from France. He proceeded to examine me, and, for the first time, the problem was identified; a diagnosis was finally made, followed by a treatment plan. Because of the severity of the diagnosis, the short length of this physician's stay on the island, and his desire to perform the surgery himself, there was no time to procrastinate. At nine o'clock the following morning, I was prepped for surgery, and a tonsillectomy was performed.

I was kept on a liquid diet for 24 hours, followed by a soft-food regimen until I became able to tolerate a regular diet. As if the pain of the surgery was not enough agony, the French doctor ordered 20 injections of penicillin, one shot per day for 20 days. A nurse came to the house every evening to administer the injection and, even though the sites were rotated daily, I hid as soon as I heard the nurse's voice greeting my parents. Eventually, I completed the series of injections, started to gain weight, and the symptoms disappeared.

Because the illness erupted at the beginning of my teenage years, I was a late bloomer. I had my menses for the first time at the age of 17 and finally developed breasts in early adulthood. It was again not until my nursing studies that I realized that I had suffered from juvenile rheumatoid arthritis, which explained the general malaise and joint pain. I finally understood why I needed a tonsillectomy. My tonsils were harboring a bacterium called beta hemolytic streptococcus that was infecting my blood, thus the explanation for the chronic fevers.

The clinic was giving me penicillin injections; however, the dosage and frequency were insufficient to kill the bacteria that was recolonizing as soon as I finished a round of antibiotics. The medicine relieved the symptoms but did not eradicate the problem completely. I suffered with recurring infections exhibiting the same symptoms repeatedly. My illness was a mystery not only to my moderately-educated parents but also to the Haitian doctors who examined me. At last, I fully recuperated and continued to shine in my schooling.

After she completed her schooling in Haiti, my oldest sister Ritza applied to the nursing program at Misericordia Hospital in Canada. When she was accepted, a door to the rest of the world was suddenly opened for my family. Ambroise sold everything he could, including the tires of his car, to cover the expenses of sending his and Francesca's oldest daughter to Canada. Within four years, Ritza was a licensed nurse working abroad who was able to send money home to assist with the expenses of raising such a large family.

Once Ritza completed her studies in Canada, she moved to the United States and worked at Misericordia Hospital in the Bronx, New York. Because my sisterly bond with Ritza was especially strong, we communicated via hundreds of letters during the four years she studied abroad, and she later asked me to join her in the United States. Once again, the stars seemed to be aligned for Ambroise's lucky child, his angel of the sun. However, was it luck that had pushed my sister to skip three older siblings and ask *me* to join her in America or was it my charming personality? Does being born lucky mean being born with lovable character traits? This would explain what had attracted Lucienne, Madame Emmanuel, and my Grand Ana to dote on me when I was growing up, and now my oldest sister was selecting me over the others. But what about Lucienne and how lucky I had made my parents? What was it about this mysterious child? Was there really a special angel in my life, or a special sun that shined on me? Should we really believe that the star that was so bright and so visible in the sky the night before my birth had anything to do with the course my life had taken?

Unbeknownst to me, my parents urged my oldest sister to get me out of Haiti as soon as possible. It had become a joint obsession for both of them. In fact, I left Haiti within a few weeks of my high school graduation. In my last year as a teenager, in the mid-60s, I arrived in the United State of America on a visitor's visa to attend the World's Fair.

Why were my mother and father so anxious to push their little angel of the sun out of Haiti? Had I changed into a devilish girl during my late adolescence years? Were my parents having problems with my behavior once I was no longer debilitated by my illness? No. I had not changed—our Caribbean island had.

There was political unrest once again in Haiti. The Haitian president, François "Papa Doc" Duvalier had created his own army similar to the "chefs de section" that existed under President Élie Lescot. Under Duvalier's regime, the "Tonton Macoutes," a Haitian paramilitary force, had taken over Port-au-Prince. They were, for the most part, uneducated men with guns, who used their power and intimidation to seduce and even rape girls; they were very attracted to beautiful, young girls with long hair, pretty faces, and firm, hourglass bodies. Because I fit these characteristics, I became the perfect prey for the "Tonton Macoutes." Ambroise and Francesca feared that I would be killed, particularly because of my strong personality: I was a bold, in-your-face type of child who disliked the current government and was not shy at expressing these controversial feelings, even though the dictatorship required silence and obedience.

Exile was the only lifesaving choice. As soon as Ambroise was able to secure a visa, my sister sent a plane ticket, and off the island I went, on my way to live in New York City. I had not seen my sister for a long time; she was, by now, married with two children. This time, Ambroise did not have to make any major sacrifices to meet the travel expenses. They were all covered by my sister, the licensed nurse, who brought a lot of pride to the family back home in Haiti.

I was a teenager boarding an airplane all alone, heading to an unknown destination. As much as I wanted to leave Haiti, and as anxious as I was to join my sister, brother-in-law and two young nieces, there was still the sadness of leaving my parents, siblings and all my friends. As I walked on the tarmac, I stopped after every few steps, turned around and waved at those who had accompanied me to the airport. Tears streamed down my face, and I knew that my parents' hearts, too, were breaking as they watched me walk away from them. They were caught between a rock and a hard place: they wanted to save my life—their primary reason for sending me abroad—but they also worried that my illness would recur with the cold weather in New York. Were they sending me to my death after all?

I entered the United States on a visitor's visa, since it was the fastest way to get me out of Haiti. The flight from Port-au-Prince to John F. Kennedy Airport took no more than four hours, but to me, it felt like an eternity. I kept my hands on the armrests, with my seat belt buckled for the entire duration of the trip, out of fear I would fall if I unfastened it. Thankfully, the airplane landed safely, and I found myself in a long line, waiting to face an immigration agent who would verify that I met all my passport requirements. I had no idea what my next move should be, so I followed the crowd exiting the immigration area. The corridors were long, and my carry-on bag was heavy; yet, I managed to stay with the other passengers for fear of getting lost in this big and unknown place.

In the large, open area full of suitcases, I recognized and grabbed my checked bag easily, as my sister had asked me to tie a ribbon on the handle of my suitcase for ease of identification. Once again, I followed the crowd to Customs. This step in the process was not expected. One by one, suitcases were opened, and items removed by the customs agent: mangos and bananas, sugarcane, and all kinds of leaves for bush tea were excluded from entry into the United States and discarded by the customs officer. Anxiously, I waited for my turn until I was asked to give my customs form to the agent. He allowed me to go through without requesting that my suitcase be searched. Even though I was not carrying any of the excluded items, I considered my luck to have struck again. Or was it my naïve and innocent look that the officer trusted?

Suddenly, a glass door opened in front of me, as if by magic, without anyone touching it. A mass of people waited on the other side of this big glass, greeting their loved ones as they appeared. Not until that moment did the anxious crowd know that a relative had arrived on that airplane, as there were no cell phones back then, and communication took a long time to travel. I quickly spotted my sister Ritza and my brother-in-law Peter who had stepped out from the crowd as soon as they noticed me. There were lots of hugs and kisses until my brother-in-law grabbed my bags and whisked me away toward their car.

I complained about being hungry, because I had not eaten the food on the airplane. So, once my bags were safely secured in the trunk of my brother-in-law's car, we returned to the airport in search of a restaurant. As Peter ordered in English, I thought, *Here I am, at a vulnerable age, fresh out of Haiti, in a new country, with a new family, expected to speak a different language.* How would I survive with no friends? How was I going to adjust to this new life? My head spun with questions and anxiety. I knew my brother-in-law in Haiti, but had never lived with him. I wondered, *how is he going to accept me? Am I going to be a third child fighting for my independence as a young adult?*

The restaurant was busy with travelers grabbing a meal before they boarded their planes, or some, like me, who had had a long day and had finally arrived. Waitresses were carrying big trays of food to the tables, all filled with plates piled high with hot food. I wondered how I would be able to choose something to eat. It all looked delicious. The smell in the restaurant made my mouth water. I was looking forward to my first American meal. But, then, the maître d' said something with a sharp tone of disapproval, shook his head, and waved at Peter dismissively. Peter looked surprised and said something back in an equally strong tone of voice. He shook his head at the maître d' and turned to us.

"Come on," he told us. "We have to find somewhere else to eat."

"But why?" I wanted to know.

"He says they have a dress code. We cannot wear jeans in this restaurant. I don't think that's the issue though. I think it's because we're black." When I looked at the patrons, many of them were wearing jeans also. They were not dressed any better than we were. I saw right away, Peter was right. We had been refused service because of our skin color. As I looked at the people sitting at the tables, eating their meals and laughing with the families and friends, I noticed one thing: every face in that restaurant belonged to a white person. There was not a single brown or black family in the dining room.

We found another restaurant in the airport right after this, but it was difficult to swallow my meal. My first encounter with America did not help my anxiety about fitting into my new surroundings. It was not just the language that was going to be difficult in this new country. The language, I knew, I could learn if I studied it and practiced pronunciation to coax my tongue into mastering the strange sounds of English. But there was nothing I could do to change the color of my skin. If this was my first welcome to America, what lay ahead for me? Was there any future here for me at all?

For the first time in my life, in my sister's apartment, I had my own room. It was a small space, about the size of a large closet, but it was mine, and mine alone. Even though I feared the unknown, I entertained positive thoughts as well: no longer would I have to adhere to Ambroise's harsh, autocratic rules. I had no schoolwork—not yet—just two babies to play with, and that made me happy. My brother-in-law put me on a babysitting payroll, and my sister showered me with shoes and clothes, because she was very happy to have my company, and my help with her two girls Lynda and Ingrid, who became my goddaughter.

Life was good, but, as usual, before long I wanted more.

Having taken English in high school as an elective, I thought that I could speak the language. I quickly realized that I had no English comprehension, and that the English vocabulary I had adopted in Haiti was foreign to the English spoken on the streets of New York City. A simple word such as *perhaps*, which I had learned in school, was replaced in New York with *maybe yes* or *maybe no*. This new way of speaking increased my frustration and added a certain level of isolation to my adjustment period. I had been a chatterbox all my life; not being able to express myself and understand what was being said on the television became a very painful and frustrating experience.

Although I felt generally happy around my sister and my two nieces, I was also terribly homesick and had major episodes of crying spells when I was alone in my room. Unbeknownst to me, my sister heard me crying at night but chose not to discuss it, hoping that I would get over it. Deep down, however, she could sense that a day would come when I would ask to return to Haiti. When I did, she was armed with an answer: because I had not returned to Haiti before the expiration of my visitor's visa, I was now considered an illegal alien. If I were to return home, she explained, I would never be allowed to reenter the United States.

"You don't want to be stuck in Haiti, do you?"

Reluctantly, I nodded no. She promised to hire a lawyer who would assist her in sponsoring my request for a permanent residency visa, so that I could live legally in the country.

Within months of my arrival, I turned 20, and my sister planned a big celebration. Since I had no friends in the country, however, all the guests were friends of my sister and brother-in-law.

I had been babysitting for my nieces, for which my brother-in-law was paying me $20 a week. Now that I was 20, I wanted to get a real job—get out of the house and go to work. My desire to gain employment was not about money; I just wanted more for myself, and was becoming unhappy and restless. Although I did not speak the language and my "illegal" status in the country made it even more difficult to thrive, I was not ready to give up.

My sister managed to find me a temp position, but we both knew full well that what she had found would not appease me for long. In the meantime, the babysitting responsibilities were shared among the three adults in the house to accommodate our respective schedules: My sister Ritza worked as a nurse the early morning shift; I worked the evening shift; and my brother-in-law Peter worked the night shift.

MAKE IT WORK FOR YOU!

Rule #6: Keep Your Feelings in Check

Reflection: Tuck it in!

Turtles have a built-in defense system that evolved over 200 million years ago when their shells developed from their ribs, shoulders, and backbones. When threatened or overwhelmed, most turtles can tuck their arms, legs, and heads inside their shell and wait for the danger to pass.

- When you find yourself provoked or feel the urge to cry because of something someone has said to you, take some deep breaths and name the emotion you are feeling to yourself silently (e.g., "I am angry" or "I am hurt"). Take as long as you need to gain control of your emotion before responding. Count to ten, and then smile. You do not have to say anything if you cannot say something positive right then, and, in some cases, the best response is no response at all.

- Try keeping a journal to help you track your emotional state and any major upsets you are experiencing. After a week or two, look back over the journal entries and see if you notice any patterns. Are there some people who seem to provoke you consistently? If you find someone is robbing you of emotional strength, first, figure out if they are worth your time. If they are not adding joy to your life, it may be time to let them go. But, if they are important to you, you may need to have a talk about the problems you are having in communicating. One thing that always worked well in my family was to find a public place like a restaurant for serious discussions. You are less likely to lose your cool if other people are around.

Rule #7: Remain Focused

Reflection: Turn Around and Keep Going!

If a turtle is diverted from the direction they are heading, they pull into their shells, turn back around, and get right back on track. They do not meander from their desired direction. It may be slow at times, but steady, slow progress is still progress.

- Make a list of goals you want to accomplish. Start with a list of 10. Then, go back over the list, and prioritize them. Find the three most immediate goals you need to accomplish first and work on those until you achieve them. Then, work on the next three goals. Sometimes it is best to work on the easiest goals first. This gives you a feeling of accomplishment as you tackle the harder goals on your list. When you accomplish a goal, reward yourself in some small way.

- Create a vision board to help you visualize your intentions. Find some images that relate to your goals and create a collage on poster board to help remind you of what you are working on. Hang the board somewhere you will see it each morning, like over your coffee pot, or on a wall in your bedroom. If you find yourself getting distracted, spend some time looking over the board to remind you where you want to focus your energy.

Rule #8: Be Willing to Make Sacrifices

The Iroquois Indians have a story about a turtle who sacrificed his own comfort to build the world. In the Iroquois Creation myth, Sky Woman fell to the Earth and found there was no land beneath her: the world was a vast ocean all around her. Without land, she would die. There would be no crops to sustain her people. With the help of other animals such as Toad, Sky Woman gathered mud from the bottom of the ocean and spread it across the back of a turtle. On its back, she planted trees and crops for food, and the Earth flourished. And, so, the turtle carries the weight of the world on its back in order that others might survive, and Earth is known to the Iroquois people as "Turtle Island."

- Once you have made your list of goals from rule #7, look at your first three priority items. Are there any obstacles to meeting those goals? If so, is there something you need to give up to achieve them? Sometimes, small sacrifices make a big difference. For example, if you want to buy a car, making more meals at home rather than eating out will help you save money.

- Pay attention to those around you. If you see someone needs help, offer your assistance. Sometimes, the elderly neighbor who needs help unloading her groceries will turn out to be a source of wisdom, and sacrificing a few minutes of your time will make you both happier.

RULES TO LIVE BY

In this chapter, I found out that life in the United States was going to be difficult for me, at least while I adjusted to a new language and culture. At times, I just wanted to give up and go back home to my parents in Haiti. It was not easy, but I stuck it out, because I knew hard work and education are important foundations for success. I also learned to swallow my pride.

Rule #9: Value Hard Work & Education

I come from a family of hard workers: working hard is something built into my bones. As you read earlier in chapter two, I made education a priority even when I was terribly sick; through the worst of it all, I worked to be the best I could be. In chapter three, my sister and her husband worked hard to build a good life for their family, and, once I moved in with them, I chipped in to help take care of the children. I even took on jobs I hated in sweatshops for very little pay (see chapter four). It was not what I wanted to do at the time, but I still managed to learn a lot while I waited to reach my goal of getting a formal education. I knew if I stuck it out, I would get to college, and things would be easier once I had my degree.

We never stop learning in our lifetimes. Even after I had earned my degrees and built a successful career, I still made sure to educate myself on the latest trends and changes in my field. It is important to feed your mind new knowledge, and there is always something new to learn.

Rule #10: Swallow your Pride

It is important to be a team player. In chapter four, you will see that, even though I disliked my factory job; I kept my complaints to myself. I found it easier to get through the day once I opened up and made some friends.

You will also see how I hated the idea of becoming a nanny. The last thing I wanted to do was give up my job at the hospital, leave my sister's home, and go live with another family, taking care of someone else's kids. But I never let my employer, Mrs. Silverman, know what I was thinking. I became part of the Silverman family by embracing the reality of the situation. I projected the kindness in my heart and opened up to Mrs. Silverman about my aspirations for the future. But I worked hard to make sure their children were well cared for, and, in the end, I did not just gain an employer, I gained a second family that helped me reach my goals.

4

Joining the Workforce

My first job in the United States was in a clothing factory, which required that I sit behind a machine for eight hours every day to sew two
pieces of fabric together to make a skirt. I was paid five cents per skirt. I carried
a small pink pillow to sit on, but my bum was still very sore by the end of the
shift. I was surrounded by other illegal immigrants who had no choice but to
devote hours and hours to this menial and underpaid job. With their residency
statuses in limbo, there was no other option for them. I was convinced that
I did not belong with them. In contrast to my co-workers, many who could
not return to their countries of origin, I had a choice: I could return to Haiti.
I had a country that wanted me. In Port-au-Prince, people understood me
when I spoke, and, most importantly, I was documented. Many people loved
me there. In the United States, I was still struggling with the language and had
only a small group of people I could converse with. Even after listening to my
sister's explanation—*You'll never be able to return to the United States*—I still
could not understand why I had to persevere in such a drab and back-breaking
environment when I could easily return home.

After 30 days in the factory, I made it clear to my sister that I was not going back
there to work. Once again, I resumed my babysitting duties for twenty dollars
a week. But soon, I became restless again, and impatient in the house with my
nieces. I wrote to my godmother, Lucienne, and expressed my frustration and
desire to return home. She, too, advised me against leaving America, as the
political climate in Haiti was "too risky." Ritza found me yet another factory
job, where, this time, the sewing machine was upright; I stood all day with my

right foot on the pedal, sewing zippers on suitcases. I had substituted the pain in my buttocks for the pain in my legs. In the factory, my hands grew rapidly tired of handling the zipper under the needle. I was miserable, and everything got on my nerves.

As they worked all day, some of the factory workers sweated profusely. Some of them lingered in the bathroom at the end of their shift to wash their faces and apply a lot of makeup and bright red lipstick before they went home. The funky smell was the worst—a strong mixture of perspiration and cheap perfume. The distinctive odor was nauseating. I showered as soon as I arrived home for fear that I, too, would start to carry the funk of the factory bathroom. That scent lingered in the olfactory portion of my brain for years after I left the zipper factory. I lasted two whole months there—only because I met another Haitian worker in a similar situation. Even though her father was a physician in the United States, he could not help her gain residency, because he was not an American citizen. As they say, misery loves company. Fofo and I became best friends and created a support system for one another. Although life later took us on separate paths, we have remained friends to this day: we talk on the phone, connect on social media, and even travel to see each other in person, now that our legal status has changed and that we can afford the expense of travel.

I remained undocumented for longer than I would have liked. Towards the end of my second month in the suitcase factory, the lawyer hired by my sister succeeded in obtaining a temporary work permit on my behalf, which was a great victory. Around the same time, a nurse's aide position opened at Misericordia Hospital in the Bronx, where Ritza worked in the Maternity Department. Because we lived within walking distance of the hospital, both my sister and her husband, Peter, encouraged me to apply. I already knew my way to the hospital, as I had, on numerous occasions, gone to meet my sister with the children during her lunch breaks.

"It will be safer," Peter said.

"The work will be less taxing," Ritza said. "You'll be happier." She worried a lot about the difficulties I had experienced adjusting to my new life.

Just the thought of not having to settle for another factory job gave me hope and, when Ritza arranged an interview at the hospital, I prayed with conviction for a successful outcome.

I dressed early for the appointment, elegant and industrious in a navy-blue pencil skirt, a white blouse with a floral brocade and matching cap, and a long-sleeved navy-blue jacket. I walked in confidently, ready for my first real interview and my first real job. Only when the hospital employee escorted me to the waiting area did I start to feel nervous; suddenly, my hands were sweating, and my mind wandered between the funky smell of the factory bathroom and that of the hospital—each a distinct aroma that carried a weight of hope and disappointment.

A very tall, very big white man in a dark gray striped suit invited me into his office. He sat in a plush chair behind a beautiful mahogany desk, and I pulled one of the two chairs in front of his desk to sit down across from him. I answered all his questions as well as I could and left the interview quite proud of myself.

"I nailed it," I told Peter when I got home. "I can't wait to start my nurse's aide position in the nursery of that big and beautiful hospital."

Later in the day, I received a call from my sister. She was still at work, and I thought she might be calling to congratulate me.

"Sol," she said, calling me by my *petit nom d'amour*—the endearing nickname she often used. "You did not get the job."

My disappointment at the news made me scream. "Why?" I did not understand.

"The director asked you to close the door behind you when you walked into his office," she explained. "Instead, you sat down. He feels that, even though you will not be talking to the babies in the nursery, you need to speak enough English to be able to converse with the mothers in the postpartum unit."

What a blow! It seemed that I was faced with only two choices: either go back to the factory or return to Haiti.

I cried for hours. Stopped. Cried a little bit more. Fell asleep, exhausted, only to wake up in tears again. The pity party lasted for several days—until I found, deep within myself, the resolve to make the firm decision that would change the rest of my life forever: I decided to be successful in all endeavors, regardless of the degree of difficulty. Yes, I realized that I had a mountain to climb. Yes, I was ready for the challenge. I knew that nothing would come easily, but I promised myself to get a handle on my own life. I had to grow up fast. No more sitting around feeling sorry for myself. I had things to achieve.

My first plan of action was to learn enough English to pass my next interview.

"We'll continue to support you until you find something," Ritza said with a hug. "You're still our favorite babysitter. Our 20-dollars-a-week arrangement still stands."

For the next two months, I stayed home to care for my nieces. This time, something was different: I actively focused on learning English while watching children's programs on television; also, instead of speaking French or Haitian Creole, I made a conscious effort to use English when addressing my two nieces, my sister, and my brother-in-law, and I studied day and night. By the time another nurse's aide position opened, I had mastered enough of the English language to successfully pass my second interview with the same director who had passed me over previously.

I was welcomed into the preemie nursery at Misericordia—the youngest person on staff working the graveyard shift and, before long, the darling of the other workers.

My primary responsibilities involved cleaning and feeding the babies and taking them to their mothers in the postpartum unit at visiting time. Many of these younger mothers, in search of a name for their daughters, were fascinated by *Solange*, which they found unique and original. While this name was practically unheard of in the United States, it was quite commonplace in Haiti—so popular, in fact, that on average there could be three to four Solanges in a room at a time. As a youngster in Port-au-Prince, I hated my name, and often complained to my mother: "It's so common. Why did Lucienne choose it?" There were at least two other girls with this name in my class. It was so common that, when applying for my passport to travel to the United States, I had added an "s" at the end of it, to distinguish myself from all the other girls also named *Solange*. It was not until I started working at the hospital that I came to like my name. Besides, the extra letter gave it an edge.

I thoroughly enjoyed working at the hospital. I fell in love with the babies and I loved to dress in my white nurse's aide uniform. At home, I often wore my sister's nursing cap in front of the mirror and daydreamed about becoming a registered nurse someday. Or even a doctor. Even though the reality of this dream seemed out of reach, I was convinced that, like a turtle, I must stick my head out of my shell in order to move forward. Slowly and deliberately, I was focused on the word *success*. Oh, so focused!

Someone was yelling my name—breaking the silence in the preemie nursery.

It was one o'clock in the morning, and I had fallen sound asleep in the nurse's lounge during my break.

One of the nurses on duty during the graveyard shift barged in. She found me in a stupor, my eyes crusty with sleep.

"There you are," she said. She had been looking for me persistently. "You must come quickly!"

I jumped to my feet, still half-asleep. "What is going on?"

"Come, come!" the nurse insisted as she led me to a glass window in the nursery.

And there it was.

My first snow.

The streets, the trees, the cars, the buildings … all covered with white snow. I had never seen anything like it before. It was magical. Everything looked soft and shimmery and twinkling from the streetlights refracting through the falling snowflakes.

The staff laughed at the awe they read on my face. I thought it was so beautiful and yet overwhelming. I was both excited and a little bit frightened at the sight of this white winter wonderland. How would I get home? I could not imagine walking in the snow. Thankfully, my sister came the rescue. She arrived for work earlier than usual, at the end of my shift, and we met for breakfast at the hospital coffee shop. She had brought me a pair of boots.

She convinced me to get home by foot. "I just walked in the snow myself," she said.

So, I did. I walked home and played in the snow all the way there, thinking how much happier I was working at the hospital than in the brutal environment at the factory. My current salary was excellent in comparison to that of the factory jobs, and I received health insurance and other benefits from the hospital. My English skills had greatly improved, even though I still had a very strong Haitian accent that made it a little difficult for others to understand me.

I was learning to navigate trials and tribulations.

Life was getting better.

A big chunk of my paycheck went to my sister so that her lawyer could finally get me a permanent residency visa. I was very intimidated by the lawyer, Mr. Rozensky, a big white man who looked just like Buddha. In fact, on his desk stood a statue of Buddha and, as I sat across from him, my eyes often went from his face to the statue. *Uncanny,* I thought. The man stared at me the whole time he was addressing my sister.

During one of our visits, in a very soft voice that did not fit the size of his body, Mr. Rozensky said, "I have bad news."

We froze. Ritza was petitioning as my sponsor with the Immigration and Naturalization bureau and, at this juncture, I sometimes felt that my very existence as a human being had become an accumulation of obstacles and challenges to overcome.

Directly addressing my sister—but still studying me—he continued, "Immigration rejected your petition because you are not an American citizen."

"What?" my sister said, defeated. "Does this mean that Solanges has to go back to Haiti?"

A tear rolled down my cheek.

"Yes," Mr. Rozensky said, "unless … " He took a deep breath. By then, I was sobbing. He continued, "Unless she agrees to what I'm about to propose."

Ritza frowned. "And what is that?"

"Leave it up to me," the big lawyer said. "I will help her."

"How?" my sister insisted.

"She will have to work as a housekeeper for an American family. They will petition for her visa." The big lawyer appeared sincere in his desire to help, seeing how disappointed we were with his news that Ritza's sponsor petition had fallen through. "I will work on it, and I will call you," he said.

We left his office in a state of shock and took the subway home. As no words were exchanged between us, the ride seemed much longer than it ever had before. I did not want to leave my babies at the nursery, and the thought of working as a housekeeper gave me palpitations. Such a title, I believed, came with a loss of identity: I would be surrendering my pride to clean a stranger's soiled toilet, pull out hair stuck in the shower drain, and wash stained underwear. Because I had grown up around housekeepers and *restavèks* (servants) in my parent's home, I understood power structure. Ambroise had impregnated one of my mother's live-in maids. She probably could not have declined if she wanted to; he had all the power in that liaison. How do you say no when you are between a rock and a hard place? This job was terrifying … and beneath me.

The *restavèks* were at the very bottom of the food chain, and I did not want to become one of them. When I was in high school, a young servant named Ti Carmen carried my midday meal to the school each day, so that I would not have to walk home at lunch time, only to return to the school once again for afternoon classes. *Ti* meant small, irrelevant—invisible. Ti Carmen and I were about the same age, but we belonged to different worlds. She might have had dreams; she never shared them with me. Even if she did want a better life for herself, any dreams she had would be stifled by the many needs of others, including my own. For the rest of her life. I used to think about it as the *restavèk* unfolded a white linen tablecloth on the teacher's desk to set my plate and silverware; she then opened the four-compartment stainless steel container and served my food to me. At times, I shared my meal with my best friend Claudette who also stayed at school during lunchtime, but whose family was too poor to provide her with an afternoon meal, let alone with the services of a *restavèk*. As Claudette and I ate, Ti Carmen watched silently, and I realized now that not once had I offered her any food. When we were through eating, the *restavèk* cleaned up and walked back home with the empty food basket.

Maybe I was paying for my parents' sins, for my country's sins—for the abuses of a system that required lifelong servitude for so many.

"You're no longer in high school," Ritza reminded me when we reached home. "You're a young woman, and you need to take charge of your life. If it takes cleaning up houses to get your green card, so be it."

Working as *restavèk*, a servant, a maid? *No,* I thought. *This can't be for me. Not for this girl.* Returning to Haiti had never been so appealing.

I went straight to bed, since I had worked the night shift and needed to rest before returning to the hospital. In my room, I prayed fervently to the Immaculate Conception, the mother of Jesus, who had helped me through all my prior challenges. I fell asleep in prayer and in tears.

Waiting for a phone call from the lawyer was agonizing.

We did not hear from Mr. Rozensky for days, then for weeks, and then not for a couple of months.

Finally, one day, my sister heard from "the big lawyer," which was how we both referred to him. "He wants us to come to his office. He has a family he wants us to meet next week."

The Sunday prior to the appointment, my sister and I attended church together, as Haitians believe that prayer helps them in overcoming all obstacles. After Mass, we stopped for a meal at a restaurant to discuss "going forward with my immigration problem." The dilemma was taking its toll on me. A final decision still needed to be made: Would I agree to become a live-in maid in a stranger's home—a Ti Carmen of sorts?

At that point, I was way past the stage of denial. I was floating somewhere between anger and bargaining. Stubbornly, I said, "I do not have any *immigration problem.* I'm going back to Haiti. I have made up my mind—and you need to help me get back there." My voice had an edge to it. I could barely keep my ambivalent emotions in check. I was confused, and I was a wreck.

My sister could not bear the thought of my return to Haiti, where young women were getting raped, and others thrown to jail for speaking their minds. Ambroise and Francesca were adamant: their Solanges was not to return home. My godmother and my sister agreed with my parents.

"Everyone is trying to find a way out of there," Ritza said. "Don't be ungrateful."

I had to admit that the thought of returning to Haiti had become painful to me as well. I had established roots at the hospital, doing a job I loved: caring for the babies. I would miss my friend Fofo from the factory, my two nieces, and Ritza and Peter. Going back meant leaving them all behind.

"Mr. Rozensky says that it's a nice family," Ritza said, "and they're willing to sponsor your visa."

As Ritza awaited my response, the silence between us became deafening. I continued sipping my coffee but did not make eye contact with my sister.

"So, what do you think?" She spoke softly. "Will you say yes to them?"

Still without lifting my head, I asked, "When?" I imagined myself on all fours, scrubbing mold, mildew, and someone else's dead skin and pubic hair from a tub.

"Tomorrow," my sister said.

"What? Tomorrow? What do you mean, tomorrow? Already?" I was talking louder than my sister had ever heard me speak in public. Caught up in the moment, I had forgotten we were surrounded by people trying to eat their Sunday meals in peace.

With a very gentle voice, careful with her every word, my sister tried to assuage my anxiety. "You are not going to work tomorrow. You are going to meet the family at the big lawyer's office."

We were quiet once again, as I needed to digest what I was hearing.

"Can we go home now?" I asked, reverting to a conflict-avoidance approach. I lifted my head to make eye contact with her. "I'm finished eating."

"I have to pay the bill," Ritza replied in a stern voice.

She understood my reticence, and I would learn later that she, too, was struggling with the idea of her little sister in servitude in a stranger's home. Just like me, she imagined the back-breaking work, the disrespect, the lustful stares. She was working very hard at hiding those feelings, however, in order to make it less painful for her baby sister.

The ride home from the restaurant was another silent trip. There was no more discussion about the meeting. When we arrived home, I played with my nieces, then returned to my room where I wrote a letter to my parents, expressing my pain and sadness.

Just before bed time, I went to talk to Ritza who had already retired to her room, getting ready to end her day.

"At what time is the meeting?" I asked. The edge had returned to my voice.

"One o'clock."

"One o'clock? Aren't you working tomorrow?" I asked angrily.

"I took the day off so that I could take you to the meeting."

My eyes, I knew, were throwing daggers. "So, you really want to get rid of me, right? You want me to get out of your house. Is that it? Is that what you want?

You want me to be a domestic?" I was crying with the grief of someone who had lost a parent. It felt that painful.

Because she was a nurse, my sister understood my need to grieve and to vent. She allowed me to have my temper tantrum, before she held me against her chest. When I finally calmed down, we sat on her bed to discuss the departure time and what I should wear. We agreed that I should not accept the job if either of us did not feel comfortable during the interview with the family.

In the lawyer's waiting room, in order to calm my nerves, I listened to my sister make small talk with a young, pretty woman with blond hair and shockingly beautiful blue eyes. Dressed in a designer pantsuit and high-heeled shoes, she reminded me very much of my godmother Lucienne. The receptionist escorted her in first, and Ritza and I continued to wait our turn. To my surprise, when we entered Mr. Rozensky's office, the woman with the blue eyes was waiting for us. We were then formally introduced. The woman's name was Mrs. Silverman, and her family needed my help.

Ritza, the lawyer, and Mrs. Silverman did all the talking, while I sat there, mesmerized by the woman's beauty and classy look, wondering whether she was as nice as she appeared—maybe even as nice as my godmother. I was staring at her, and I could tell that she wanted to talk to me, but I was embarrassed by my heavy Haitian accent and afraid of saying the wrong thing. Because of my enduring limitations with the English language, I missed the meaning of some of the conversation. What was clear to me, however, was that my sister was comfortable, not only with the lady herself but also with the arrangements that were being made. On numerous occasions, Ritza turned towards me to nod or to explain a few details in Haitian Creole. She wanted to make sure that I agreed with some of the collective decisions.

At the conclusion of the meeting, we agreed that I would visit the woman's house and meet the children before I accepted the position. Due to my sister's demanding schedule at the hospital, the visit would not happen for another few days, when Ritza was off from work. We would make the trip together, as I did not know my way around New York and had difficulty navigating the city's transit system. In any case, my protective sister would never have let me go alone.

The train ride home was a much happier trip than the previous ones. I learned that I was not going to be a domestic after all. By our own standards, this family was terribly rich ("*Very, very* rich," Ritza said,) and a woman named Pearl was already in charge of cleaning the house. Another employee came in for the laundry. It all sounded like my prayers were being answered: No more talk of *restavèk*—a term that was still offensive to the ambitious, goal-oriented young adult. I considered myself to be a visionary and a dreamer. My job would be to look after the family's two children: a daughter who was almost three years old, and a son who was almost two. I would be their "nanny," a term that was new to my vocabulary. The angel of the sun would bring a lot of warmth to two little children.

This time, Ritza and I were both animated as my sister recapped, in both French and Haitian Creole, what I might have missed during the conversation. She repeated all that was said in the lawyer's office in an attempt to fill in the gaps. We talked nonstop the entire ride from Manhattan to the Bronx, where we lived. This time, the trip seemed to go by very quickly. My sister had such joy in her voice. She was smiling broadly, and I knew that she felt great relief, as my "illegal" status in the country had been nothing but a burden. Mr. and Mrs. Silverman were willing—and able—to complete all the requirements, so that I would become a permanent resident of the United States of America. No more talk of my "immigration problem." For too long, I had been living in fear of being deported by Immigration and Naturalization Services—a fear that had been very real in my mind. So many nights I had imagined uniformed officers barging into the apartment with batons and handcuffs, ready to deport me, forcing me to return to Haiti with the threat of the "Tonton Macoutes" of President Duvalier.

I was all smiles, beaming from ear to ear.

On a Sunday morning, my sister and I took two different trains to 34th Street in Manhattan, and then traveled to the Greyhound bus station. We had never taken this particular trip before: we were on our way to East Orange, in New Jersey, to meet the rest of the Silverman family. It was a bright and sunny day, and the bus was gigantic. With more than 50 passengers, the vehicle had a restroom, which was another first for me. I never imagined that a bus could be equipped with a toilet. I did not understand the mechanism: Where did the stool go? I thought it was weird and had difficulty comprehending the process.

The bus ride seemed endless. I was eager to reach our destination. Once we exited the highway and started making a few stops, the environment changed. Even though the bus was traveling on the main road, I could not help but notice and appreciate the side streets with their majestic oak trees and their beautiful houses with gardens of magnolias and tulips. When the driver announced, "Ardmore Road," I checked the address on the piece of paper I carried in my purse. It was our turn to exit the bus. We had arrived at our destination.

I was nervous as we set out on Ardmore Road. It was spring, and the grass was green, the lawns beautifully manicured, and the violets were in full bloom. Ritza and I were a bit overwhelmed by the sight. The enormous houses were detached and fancy, with two-car garages. I thought about the tall buildings of the Bronx—about the dry asphalt, the lack of greenery and flowers. And, oh, the noise! The buses. The trains. The never-ending chatter. By contrast, Ardmore Road was deserted, except for a car or two that passed quietly by us on occasion. A truly different world. My head was spinning. I thought about my grandmother's house on Rue Magloire Ambroise, about my parents' house on Jean-Jacques Dessalines Boulevard, about Lucienne's "château" in Lalue and about Ritza's apartment in New York. Nothing compared to East Orange, New Jersey. We stood in awe on the street outside the lovely Dutch colonial home that bore the number 12. It was surrounded by perennials and bluestars. I was asking myself, *Is this really the house?*

I was still gathering the courage to climb the steps and ring the bell when the door opened. Beset by a nervous excitement, the lady of the house had been seated by the large bay window in the kitchen, looking out for us, "the sisters." Mrs. Silverman had prepared the children for our arrival, and they, too, were excited. There was a warm feeling about the foyer. The Silvermans seemed so happy to see us. The spacious room was bright and featured hardwood floors and a gorgeous stone fireplace. It was generously furnished with a large sofa, a large television, several chairs, a coffee table, and two side tables that held intricate lamps and beautifully framed pictures of the two children—Jodi and Jeffrey.

After the mother introduced us to the children, she took us on a tour of the house, a perfect mix of old and new. I was not to live in a shack, like the senator's help did in Haiti; instead, my living quarters were inside the main house, which had so much class, it reminded me of my godmother's home. As

I looked around, I caught myself daydreaming. I imagined owning a big house just like this one, or just like my godmother's. *One day,* I thought. *There is time. I'm barely 20 years old.* In the meantime, I was in awe at being so lucky to even live and work in such a beautiful home. I would use the experience I had gained caring for my nieces and look after the Silverman children. The family, I knew, would adore me. How lucky was I to land this job? Forgotten were my fears that working for the Silvermans would turn me into a *restavèk.* I would be a princess in her castle. Twice a week, in the evening, the driver would take me to school for an English class. The Silvermans were also willing to pay for driving school. The stars were once again aligned for this little angel of the sun.

"Of course, your room and board will be free," Mrs. Silverman explained.

So, my expenses would be minimal. *What a great deal,* I thought. I would be paid $50 a week, which made me happy, as I was eager to contribute to the money that my sister sent home to support our family in Haiti. Ritza and I had discussed the possibility of assisting some of our siblings in immigrating to the United States as well. The focus right now, of course, was on my own status, but Mr. Rozensky had convinced us that this arrangement with the Silverman family was the best way for me to get my green card. I finally felt relaxed, and almost at home.

The Silverman children were very warm towards me, even though I was a stranger to them. The boy, Jeffrey, wearing only a diaper, was much too young to figure out who I was or take part in any conversation. The little girl, Jodi, stayed very close to her mother and, at times, as she was carried with her arm around her mom's neck, she whispered in the young mother's ear. After one of those long whispers, the mother said to her baby girl, "Can you say *Solanges?*" Jodi shook her head from side to side. No. It was obvious to all of us that this name was too difficult.

Mrs. Silverman then said, "So, what should we call her? She's coming to live with us, you know."

"Kiki," the little girl said. She was so beautiful with her curly blond hair.

And from that point on, everyone in East Orange would come to know the new nanny as "Kiki."

Although I worried that, with the name Kiki, the angel of the sun would lose part of her identity, I basked in the mutual sense of acceptance in East Orange, a sense that this might work out. The little girl wanted her Kiki to stay and play with her that day, which made the mother very happy. When Mrs. Silverman looked at me, her blue eyes were full of hope. "Kiki will return soon," she said.

Indeed, I would. There was a lot of paperwork to be completed and processed, but I had made up my mind. I could not move in that day. Before I could move to New Jersey and work as a live-in nanny, I had to formally resign from Misericordia Hospital.

Pearl, the housekeeper, came every Tuesday and Thursday. In addition to cleaning the house, she sometimes cooked dinner, depending on the activities the Silverman family had carefully planned. Then, there was Sarah, who came in to do the laundry; she was very organized and meticulously arranged the clean garments in the large closets and drawers. Paul, the driver, reminded me of stories my father often told me, about his days as the senator's chauffeur. Dressed impeccably in a black uniform and a black hat, Paul sat behind the wheel of a black town car, ready to take us on outings. The Silvermans and I often had dinner at renowned restaurants; I met many famous actors and actresses at the country club, where membership was synonymous with money, and I managed to even have my picture taken with a few of them, albeit in my white nanny uniform. There I was, blending with all the servants at the club, but also people watching. I was not born rich but, in this job, I learned how the rich live and about their powerful connections. Paul also took us to the airport, as the family traveled to many beautiful resorts and stayed at five-star hotels. On all these trips, the nanny from Haiti, who was still learning the English language, "Kiki" was the perfect addition to the family. They took me everywhere they traveled with the children. The kids loved their Kiki so much that they no longer cried when Mr. and Mrs. Silverman left for the day. Instead, they happily waved and threw goodbye kisses at their parents.

Mr. Silverman was as much fun as the children. He was very playful and participated in our games when he was not at work. On one of the trips at the Diplomat Hotel in Miami, he purchased water guns for us all. As we returned to the hotel from the beach, a water-gun fight erupted, with everyone shooting at each other and running all over the suite. Cornered by the children's father on the balcony of the hotel suite, I was being soaked with water. My own gun emptied, I was defenseless. The more I screamed, asking him to stop, the more he laughed hysterically and continued to shoot at me playfully. When his gun finally ran out of water, I ran past him, straight to my bathroom, slammed the door and started to cry. I did not know where the anger and sadness came from, but I was livid.

When the children realized that their Kiki was crying, they called their mother, who came to the locked door. "Kiki, Kiki, come out. I still have my gun. Let's go get him."

But I refused. This reaction was very unusual. I had always been a good sport with their rambunctious games. I guess I missed the Bronx. I missed my family in Haiti. I missed my godmother. It was all of it.

Mrs. Silverman was now screaming at her husband. "What did you do to her? What did you do?"

The father was, I assumed, in a state of shock, baffled by my unexpected behavior. He must also have been mortified to think he had somehow hurt me.

After I showered and changed into my house robe, I finally came out to have dinner in the suite with the children, as the parents were ready to go out on a date. To my surprise, before they left, Mr. Silverman handed me a package. He had gone down to the gift shop while I was getting ready. Wrapped in the box was a beautiful gold and rhinestone necklace, with matching earrings. He apologized for upsetting me. He admitted that he was having so much fun that he did not realize that I was no longer playing. The Silvermans were in their thirties, and I was in my early twenties. The truth is, in that household, we were all kids at heart—or by age—having fun. They often played loud music and the five of us ran all over the house, chasing each other and dancing to the beat.

One day, at breakfast, I learned that a third child was on the way.

"It's all because you're our nanny, Solanges," Mrs. Silverman said. "You've created such a great atmosphere in the house that we've been encouraged to have another child."

One year had passed. A second year was nearly ending. The finalization of my residency papers was taking longer than I expected, and just the idea of not being a resident in the country continued to be an issue for me.

"I love taking care of the kids," I told Mrs. Silverman. "But I hope you understand that, as happy as I am here, I do not see myself as a nanny for life."

"Of course," she said. "Tell me about what you want."

As a teenager, I had had multiple goals and aspirations. At one point, I wanted to be an airline stewardess. I had no idea what the duties entailed, but I knew that flight attendants were respected in Haiti. I loved their uniforms, particularly the hat and the gloves, and I wanted to fly all over the world. "This position is no more than a glorified maid," my godmother had said, discouraging. "You're smart. You should aim for a real career." And now, after spending time at the hospital as a nurse's aide in the preemie nursery and interacting with the registered nurses, I thought that nursing could be a career path for me. I wondered: were nurses glorified maids as well? Was a nanny a glorified maid? As a young adult looking ahead at my future, I had many questions.

Whatever I chose as a career, I knew that my primary focus had to remain on helping my family back in Haiti. I had been committed to them from the time I was in utero, when my father had met Lucienne who would eventually become my godmother and a major support to the young couple with numerous children. Once I started to work, I would make it a point to continuously provide for the sisters and brothers who still lived in Haiti. My sister Ritza had helped me; I was now eager to help my second oldest sister, Paulette. She was married with children, and she hoped to one day leave Haiti for the United States, in search of a better life.

Mrs. Silverman listened to all this, nodding as I made it clear: legal residency would allow me to attend school and be on my way to meeting my goal, becoming a registered nurse. In the meantime, I was content with my life in East Orange with the Silvermans. At this point in the relationship, I was more like family than an employee, and Mrs. Silverman promised that she, herself, would drive me to the pre-entrance exam once the time came for me to apply to nursing school.

And she kept her promise.

My second year as a nanny ended and, as the third year began, all my paperwork had been processed. I obtained my residency, something that I had been waiting for since my arrival to the United States. What a glorious moment! With my green card in hand, I could live without fear of deportation. I was free to travel back to Haiti to visit my family and friends, and I could finally attend nursing school.

MAKE IT WORK FOR YOU!

Rule #9: Value Hard Work and Education

Reflection: Hard Lessons Build Muscle

When baby sea turtles first hatch from their shells, they are still too weak to swim. They MUST make the perilous journey across the sand to the beach to build the muscle they will need to survive in the open water. They have to fight the waves crashing against the shoreline to reach deep water and begin their migrations. Otherwise, the very ocean that they are struggling to reach will kill them. Turtles *must* struggle in order to be strong enough to survive.

- Journal it: make a list of your proudest accomplishments. Pick ones that did not come easily. What held you back from achieving them? Next to each of those accomplishments, jot down a few of the skills you developed. How were you stronger as a result of the lessons you learned?

- Find a new skill you would like to learn and sign up for a class in your community. It does not have to be related to your career goals. Maybe you always wanted to learn how to make pottery or paint. Try something new, such as learning to perform CPR or to dance salsa. The point is to show yourself that, once you struggle with the new skill, it becomes easy with practice.

Rule# 10: Swallow Your Pride

Reflection: Go with the Flow!

A turtle's hard shell protects its tender parts. From the outside, a tucked-in turtle looks like a pretty painted rock to a predator, though, inside the shell, the turtle may be filled with fear. It is all contained inside an impenetrable carapace. Turtles also allow themselves to move with the currents instead of expending valuable energy fighting against it. Follow the waters that make you feel warm, and do not be too afraid of getting swept into the flow!

- The next time you are invited somewhere (maybe a party with people you do not know) and you have doubts about attending, take a deep breath and let it out. Shake your arms and legs and imagine all the anxiety is leaving your body. Remind yourself that you can always leave if it gets dicey. But, also, remind yourself that you never know who you might meet if you go. Opportunity is all around you.

- Journal it: think of an occasion where you took a risk and the end result was not as bad as you imagined it would be. It might be something like sticking up for someone who was bullied in middle school, or getting over your fear of jumping from the high dive at the community pool. Feel free to write about the experience. How did the initial dread feel in your body? How did accomplishment feel once you did it despite the dread? What did you learn from the experience?

RULES TO LIVE BY

In chapter five, you will read about an assault I suffered by a man I believed I could trust; he held tremendous power and used it to his advantage against me. I shook that off and put it behind me, because I had reached my goal of attending nursing school, and nothing was going to stop me once I got there. I learned to protect myself, but I also learned to open up, make new friends, and take some calculated risks for my own health and wellbeing.

Rule #11: Take Calculated Risks

If it does not harm anyone else, and the stakes are high, it is sometimes wise to break the rules. You will read in chapter five about how I broke one of the rules at the Manhattan State Hospital School of Nursing. I could have gotten into a lot of trouble if I had been caught cooking in the dorm, but my health was at stake, so I knew that the rules had to be broken in that instance. Throughout my life, I have had to take calculated risks. It is always smart to weigh the risks and act wisely. You will read much later in the book about how my friend Ana called me out of the blue from an airport one night, asking if I was interested in becoming part owner in a hospital on the verge of bankruptcy (see chapter 15, "Out of My Way"). A lot of people would have laughed her off and hung up the phone. I did not. I listened to what she had to say, got some advice from people I trusted, and went with my gut. I bought into the hospital, and, a few years later, we made a small fortune when the hospital sold at a profit. It was a risk that paid off.

5

Nursing School

With the assistance of the Silvermans, I found a family willing to fill out the immigration paperwork that would allow my sister Paulette and her husband Emanuel to enter the United States legally. To handle Paulette's application, I hired the same big lawyer who had been so instrumental in securing my green card. I made several trips to Mr. Rozensky's office in Manhattan to discuss my sister's status and to deliver or collect the completed petition forms the family needed to sign. During one of those visits, I sat in the waiting room for more than an hour, because, according to his secretary, Mr. Rozensky was very busy. It was midday when he finally popped out of his office and apologized for having me wait for so long.

He said, "I have to go to lunch. Come. Let's go get something to eat."

I followed him to the elevator, and then to the street. There were many restaurants by the office, but the lawyer did not seem interested in any of them. He walked with a purpose and a direction I could not have fathomed at the time. As we talked about my family in Haiti, about Paulette, and the Silvermans, we walked for a couple of blocks, then turned on some of the side streets. We reached a semi-residential neighborhood, and, by then, I had no idea where we were in relation to his office. We entered a building, and it was not until he opened the door of this first-floor apartment that I realized that we were in his personal unit. Apparently, going to a restaurant had never been the plan. It became obvious to me that he had anticipated coming to his apartment for lunch, and he planned to have company. In his refrigerator were some pre-made sandwiches which he quickly placed on his dining room table with two cans of coke and a couple of glasses. Looking back now, I can see the way he had set things up for what transpired that afternoon, but at the time, I was blindsided by what he had planned for me.

He stared at me, as he did whenever I met with him in the presence of my sister, before I could even understand the conversations. I had always been intimidated by Mr. Rozensky—he held my fate in his hands—but I looked up to him. I could have never guessed he would use his power against me. He had acted as my protector in the past by securing me a welcome place to work. To me, he had always been the "big lawyer" who helped me with my "immigration problem," my savior, someone I respected. The way I saw him, he had the appearance of a Buddha. He was nearly identical to the placid statue he kept on his desk. His voice had always been soft, out of place with how large he was physically. He had taken care of my legal issues and placed me with the Silvermans, who had taken me in as part of the family and had been instrumental in helping me build a good life in the United States. I had no reason not to trust him. I did not know what to do but to follow his directives. I could have left right away, but I did not even know how to return to his office. Besides, we needed to discuss Paulette's future. She was the mother of three young children and so desperate to leave Haiti.

So, I agreed to eat lunch with him and, when it was time to return to his office, instead, he forced me into a bedroom and proceeded to rape me on a waterbed. It all seemed to change so quickly. One minute, we were eating. The next, I was pinned under him on the bed. All the while, he kept on saying, "You are so young. You are so beautiful. You are so firm." I closed my eyes, felt every violation expand into the next until he was done and quiet. The incident left me screaming inside.

I was still trying to understand what had just happened when I heard the zing of a man zipping up his pants. He warned me against ever discussing the event with anyone. He was a powerful man, he reminded me, and the fate of my sister Paulette and her family were in his hands. And I believed him. After what he had just done to me, who knew what else he was capable of? Bruised in places I could easily cover, I followed him back into the streets, until everything around me again was familiar. I was not only young, I was also very naïve:

never in a million years would I have imagined that this man could ever hurt me. I will never comprehend why he did that to me.

I never did tell anyone. Women are sexually abused by powerful men and forced into submission for many reasons. In my case, I kept silent because of my fear of deportation, since my papers were not yet final when the incident took place. I kept silent, because I needed him to finish Paulette's papers. I kept silent, because the irony of my situation was not lost on me: I had come to the United States to escape the threat of the depraved "Tonton Macoutes," well known for their sex crimes, only to meet Mr. Rozensky, who behaved just as brutally. He knew my situation, and he took advantage of it. The lawyer haunted my nightmares and, in my feverish sleep, I relived the event over and over. In the morning, the memory turned my stomach, and I found myself hurling into the toilet. There was only one way I could describe the mental anguish: an ache so empty it wanted to explode, so full it wanted to swallow me whole.

When I saw Mr. Rozensky again about Paulette, we acted as if nothing had happened. He was very professional, and I was determined not to allow the incident to ever play a negative role in my life. I decided to block it out and move on. My goal was to help my sister enter the United States legally, and Mr. Rozensky was successful in helping her gain permanent residency. It was all that mattered, and I was glad. Mission accomplished: my sister Paulette and her husband arrived in New Jersey in 1967, and I was close to family once again. I no longer felt alone. Unfortunately, I had paid a hefty price for this transaction. The experience left a deep internal scar, and I have kept this secret from everyone—until now.

These days, it is much easier for women to come out about abuse, not that it is ever easy, but we have made a lot of progress since I was raped. Today, at 73, I can finally feel vindicated by the brave women speaking truth about the abuse they have suffered at the hands of powerful men. I have been watching the media coverage of the Me Too movement, and those voices often feel like my voice, speaking—no, roaring—out of silence and indignation at the injustice of being made to feel powerless and trapped in fear. I know the plight of violated women. I know the mental anguish of immigration. At least, in America, there is hope: we are not stifled in a culture that has no intention of changing. We go on, sometimes, when there is no alternative, and I was helpless to change what had happened to me, but I was not about to let it hold me back. Head out of my shell, like a slow turtle, one step at a time, I moved past it. But I never forgot.

As fate would have it or, should I say, as the stars once again aligned in my favor, I struck gold.

On a bus to visit Ritza in the Bronx, I sat next to a lady who seemed to be of Caribbean descent. She was intrigued by my air of strength and superiority. On the hour-long ride to New York City, we shared life stories and pledged to become friends, since we were both nannies working within walking distance from each other. As friends, Erith and I pledged to attend nursing school together, and we worked very hard toward that goal. Eventually, we applied to the same institution and were accepted into a three-year diploma program at the Manhattan State Hospital School of Nursing in Manhattan, New York. I was ready to start the next chapter of my life: that of a student of the science of nursing.

On a clear Sunday morning, the Silvermans drove me to Manhattan. It was a glorious day, one that I had been waiting on for a long time: Finally, I was moving into the nursing school dormitory. A warm feeling in my heart was pouring out from my pores, like steam escaping from a chimney. My dream to become a nurse was about to begin, and Mr. and Mrs. Silverman were in the grip of strong emotions, as though they were taking their firstborn to college. It was an exciting moment, but one tinged with sadness, too. Jodi and Jeffrey were also very sad that their Kiki was leaving them. I promised to visit whenever I was not at school, and they promised to keep my suite at the house available.

I must admit, in the midst of all this joy, I was a bit anxious and apprehensive, as I had no idea what to expect or what the future held. During that transition, I often reflected on how lucky I was to have found a family as gracious and generous as the Silvermans in my time of need. It has been said that you reap what you sow: I am thankful to my dad for having been such a gracious man to a stranger in the night. His gesture of kindness yielded a healthy, positive and nurturing relationship between Ambroise and Lucienne's families, and it all had a domino effect that tumbled into my life and shaped the positive direction it had taken.

Cars were parked everywhere as students, parents, spouses, and friends arrived at the school. It was a bit chaotic, all hustle and bustle of parents and students rushing by, trying to find their way around. It was overwhelming for this small-framed Haitian girl; I found myself moving slowly down the hall, through all the chaos around me, making my way to the housemother, an older woman on the plump side, with short, salt-and-pepper hair, light skin, and a very stern face. The housemother stood at the entrance, directing students to their rooms. As I walked down the hallway, after getting my room number (202), I spotted Erith from New Jersey. Seeing a familiar face brought me joy. She was still in line to get her room assignment, and I waved frantically.

"Where are you?" I asked Erith the minute she got off the line.

"Second floor," she said. Then, she announced her room number: also 202.

We dropped our bags to the floor, ran towards each other, hugged, and jumped up and down, screaming so loudly that we attracted the attention of the other students. They looked at us with envy; Erith and I had been assigned to the same floor and to the same room, a request that neither of us had made. Once again, my luck was right on point. I would have a good friend close by to keep me company and help me figure out how to proceed through the daunting task of fitting into this new environment. We shared the same front door. Beyond the door, the suite was separated in two individual rooms—mine to the right, and Erith's to the left—with a shared bathroom at the center of a short hallway. We quickly unpacked our bags and went to a meeting point assigned to us at registration.

The school was located in midtown Manhattan inside a psychiatric hospital. It was a state-sponsored nursing school with no tuition fees. In fact, students received a monthly stipend of fifteen dollars, which, in the late 1960s, was a lot of money for someone with no other income and no major expenses. Even the cost of books was covered by the city of New York.

There was much excitement in the auditorium as students met new faces and made new friends. The housemother served as the moderator of this quick mini orientation. The most important of all the instructions were the location of the cafeteria, the meal times, and where classes would be held the next morning. Erith and I stuck to each other like glue. As we watched other students who appeared lost and alone and sad, we felt privileged to have each other. The road ahead was not an easy one. Attending nursing school meant going through three years of intense learning and, then, after graduation, a candidate for licensure had to pass a national examination to obtain the license to practice as a registered nurse in the State of New York.

I worried that my difficulty with English as a second language would continue to be a struggle. After living in the United State for about four years, I clearly understood the language and believed that I possessed enough skills to comprehend my instructors and read the assigned material. I was confident that I could speak well, too. However, my heavy Haitian accent was an obstacle that led others to assume that I had difficulty with the English language, as they could not understand me when I spoke. In order for me to keep up my grade point average, I studied twice as hard as my friend Erith who was from an English-speaking Caribbean island. I woke up at four o'clock every morning to study before getting ready for my eight o'clock class. I was still living with my Haitian school days' mentality, convinced that I must hold a high-grade point average to be in front of the class, even though the rigid structure I was used to in Haiti was much different in the United States. It was much less competitive. None of that mattered to me. Being ahead of the class was very important to me, and I did whatever it took to be there.

If dealing with a language barrier and a demanding schedule were not hard enough, adjusting to the cafeteria food was another thorn in my side. For three years, I had been well fed in the Silverman home and, by comparison, the cafeteria food was unfit for human consumption. More often than not, dinner was a spoonful of potato salad served cold, slices of American cheese and Bologna, and a scoop of cottage cheese with two saltine crackers. The thought of eating it made my stomach turn. The white plates were clean but very dingy; they looked as though they had been washed a million times. Most times, I simply grabbed the two packets of saltine crackers for dinner and returned to my dorm room.

Because of poor food intake and sleep deprivation, I lost a lot of weight and soon developed malnutrition and dehydration. I was exhausted. Before long, I became a patient at Manhattan State Hospital, the same hospital where I was a student. The episode scared me enough to make me realize that my lifestyle had to change if I intended to complete the program and reach graduation successfully. So, I started to cook in my room, using an electric pot late at night once the housemother was not around. This was a major violation of school policy that could have resulted in my expulsion. It was, however, a risk that I was willing to take for fear of rehospitalization. I used every opportunity to visit the Silvermans in New Jersey where I was guaranteed several nourishing, well-cooked meals during my stay. Mrs. Silverman also took me to the market before dropping me off at the bus stop; she made sure that I had a big bag full of food items to take back to my dorm in order to complement whatever I did get from the school cafeteria. On the weekends, I sometimes visited my sisters and their friends to get a good meal. I did what I had to do to climb Maslow's hierarchy, since good health was vitally important, if I were to meet my goal of becoming a nurse.

Not only did life on campus become bearable, it was also enjoyable and fun. I had a great community of friends who made my life fuller and less lonely. On initiation night, I was assigned a big sister named Phillis, a senior getting ready to graduate. Phillis had a younger sister named Sue who was a freshman in my class and, since we shared the same big sister, Sue and I became good friends. Sue was tall and very skinny with striking blue eyes and a bob haircut. I could easily spot Sue, because she always wore a cap sleeve sweater for warmth and comfort, even when the temperature was too warm to wear one. She was a soft-spoken young woman with a charismatic personality and a beautiful smile. A genuinely nice person.

I also made friends with Stella, who was older than all of us freshmen and, therefore, thought it her duty to teach the "younglings" about life. She was a slim, fearless, and somewhat bossy African American woman who wore her hair permed with curls she obtained by sleeping in pink sponge curlers. In our spare time, several of the other students and I congregated in Stella's room to hear all about her sexual escapades.

Then, there was Peggy with long brown hair. She came from a rich family that lived in Upstate New York. There were those who wondered what she was doing at a school for the lower class whose families could not afford University tuition. As time passed, Peggy and I became the best of friends. She was the first to travel to Haiti on vacation with me. Yet, I still do not know why she chose that school.

Finally, there were Carlos, Perez, Colon, Terrance, Elizabeth and a few others who, together, were affectionately called "The Spanish Diaspora." Hanging out with them was a blast. This group celebrated if they passed an exam and celebrated harder when they failed an exam. They did not need an excuse for a party. They were the happy-go-lucky group that drank a lot of alcohol and smoked a lot of cigarettes and anything else that would keep them happy. Although I traveled in their pack and was considered their friend, I was careful not to participate in the drinking and smoking and returned to my dorm room well before curfew.

It was the '60s, a period characterized by afro hairdos, hot pants, hippies, loud music, late-night parties, and some promiscuity. Things were a lot wilder than what I was used to. I was no longer the naïve little angel girl from Haiti. By then, I was my own fully-grown woman, surrounded by a lot of other people whose behaviors were in contrast with the principles and manners taught to me by my godmother and Mrs. Silverman. I had been brought up to be a proper lady. My classmates thought it weird that I placed a napkin on my lap on the rare occasions that I sat down for a meal in the cafeteria. I had learned proper eating etiquette at the home of Lucienne and then, again, as a nanny for the Silverman children. My peers felt that I was just too formal. I would never use a four-letter word, which prompted Stella, the oldest classmate, to summon me to her room one day for a crash course on four-letter words. In addition, I acquired new slang terms such as "hanky panky," "busting one's cherry," and "having a quickie." I learned all kinds of things in nursing school—some of the lessons more practical than others.

The freshman class teacher, Miss Viskovish, was a tall woman with straight red hair, who wore her spectacles perched just on the tip of her pointy nose. A matronly woman, she had never been married and had no children, and the rumor on campus was that she would die a virgin. She was a Florence Nightingale-type figure and continuously reminded us that, as nurses, she expected us to always be nice but firm—a lesson that I practiced as a RN and, later, as a leader in the health care system and as a professional business woman.

Ms. Sullivan, the Dean of the school of nursing at the Manhattan State Hospital, had little faith in my ability to complete the program, because she believed that my English level was not good enough. I had a strong Haitian accent and, no matter how much fluency I had gained, people still thought that I could not speak English. At this point in my life, however, after living with a white American family and speaking only English with small children for three years, I knew that I had enough English to survive the program. I continued to apply myself and studied even harder. Ms. Sullivan was surprised when I ended my freshman year with a grade point average in the 98th percentile. She decided to send my grades to Albany, New York, along with a couple of other students', requesting that we be awarded a practical nursing license that allowed us to practice nursing without having to sit for the national examination. The practical nursing was only an entry-level license to practice nursing in the United States, however. I needed to stay in school for two more years to become a registered nurse.

My life was full of laughter and happiness, having completed the first year of my nursing program that culminated with a capping ceremony. I earned the nurse's cap that I had been dreaming of from the time I worked as a nurse's aide at the hospital—and it looked fabulous on my head. It belonged there. Ritza and Paulette both attended the ceremony, along with their husbands, several relatives, and friends. Also in attendance were the Silvermans, including the three children, who were proud to see their Kiki become a nurse. I remained a true member of the Silverman family, and they loved their Kiki so very much that nothing could have kept them from attending my capping ceremony.

My roommate Erith had traveled back to her country, the island of Antigua, to marry her high school sweetheart. Upon her return, she moved out of the dormitory to an apartment with her new husband who had joined her in the United States. I remained good friends with Erith, always happy to see her every morning in class. Sue became my new roommate and we, too, have remained friends throughout our lives.

As a licensed practical nurse at Columbus Hospital, in Manhattan, I worked the evening shift and attended my nursing classes during the day. One evening after work, I was invited to attend a wedding celebration in honor of Erith and her spouse. Erith was introducing her new husband to her family in the United States and to her close friends and classmates. Once my shift was over, I quickly wrote my report, folded my white nursing uniform, and changed into a white crop top with red embroidery, capris pants, and open-toed red pumps to attend the party. What an experience that was! It was just about midnight when I arrived at Erith's apartment. Feeling cute in my little party outfit, I was on my way to have big fun, forgetting that I had just been on my feet for an eight-hour shift. I had one glass of punch and woke up the next morning in my bed at the dorm, with a throbbing headache and no recollection of ever being at the party.

It turned out this was not any ordinary punch, but instead a Caribbean rum punch, which should have been consumed slowly and in small quantities, preferably on a full stomach. Not realizing how strong the concoction was, I had drank a water glass full of punch to quench my thirst. This was my first (and last) experience with inebriation—a lesson learned on the power of alcohol and my low tolerance of this substance. From then on, I only consumed alcohol in very small quantities, if ever. I did not enjoy the feeling of helplessness and lack of control.

As a second-year student, I had to report to the Montefiore Hospital in the Bronx for clinical practice in addition to attending my didactic classes. At the hospital, I met a Haitian physician and fell in love. Luc was already in private practice and had a beautiful house in Scarsdale, New York. He had never been married and had no children. We dated for a couple of years, and the relationship grew to the point that everyone—friends and family—would say, "Those two will be married right after her graduation." Everything seemed to me to be pointing in that direction also. I was happy, head over heels in love with a wonderful man who, it appeared, loved me back. But, sometimes, things go in a much different direction than what you expect.

I continued to have a very close relationship with my New Jersey family. One Sunday afternoon, I attended an ice-skating birthday party for their youngest daughter, Wendy. While ice skating, I fell and sustained an injury to my right arm. I was rushed to the hospital. Mr. Silverman followed the ambulance so that he could be with me in the ER while Mrs. Silverman remained at the skating arena with the birthday girl and her little friends. At the hospital, the X-ray revealed that I had sustained a fracture of the right wrist and my right arm was placed in a cast. As it turned out, Luc, my physician boyfriend, was an orthopedist in private practice; he became the primary care physician for my broken wrist.

I was distantly amicable with the office assistant at Dr. Luc's office, and our relationship grew stronger as my visits became more frequent during the time Luc was caring for my broken wrist. When I came in for my last official appointment on cast-removal day, I was in a great mood, almost euphoric about my freedom from the cast. The recovery from this broken arm had been very difficult, because I am right-handed. It was with great struggle that I managed to meet my activities of daily living.

After I greeted the secretary, we engaged in small talk. She casually asked, "Are you going to Doc's wedding tomorrow?"

What? Luc is getting married? To whom? He hasn't proposed to me yet. The news came as a shock to say the least. I automatically went into self-defense mode and showed no emotion. Without blinking an eye, I told a bold lie. "I will have to miss it. I'm part of my girlfriend's bridal party." Like a real trooper, I held my composure, with many questions still running through my mind.

How in the world was he about to marry another woman when he was still acting as though he was in love with me? He was at my apartment last night … How come he did not have the courage to tell me that our relationship was over? What was he thinking? Was it his plan to have a wife and a girlfriend?

I walked away from her desk to sit in the waiting area until it was my turn to see the doctor. Truth be told, I was in a state of shock. My heart was pounding rapidly, and my hands were shaking. But I did not want to give away to the secretary that she had just broken the news of my boyfriend's impending marriage.

I was confused, hurt, and angry all at once. However, I decided not to let him know right away that I was aware of his secret. As he removed the cast, we talked casually, and never did I let him know that I knew of his wedding plans. Nor did he offer any information.

Just as I was getting ready to open the door to exit his office, I turned around, looked at him, and said, "Oh, by the way, have fun at your wedding tomorrow." I was hurt and humiliated.

As his eyes opened widely, he reached out and pulled me back in his office. "I can explain. Please, listen to me. I can explain."

He sounded like a cliché character from a bad chick flick and, at that point, no doubt could remain. He was not the man I thought he was. I found myself once again dealing with a major disappointment—a different kind of challenge than what I had had so far.

"My secretary told you, didn't she?" He was now getting angry and ashamed at the thought of his secretary sharing his well-kept secret. He would have told me eventually, he said. He regretted the way I had found out, and it made him furious that she had broken the news to me. As if her honesty was the problem in this situation and not the fact that he was about to marry someone else.

By then, I had one objective: getting out of his office as quickly as possible.

"I got someone else pregnant and, because of her family, I have no choice but to marry her."

"How interesting," I responded. "I did not know that you had another woman." My tone was sarcastic.

I stayed in his office for a while. He looked remorseful as he tried to explain that he had been forced into this situation. It was the pitiful story of a man trapped by a misguided decision and forced to marry a woman because she was pregnant. A woman he did not love—at least, according to him.

As I listened attentively, I felt sorry for him, but my stomach churned. I wanted to puke. I just could not understand how he could plan to get married with a woman expecting his child and, at the same time, tell me how much he loved me. I had to get out of there. I looked him in the eyes, wished him the best of luck, and left the office.

I cried all the way home on the train. The next day was Luc's wedding and, needless to say, a very sad day for me. That evening, Morris, a mutual friend of ours, who had attended the sumptuous wedding, called to say that Luc had walked out of his own wedding reception to tell him, remorsefully, that he had just made the biggest mistake of his life. "I married the wrong woman," Luc reportedly said.

I would later find out that the woman in question had been one of my high school classmates in Haiti. Their marriage only lasted a few short months, but, in hindsight, our breakup was the best thing that could have ever happened. As much as I loved him at the time, and had imagined a beautiful life with him in his nice house in Scarsdale, Luc was not right for me and, by his behavior, he had freed me from a loveless future. Even at the lowest moment in my life, the angel of the sun was shining a bright light of protection over me. I would have missed out on the life that I enjoyed with the man I married later had Luc not been dishonest. There is a lesson to be learned from every life experience.

I completed my nursing program, graduated, moved into my own apartment, and secured a registered nurse position at the Mount Sinai Hospital in New York City. I was in the prime of my life, earning a very good salary, which enabled me to send even larger amounts of money to help my family in Haiti, where the economy was still insufficient to meet their needs for work and security. As my personal quality of life improved, it was important for me to support the family who had raised me, so that their quality of life could improve as well.

I was so admired and trusted as the evening charge nurse at Mt. Sinai that I was soon transferred to be the charge nurse on the morning shift. Before long, Lucille, the head nurse, promoted me to the position of assistant head nurse. She thought that I was an excellent young nurse with a lot of leadership potential. As a member of the leadership team, I no longer dressed in a nursing uniform. The new position required that I wear business attire to work. I wore very nice designer suits, mainly, pantsuits with high-heeled shoes. Going to modeling school was simply part of the plan that was started many years ago.

While working as a nurse, I attended the Barbizon School of Modeling and started to freelance as a model in New York City. I became a true fashionista, and my sense of fashion remained throughout my adult years. Friends and employees would wait every day to see what I wore to work and, even in my nurse's uniform, I looked like a model with my hair impeccably groomed and my makeup perfectly applied. I credited my godmother for my fashion sense, as she took pride in dressing me when I was an infant all the way into my teenage years. Madame Emanuel and my mother also made sure that I was always presentable.

In modeling school, I learned that you are seen first, and then heard; therefore, a good impression starts with one's appearance. Like Maya Angelou said, I walked as though I had diamonds between my legs. I wore a permanent smile on my face as though I had no worries. I had faced so many challenges as a young adult that I considered my new life a gift from God. Every day is a day that the Lord has made, and I will always rejoice and be glad in it.

MAKE IT WORK FOR YOU!

Rule #11: Take Calculated Risks

Reflection: Know When to Stick Your Neck Out!

When a turtle senses danger, they do what they need to do to protect themselves. They pull their heads and legs into their shell and wait until they think it is safe. Before sticking its neck back out, a turtle will assess its surroundings. If they are calm, there is a good chance the danger has passed. There is also a chance that a predator is lying in wait for the turtle to emerge from its shell. But a turtle cannot remain in its shell forever. If it stayed all tucked in forever, it would never move forward.

- Start small. The next time you see someone you would like to make a connection with but are afraid they might brush you off, take a moment to examine your fear. Often, we pass up opportunities to make a connection because of insecurity. Be bold. Have some faith that you are a person of value. Walk up to the person, stand tall, and introduce yourself. You might meet someone who will change your life. Get comfortable with stepping out of your comfort zone.

- If you are presented with an opportunity that has some risk attached to it, take your time figuring out if the risk is worth the reward. Make a list of positives and negatives. Ask people you trust for advice. Sleep on it. And when you are ready, listen to the instinct in your gut.

RULES TO LIVE BY

In chapter six, I started to pick up steam on my journey toward a successful career. I had my nursing license and was working at a job I loved. But, then, things got a lot steamier. I met the love of my life, Keith, and he pushed me to stretch myself further than I could imagine, in pursuit of a successful career and a happy life. We had our differences, and it was not always easy, but he held me together when I needed support and guided me when I was unsure of which direction to take. I learned to balance the good with the bad.

Rule#12: Remember It Is All Peaks and Valleys

It seems that each time something sweet came into my life, something sour followed. I was accepted into nursing school but had to leave the Silvermans behind. I met the love of my life, but he did not want to be married. Life is full of peaks and valleys, and, while we make gains in our progress, we also must mourn what we leave behind. One of the hardest things to learn is how to accept the bipolarity of existence. When a shadow passes, we learn to appreciate the light. We appreciate the good more when we also accept the hardships and persevere. There is a balance to life that is mysterious and makes our laughter richer for having survived tribulation.

Rule #13: Embrace Change

Life does not allow you to get very comfortable before something comes along and shakes you up, and, if you plan to have a good life, you will need to go with the flow to survive the surprises it has in store for you, because they are bound to happen whether you anticipate them or not. We all tend to cling to what is safe and familiar, but clinging to anything too long just leaves you stuck in one spot, hanging, and that is no way to move forward. Learn to let go and trust that whatever changes life hands you, they are meant to be. Whether it was leaving my homeland and learning to live in a country with a different language or adjusting to a new city or keeping up with new practices and changes to policies in my profession (see chapter six, "Sweet & Sour"), I learned to embrace change and find something positive in the turmoil it sometimes brought into my life.

Rule #14: Preserve Relationships

Preserving relationships with people I value and who value me has enriched my life. After I immigrated from Haiti, I made sure to keep in contact with my family members and godmother while simultaneously making new professional connections and friendships. It is important to form a variety of relationships and to be open-minded about whom you form bonds with. Life is a lot more interesting when you meet many different kinds of people. When I started college, I found myself part of a diverse group of students. I was careful not to prejudge them based on their backgrounds, which was a courtesy not always extended to me (see chapter five, "Nursing School"). Many of the friendships I made while in college have lasted many years and continue to make my life richer. Maintaining relationships over distance can be difficult, but you can do it. Keith and I hit some rough spots when we were living in separate households, but we learned how to maintain our connection despite the distance. It was much easier to keep our relationship healthy when we saw each other every day.

We can extend that thinking beyond a romantic relationship to all the relationships we form over the course of a lifetime, whether they are personal or professional. Some of them will require more tending than others. In business, It is good practice to learn what you need to do to make every professional relationship blossom. In an era where remote work is becoming more common, this is an added challenge. Nowadays, people may work in jobs where they never meet their coworkers in person. It is possible to attend college online and never meet your classmates. Relationships in those circumstances still need to be nurtured. Part of taking on a leadership role in business is learning to foster working connections with others, even with people you may never see in person.

As I built my career, I found that leaving one job for another was a difficult prospect, but I maintained connections with my former coworkers (see chapter six, "Sweet & Sour"). My former colleague, Myrtle, was key to helping me start a new business venture, even though we had not worked with each other for years. And, when it did not work out the way we planned, Myrtle was gracious, in part, because we had stayed in touch (see chapter eight, "The Fishing Expedition"). It is important to find the right partners in your professional dealings. I have struggled with this aspect of business myself (see chapter nine,

"Climbing the Mountain to a Dynasty"). One great way to preserve your relationships is to accept the person, and all their limitations, for who they are right now, not who you would like them to be. Keith and I are a good example. We loved each other deeply but had differences. I wanted to get married. He did not believe we needed to get married and was afraid marriage might change me and how we related to one another (see chapter six, "Sweet & Sour"). But, in the end, it worked out. We made sure to communicate our needs to one another, to accept each other for who we were right then at that moment, and we compromised on the marriage issue. Both of us reached an agreement in the end.

6

Sweet & Sour

When I became the assistant head nurse of Housman II, I suggested that my hospital unit be used for training and orientation. I developed a solid relationship with both the Continuing Education staff and my newly hired professional colleagues, and, as a valued member of the Staff Development Department, I was made preceptor to some of the new nurses. I happily participated in the Hospital's Policy and Procedure, Quality Assurance, and Infection Control committees. I was hungry for knowledge, and I learned the benefits of building relationships and growing a network.

My popularity at the hospital grew. That Christmas, I was invited to almost every party thrown at Mount Sinai, and I attended as many as my work schedule permitted. The hospital had multiple buildings with multiple divisions, and every department and every unit seemed to have planned holiday festivities. In fact, there were so many social functions that the head nurse of Housman III, Dorette, decided to delay her unit celebration until March, as it was impossible to find a convenient day and time in the winter.

I decided to skip the party, because I agreed to cover a 3-to-11 shift on that particular Saturday night so that one of the new hires could go to the get-together. Everyone wanted to go, particularly Lucille, my head nurse, because Gregory, her love interest, was going to be in attendance. Not wanting to go alone, she begged me to come along after my shift ended.

"Even if it's very late," she said.

"I'll think about it," I said.

I considered it, but, although I did not want to let down my boss and best friend, after working a long shift short one of my team members, I was too tired. As I gave my report to the graveyard-shift employee, all I wanted was to get in bed for a good night sleep. I headed home, exhausted. Thank God for the short distance. The Mount Sinai Health System owned several rental buildings reserved for doctors and nurses. Lucille and I were both Sinai tenants and lived in the same apartment building.

Lucille was waiting for me in the lobby in her party dress.

"Why are you so late?" she asked.

"Girl, we were short-staffed: one nurse called in sick and one had to leave early."

"I've been waiting for you. Go up and change quickly. We've got to get to the party."

I sighed. "There is no way I can make this one, Lucille. I am falling asleep."

Unfortunately, Lucille would not take no for an answer. She was intent on not missing this rendezvous with Gregory, a prospective new boyfriend, and she insisted that I accompany her. I relented, even though I was absolutely, positively *not* interested in the party. After all, more than a supervisor, Lucille was a dear friend. I only agreed because I loved her very much. Less than a half hour later, we were jumping in a taxi.

We arrived at the party well past midnight. The room was full of young professionals already drinking and dancing under the flashing lights, all having a good time. Before long, I was on the dance floor, ready to forget how hard I worked and how tired I was. Ever the fashionista, I had changed into a very short multi-colored striped dress, a perfect mix of sexy and conservative, and high-heeled pumps. My afro hair was perfectly styled. I was beautiful—and I knew it. One man after another asked me for a dance, each waiting patiently for a turn. I hit my second wind, and I was in party mode! In fact, when Gregory invited Lucille and me to another party at his friend's house, I was in.

We jumped in his car and off we went to the next gathering, where we danced until dawn.

Who could have predicted that being dragged to these parties would change my life in so many ways?

In my nanny days, the Silvermans had paid for my driving classes, because I so desperately wanted to learn to operate a car and obtain a license. The experience had been painful: despite the regular lessons, I repeatedly failed the road test that proved so easy for others. Every time, I found the driving examiner intimidating. Over and over, I failed. Each time I became more anxious—and failed again. To assuage my sadness, the Silvermans would pay for more lessons and a new attempt at the road test. In vain, I returned home in tears. After my fifth attempt, the Silvermans stopped paying for the classes and I quit trying.

At 26 years old, I had completed my nursing program, I was a working woman with enough disposable cash, but I was still not a licensed driver in New York. I wanted desperately to own a car. I had just taken a refresher driving course and practice lessons in New York in preparation of one more road test. It was scheduled on the Monday following our Saturday night frolics.

I was anxious as I waited in line for my turn to demonstrate my driving skills. My name was called, and my hands were unsteady as I opened the car door. I sat down, took a deep breath, and looked at the examiner. Surprise! On the passenger seat was one of my "Cavaliers," one of the men I had danced with at Gregory's friend's party. He recognized me, and we both started laughing. My anxiety was gone—just like that!—and I walked away with a driver's license in hand.

Was this Luck, coincidence, or my angel of the sun once again manifesting at the right time? Would this guardian angel ever reveal herself in the flesh? What was this unbelievable and mysterious force in my life, and why was this star shining on *me*?

I had only attended the party, because I wanted to be nice to Lucille—and another great milestone was achieved. I would have given anything to get my driver's license; it turned out that all I needed to do was to be kind to a friend.

I had arrived at the DMV in Manhattan as a nervous wreck; the outcome of my driving test could have been completely different, had the evaluator not had a familiar face.

In retrospect, I benefited more from these parties than Lucille did. Her relationship with Gregory remained in the friend zone. On the other hand, I got a driver's license out of the deal—and relentless calls from Dorette.

When I returned home from the DMV, I got the first call from Dorette, the head nurse of Housman III, who had organized the March holiday party for her unit. She was requesting my permission to share my telephone number with a certain gentleman.

"He met you at the Housman party," she explained. "He wants to speak to you."

I emphatically refused. "I have no recollection of any specific man," I said. "I attended two parties in one night. Thank you."

But this gentleman was persistent with his calls to Dorette who, in turn, was harassing me for permission to give out my phone number.

"I need him to stop calling me," she said, "and instead call you directly." She sighed. "It's not like he's a complete stranger, Solanges."

He was friends with Dorette's boyfriend, Eddy, and it was becoming clear that Dorette was tired of her go-between role. The calls from this man were incessant, and she was blaming me for the disturbance. This went on for a couple of weeks until, finally, I relented and gave her permission to share my phone number with Keith.

I was enrolled as a part-time student at Hunter College, pursuing a bachelor's degree in the nursing practice program while working full time as a registered nurse. In addition, I often modeled for fashion shows. In other words: I was busy. If Keith had been persistent in getting my number, he was even more persistent in calling me. Every night, he called—until I would agree to a dinner date. We already had something in common: both Keith and I had attended the Housman III party against our will, only to please a friend. Keith had gone to the get-together as Eddy's wingman. Eddy, a married man with a son, was dating Dorette on the side. He knew that Dorette would want him to stay overnight, and having to take Keith home was the perfect excuse to leave at the end of the party.

When I finally agreed to go out with Keith, I dressed in a beautiful navy-blue suit and high-heeled pumps. I was very apprehensive about this "blind date," a concept I had heard of from my friends, but it was a new experience for me. I knew that this man had been at the hospital party, because Dorette vouched for him; when we talked on the phone, he was also able to describe what I wore that night. But, even though I had danced with Keith, I had no recollection of him. I could not picture his face, so this definitely qualified as a blind date.

The plan was to meet him in the lobby of my apartment building once he had been announced by the doorman. To my surprise, my doorbell rang. There he was, standing in the hallway outside my door, and I panicked, not knowing what to do. Should I open the door? *What happened to the doorman?* I wondered. *How did he get past him?* Keith, I would learn soon enough, was both persistent and persuasive—two traits that made him unstoppable. I found it alluring, but it could also be disquieting.

The doorbell rang again—and then twice more. Through the peephole, I could see a face.

"Just a minute," I said. After I grabbed my purse, in swift motion I opened and closed the door, making it clear that he was not invited into my apartment.

He was slim, six feet four inches tall, dark and handsome. He wore tan-colored pants, and a double-breasted navy-blue blazer with a white shirt and tie, and he was nicely shaved with a tight haircut. He was from the island of Barbados and spoke very proper English with a British accent. I enjoyed the baritone of his voice as we headed to the members-only Playboy Club in Manhattan, where black and white linen covered the tables and the bar was of a beautiful mahogany. Keith turned out that night to be a real gentleman who opened the door for me, pulled out the chair for a lady, and ordered the drinks from one of the waitresses dressed in black-and-white bunny outfits. Three violinists serenaded the dinner guests. I was impressed: this guy had a lot of class, the kind of class I was accustomed to when going out with the Silvermans.

Truth be told, I had never been treated like this by any of my other dates. I agreed to continue being friends, if he agreed to stop calling so frequently.

"I need to devote time to my studies," I said.

He ignored my request and continued to call every day. He also started to visit more frequently than I would have liked. He made it clear that he had no intention of keeping his distance. "Solanges, you need to learn to study while I'm here, because I intend to be around for a very long time."

Ten years my senior, he made me his "personal project," because, he said, he saw my potential and wanted me to meet all my goals toward upward mobility. He became my mentor, my counselor, and my sponsor, all at once. He taught me how to write my first personal check; he helped me with homework; he scouted for job advertisements and other career development opportunities in my nursing magazines; he cooked dinner and even cleaned my uniforms, polished my nursing shoes, and, yes, taught me how to drink alcohol.

He loved me with all his might, he said. I was his princess and, the day he laid his eyes on me, he saw something in me that I did not even know I possessed.

My angel of the sun had dispatched him to guide me. All it had taken was for me to reluctantly play the role of chaperone as a favor to a friend, and I had gained not only my driver's license but a potential husband. Was this a case of being at the right place at the right time? Or was it really my guardian angel looking out for my wellbeing?

Keith insisted that I learn to play tennis so that we could play together on weekends; he was an avid tennis fanatic and did not want me to become a "tennis widow." He not only loved to play the sport, but loved to watch as well. If I intended to spend time in the company of this man, I had no choice but to learn everything about tennis—and other sports like football, basketball, cricket, and golf, for that matter. Unfortunately, I had the same difficulties learning to play tennis as I had learning to drive. He spent a lot of money on tennis lessons with top tennis instructors, just like the Silvermans had invested in my driving lessons. He bought me the prettiest tennis outfits, and I felt like a little girl again: he reminded me of my godmother, Lucienne, who used to dress me as a child. I eventually did become a decent player but never skilled enough to be a true partner: I was too afraid to ruin his game.

I transferred from Hunter College to Long Island University to complete my bachelor's degree in nursing and surrendered my small studio so that Keith and I could move in together into a larger apartment in the same Mount Sinai building. All was well at the hospital, where I continued to excel, until I was denied a head nurse position in another unit. There had been rumors of institutional racism at the hospital, but I refused to believe them until a Caucasian nurse, by far less qualified and certainly less experienced, was chosen for the job I had deserved. Keith became terribly upset by the hospital's decision to deny me the promotion and convinced me that leaving Mount Sinai was the only way I would climb the ladder within the nursing profession; he fervently and confidently went into "career-counselor mode" and found an advertisement for a promising position at a rehabilitation center in White Plains, New York.

"The perfect career advancement," he said. It was a good fit: since graduating from nursing school, I had worked in Urology, a branch of medicine that dealt specifically with the genitourinary system.

Although I had grown disappointed with Sinai, I was not emotionally ready to leave. I had come to suffer from separation anxiety as a result of my personal journey: I had left my family and friends in Haiti to travel to the United States, where, for a long time, I faced the threat of deportation; I had grown to love the Silvermans, only to say goodbye. I missed my college classmates. I certainly did not want to leave my friends at the hospital.

At Keith's insistence, however, I interviewed for the nurse clinician position at the Burk Rehab Center and was offered the job on the spot. "Please give me a few days for a final answer," I said.

Keith, Mr. Persistent, asked me about my decision every single day. "It's your chance to climb the professional ladder," he reminded me.

"Maybe you should take the clinician position yourself," I said, even though I knew full well that he was not a licensed registered nurse, nor was he planning to change employment.

He said I was just stubborn.

I was angry. "Do you realize what you are asking me? Let me understand this: you want me to leave my friends and a steady job at Sinai, and get an apartment in White Plains, New York. Is that what you want me to do? I don't have a car: how do you expect me to get to work? In Manhattan, I can walk … Oh, my God! No, I do not want to move." I was hyperventilating, and part of me knew that I needed to slow down. But I was overwhelmed with emotions, just like during my tantrum, years ago, when my sister Ritza suggested I accept a housekeeping job. "Now you want me to move? What is this really about? Are you staying in Manhattan and sending me away?" My insecurity and fear from separation were keeping me from freeing my future.

When I finally stopped to catch my breath, he talked in a very soft voice. "We will move together." He opened his briefcase and pulled out a pad covered with notes; he had anticipated this conversation. He reassured me that everything would be fine. We would get an apartment close to the Rehabilitation Center. "Look at this," he said, getting closer to me. "We can move to Scarsdale, Yonkers, Mount Vernon, or White Plains." A meticulous man, he had already researched the bus routes. "Mount Vernon might be best. It's closer to the city, and I can take the train to Manhattan."

"Wow, you thought of everything, didn't you?" I said.

"I think this would be best for both of us," he replied, "It will improve our lifestyle, and, on a professional level, this job will put you on a better trajectory towards your career goals."

Despite some of my anxieties, I had never been one for the status quo—and Keith knew it. I was not complacent: I tried to stay ahead of the curve, and Keith actively worked on sharpening these traits even more. He knew what was best.

It took two buses to get to the rehabilitation center in White Plains, New York, where I accepted the position as a nurse clinician in the urology department. Soon, I started to carpool with a new friend, an employee at Burk who lived close to our apartment in Mount Vernon. But, before long, I wanted my own car.

"I'm isolated from my friends and family," I told Keith, "unable to attend parties for fear of missing the last bus or the train."

Keith had never owned a car; he did not even have a driver's license. Even though he was a confident man, he also liked to be in total control of his environment. I knew he was not comfortable with the idea of a car, because it would bring about a great change in our relationship. He would not admit it, but he wanted to keep track of my whereabouts and, once I was behind the wheel, he would lose control. I usually did not mind that he was passively controlling—he was more experienced than I was, and he wanted what was best for me—but I was ready to put my foot down this time. We engaged in a heated discussion until he admitted that he, too, was experiencing isolation. "We are far from our friends," he conceded, "and getting around is an issue."

He finally agreed we needed to buy a car. In fact, in true Keith fashion, he became very involved in selecting the vehicle. He did all the research and was instrumental in getting us a good price. Fortunately, in comparison to midtown Manhattan, living in Mount Vernon had its perks: I had free parking in my building and free parking at work.

I had not driven since obtaining my license, so for the first month, I asked my colleague from work to ride with me until I was comfortable enough to brave the road alone. Keith sometimes served as my copilot from the passenger seat. On our first trip to Manhattan, my legs were shaking as I approached the Triborough Bridge, where the tollbooth area was not only narrow, it also required that I aim perfectly to drop the quarter in the basket. I was so nervous that I missed, and the quarter hit the pavement. Keith had a good laugh, as he had seen it coming. Later, he shared this anecdote with everyone whenever the topics of driving or paying a toll came up.

I truly blossomed in my position as a nurse clinician at the Burk Rehabilitation Center. I worked alone most of the time, except on the clinic days when I assisted the urologist caring for the spinal-cord-injured paraplegic and quadriplegic patients. Many of these patients required a drainage tube that carried the urine directly from the kidney into an external catheter. It was difficult to securely attach this thin tube to a larger catheter. Working with so many post-ureteral ostomy patients in danger of infection, I experimented with a medicine dropper. Using a large needle, I made a hole in the rubber end of a medicine dropper. I, then, inserted the ureteral catheter into the rubber end of the medicine dropper; a water-sealed, tight connection was made. The other end of the medicine dropper was easily attached to the collection system. My technique worked, providing a closed urinary system that decreased the possibility of contamination and infection. I presented my invention of the close drainage system at the American Urological Association's national convention in New York, and it was published in the journal *Urology*. Unfortunately, I did not have the know-how nor the finances to commercialize my invention. Subsequently, the closed system became a major money-maker in the United States and abroad. Even though I was not compensated for my creativity, I became known as a young leader in the healthcare field.

A Haitian newspaper picked up the story and, like my Grand Ana had predicted, this girl was going places. A beautiful article in the *Le Nouvelliste* mentioned my name, and my picture appeared under the heading, *Une Société américaine reçoit une haïtienne* ("An American Association Recognizes a Haitian"). For the Haitian diaspora in the '70s, this was a big story: A Haitian registered nurse had just been admitted as a member to the American Urological Association. Soon, I was asked to speak at seminars and to provide consultations on nursing issues related to the urinary system and management.

While my professional life had become gratifying, I suffered immensely in my personal life. Keith and I were madly in love; he was proud of my professional growth, and I was grateful for having him in my life. We had been living together for several years, but I wanted so desperately to be a wife and mother that I felt incomplete. Unfortunately, Keith did not believe in marriage. I lived in constant disappointment. For me, a child out of wedlock was totally unacceptable. For Keith, marriage was out of the question. God had favored me until now, and I was well aware that God has never given everything to one person, but I could not understand why He was depriving me of a child when I wanted one with all my might. I could not think of a time in my life when I had been fully happy—not even for one day. From birth, my happiness had been invariably mixed with a dose of pain or sadness. *Sweet and sour.* I was with the greatest man, but he refused to be a husband or father. Like so many young women in our late 20s, I dreamed of walking down the church aisle in a long, intricate, white bridal gown, my face covered with a lace veil, a long train dragging behind me. My happily ever after, of course, involved a beautiful baby. This was the dream of most young women in the '60s and '70s.

Something was missing in my life. I had accomplished so much despite my humble beginnings, and, yet, I was unable to convince Keith to marry me. I was miserable.

"Why won't you marry me if I'm so special to you?" I asked during one of our heated discussions.

"You know that I love you. I love you the way you are, and I'm afraid that marriage will change you." As crazy as this may sound, he was afraid of losing me. Marriage, he believed, would make our relationship so real that I would start questioning it. There was a 10-year age difference between us, and my youth made him insecure.

I started crying, promising him that marriage could not change who I was.

He still would not marry me.

This was the only point of contention in our relationship, and we argued about it frequently.

What in the world could have been so bad in his previous relationships with women—or his relationship with his mother—that he would be so against getting married and having children? I wondered.

"I love our relationship as it is. Why can't you just accept it, too?" he asked.

I just could not see it his way. Through it all, I never once contemplated the idea of leaving him. He was my hero and my champion, my companion, my mentor and advisor, my king. He had become such an important part of who I was, and I could not imagine a life without him. He was my lover and, yet, in a way, he was my surrogate father with Ambroise so far away in Haiti. He was a compelling male figure that I cherished. Leaving him was out of the question, and I never considered it an option.

Faith and religion have always played an important role in my life. I grew up attending church every Sunday, and, to this day, I celebrate holidays in observance of Catholic rites. I believe in the intercession of Virgin Mary, mother of Jesus, and I pray to her for anything that requires divine intervention.

As a teenager, every day on my way to school, I stopped at the small neighborhood church to visit the private garden and genuflect in front of the grotto with its beautiful statute of Mother Mary. Behind the statue was a skyline with rolling hills and waterfalls; in front of the Virgin stood a smaller statue of Saint Bernadette kneeling in prayer. It was a depiction of the apparition of the Immaculate Conception to Bernadette in Lourdes, France. The garden was quiet and peaceful. Just like Bernadette, I kneeled and prayed, filled with serenity and hope. As I grew up, I continued to pray to Mother Mary every day. On the morning of my 30th birthday, I was on my knees in front of a statue of Mother Mary. The grotto in the Bronx was similar to the one in Haiti, and I prayed for marriage and motherhood.

I was mid-prayer when I realized I had skipped my menses the prior month and was already late for the current month. I paused for a minute, frozen at the idea that I might be pregnant. *This can't be*, I thought, overwhelmed with joy. Then, I began counting the days. "I know that I took my birth control pills every day," I said to myself as I tried to shake the idea of a pregnancy out of my mind. But I could no longer focus on my prayer.

That evening, I did not mention my suspicion to Keith. When I arrived home after a hard day at work, I found a candlelit dinner waiting for me; two dozen beautiful roses decorated the table, next to a profoundly loving birthday card with the exact words any woman my age might want to hear. Maybe this would be the day he finally came to his senses! *He's proposing tonight*, I thought.

We conversed for a little while at the dining table over the magnificent dinner he had prepared, until he suddenly looked at me with a teasing look. "I have something for you, and I have something to tell you."

Excitedly, I asked, "What is it?"

Teasing me some more, he said, "Which one do you want first?"

"How about both together?" I smiled. "Okay, my birthday gift first."

We were flirting with each other, just as we had on our first date.

When he reached over the table, he held a small box. My heartbeat quickened, and, in that second, I was the happiest woman. Not even the thought of being pregnant at the grotto could surpass the feeling I was experiencing. I had dreamed about marriage for so long—waited for it, cried over it. And Keith was finally proposing. I took the box from him with a large smile and thanked him profusely before I even opened the gift—what I thought could only be an engagement ring. I would be getting married.

I unwrapped the box carefully.

It was not the small silver or gold band with the diamond that I had expected. Instead, I discovered a wide gold band, with six rubies and a large opal in the center. Not an engagement ring.

Yes, the ring was magnificent and, I could tell, very expensive. However, in that moment, it was the ring of death: with that ring, Keith had just killed my joy and hope. It was his way of saying, *I am deeply committed to you forever, but I am not marrying you.* He had verbalized it many times; now, he demonstrated it with the ring. Truth be told, he was a better partner than many of my friends' husbands, but, nevertheless, I was crushed. My heart bled, but I smiled, thanking him for the gift, which I wore for the rest of the evening.

"Are you ready now to listen to what I have to tell you?" Mr. No-Emotion finally appeared excited about his big announcement.

Once again, I perked up, thinking, *He has something to tell me. Could it be that he did not want to engage in the diamond fad like our friends but is still going to propose?* I lifted my face from my dessert plate. "Tell me."

"I got a letter from the OAS," he said.

"What?" I was puzzled. "What is OAS?"

"The Organization of American States," he said. "It's located in Washington, D.C. I applied for a position to work with them when we lived in Manhattan, and I just heard from HR. They offered me a position as a system's analyst. It is a good opportunity for both of us."

"You seem to be happy about it," I said coldly. "Great! So, you forced me to leave Manhattan for Mount Vernon, isolated me from my friends and family, and now you plan to move to Washington, D.C.? This is just great!"

With that, I stormed away from the table to the kitchen and started to clean up. I had had it with him for the night. I had gone from euphoria to sadness, back to euphoria, and back again to sadness—so many times in one day that I felt a little manic. While I went back and forth, collecting dirty dishes from the dining room and piling them in the sink, Keith remained almost motionless after my reaction to his offer. He was not sure what to say and what to do, for fear of an outburst. What he did not know, of course, is that I also had something to tell him, but was afraid to bring another sensitive subject into this already volatile night.

In the '70s, members of the diaspora strived to improve their financial situation. They applied for upward mobile positions in and out of states, even though they knew that those positions were rarely offered to people of color. Keith had been supportive, even aggressive at times, in pushing my career forward, so, in the end, I had no choice but to reciprocate, even though a separation at this point in our relationship was the last thing I wanted or needed in my life. Once I calmed down, we discussed the pros and cons associated with him taking the position. He was so excited; I did not want him to be disappointed or dissuade him from accepting this opportunity. I could not bring myself to stand in the way of his aspirations, so I decided not to mention the possible pregnancy, and did not discourage him from taking the position and moving to Washington, D.C.

It was almost midnight, and we both had to be up early for work the next day. We had promised never to go to bed angry at each other, no matter the circumstances; we always kissed good night and shared intimacy in bed, and that night was no exception. As was customary, we lay down in each other's arms. I kept my secret, because I did not have the courage, nor the energy, to share my suspicion. There was so much to think about. I was only in my second year at the Rehab Center, making a name for myself in a position that I loved and had no intention of resigning from. I was enjoying our new home, a large two-bedroom apartment in a cozy neighborhood that featured great mom-and-pop shops, restaurants with outdoor seating, and a little bakery where I could get delicious croissants and hot chocolate for breakfast. While

I loved the life that we had built together and wanted it to continue, I could not expect him to forego the pursuit of his own dreams and career growth. I was torn inside.

Keith was my confidante but, for the first time in a long time, I was alone in my thoughts and actions. I really did not know when or how to tell him. In the next few days, it became difficult for me to concentrate at work, and even more difficult to focus on the road home. I was afraid that the upset that started on my birthday about the OAS and Keith's move would continue. I decided to stop at church to speak with Mother Mary and ask for guidance. After dinner that night, I approached the topic of the OAS. I wanted to know more about the offer and Washington, D.C., and asked to read the letter.

True to form, Keith had already done his homework. He presented information on the metro transportation system, the buses and airplanes to and from Washington, D.C. His friend Edward, a Consulate General at the OAS, would arrange to meet him on his first trip to assist with room and board until an apartment was secured. Keith assured me that he would work in Washington, D.C., and fly home every Friday evening to be with me on the weekends. Once he leased an apartment, I would go down on some weekends and stay with him until a permanent solution was found. We discussed the expenses associated with such arrangements and the financial and emotional toll it would take on our relationship. It was clear that he had already decided to accept the position, which he deemed a great career move. He was not even gone, and just talking about it made me miss him.

On a cool spring morning, I drove Keith to LaGuardia airport to begin his life away from me in Washington, D.C. I cried all the way home. I was happy and proud of him for this big opportunity but, at the same time, I was sad that I would not be able to physically kiss him and feel his warm body against mine at night. I was relieved that I did not have to face him daily with my secret, yet I so desperately wanted to share my joy with him, even if the pregnancy remained unconfirmed.

During the day, I was fine at work, keeping busy and talking with others. I ate at work, eliminating the need to cook for one person. Keith and I talked on the phone very late at night until one of us started dozing off during the conversation; then and only then did we end the call. But bedtime remained difficult. Because we were not legally married, I could not help but wonder about the sustainability of this long-distance relationship. Would our love shatter with the distance?

I was at LaGuardia Airport, seated behind the wheel of my green AMC Pacer, waiting patiently for his flight to land. It had been delayed due to a thunderstorm in Washington, D.C. And I kept thinking, *I have to tell him.* I agonized over it and rehearsed the best way to tell him that he was going to be a father against his wishes. It had started to become evident that I was pregnant. I had to break the news to Keith this weekend, before he discovered it on his own.

When he finally landed, he was tired and apologetic, so I decided to wait, even though the suspense was excruciatingly painful. That night, I had trouble staying asleep. I turned, changed position, and then got up, had some tea, and went back to bed. Dawn came. I settled close to him and tried to wake him before he was ready for the new day. I kissed him, and we made passionate love, happy to be physically together.

Then, it just came out—unexpected to both of us.

"I am pregnant."

As cool as a cucumber, without any reaction, he asked, "How do you know?"

"I took the test," I responded.

"So, now, you are a doctor?"

"*No!* I went to Walgreen's pharmacy downstairs, purchased a pregnancy kit, took the test, and I am pregnant."

He was quiet for a moment. "So, you are pregnant. What are you going to do with it?"

"What do you mean? I am keeping it," I said with conviction.

He looked at me, and with a playful smirk on his face, he said, "Okay. I know how much you wanted this." He laughed. "I will let you have it this time, on one condition: that you will never let this happen again."

With great emotion, I said, "I'm going to be a mother, and you're going to be a father."

We kissed and tightly hugged each other, and we began a new phase in our relationship.

After I had prayed to Mother Mary, asking her to speak to God on my behalf, the angel of the sun had shined a beam of light into my womb. I was blessed. But no matter how happy I am, there is always something to rob me of full happiness. Once again, my life was both sweet and sour. I was having a child, but I was still not legally married. I tried not to let this joyous time be tarnished by the lack of a legal document. After so many years living in a common-law arrangement with Keith, I thought, I was his wife in every way that mattered; in our hearts and souls, we were connected forever.

Keith was beaming with pride and joy at the anticipation of the birth of his child. He loved to tease me about the size of my belly as it grew, calling it a coconut, then a ball, and, finally, a watermelon. He often told me how beautiful a pregnant woman I was and how happy I made him. I remained in Mount Vernon, and Keith continued to work in Washington, D.C. Our weekends were spent together between Washington, D.C., and Mount Vernon until I was too advanced in the pregnancy to travel. During the last few months, Keith hired Claudia, a live-in nanny, making sure that I would never be in the apartment alone before and after the birth of our child.

Being pregnant alone was one of the hardest things I have had to do. It is not that I did not have an active, invested partner in Keith. He loved me, and, once he accepted that there was a baby on the way, he threw all his support my way, but, most nights, I was still alone with a growing baby in my body. Even with Claudia in the house with me towards the end of the pregnancy, the other side of my bed was empty most nights. There were times I wished Keith could reach out and rub my back or put his hands around my belly. The first time I felt the baby kick, it came as a shock. I remember wanting to reach out and grab Keith's hand and put it firmly on my belly so he could feel how strong our child was and wonder with me at the movement in my womb. That first kick was a bittersweet moment. On one hand, it gave me proof that my baby was growing strong inside me, but, on the other hand, there was no one to share it with. I was sad that Keith had missed the moment, as much for him as for myself.

Luckily, our baby moved around a lot, and, later, during his visits home, Keith did feel how powerful the baby's little legs were and watched as my belly rolled with the tumbling child inside. However, I never got to share the first time with him, and it felt like an event that lost significance after the first signal from our child that they were in there and would be in our arms soon.

I still had to work through my pregnancy—through the swollen ankles, morning sickness, back aches, doctor's appointments, and hormonal changes. Keith was not with me for birthing classes. Much of the time, it felt like I was a single parent, even though the child was still inside my womb. I understood the need for our separation at this point, and knew we would eventually be back under the same roof, but, every time he left for Washington, D.C., after a weekend home with me, it felt like he was heading for the other end of the planet. I missed having someone to share the pregnancy with.

We teased each other about the name of the baby until we decided not to select a name beforehand. We agreed on a strategy: if the baby was a girl, I would select the name; if it was a boy, he would be the one to name the child. Because I did not know exactly when I had gotten pregnant, it was difficult to pinpoint an exact delivery date. The doctor worried that I might be late for delivery. He asked me to undergo a 24-hour urine analysis at the lab. This was the scientific way to calculate gestation in the '70s; the urine was tested to measure an infant's distress levels in utero. I had a belly so large that my Lamaze coach, who was also my physician, teased me about carrying twins, although we both knew that it was not true. I had gained 50 pounds, and it was all baby. That night, when I called Keith, as my doctor had done to me, I informed him we were having a set of twins.

Without any hesitation, he replied, "Oh, we are? Well, bring one home and leave the other one in the hospital."

Luckily for me, I was only pregnant with one big baby.

Desperate to deliver, I decided to move around to help push the baby out: accompanied by Claudia, I took the train from Mount Vernon to Manhattan for a shopping spree. Claudia and I had developed a very close and healthy relationship. We walked the entire day, went up and down escalators. Not in vain: at two o'clock in the morning, I finally went into labor.

It lasted over six hours.

With the use of forceps, I naturally delivered a seven-and-a-half pound and 21-inches long boy. Both mother and son were healthy.

As it was a weekday, Keith missed the delivery. Even if he had been home, he had no intention of being in the labor and delivery room. The hospital was not his favorite place. He would never meet me at work for lunch, even if his life depended on it.

Prior to discharge from the hospital, the mothers were to complete a form indicating the child's name in preparation for the birth certificate. I had to wait until Keith called that night to complete the form, since we had agreed that he would name the boy.

"Do you have a pen and paper?" he asked. "I do not want his name to be misspelled like yours."

"I have the form in my hand," I responded.

"Do not write it on the form," he insisted. "Write it on a scrap paper first, then you can transcribe it to the form."

I still did not know the name of my own son. "I hope you do not plan on calling him Keith, because I do not want him to be called 'Junior.'"

He chuckled. "His name is K.E.V.I.N."

"Oh, Kevin," I said. Kevin! That was my baby's name. This was my first time hearing it. *Kevin.*

"I did not say *Kelvin*. I said, Kevin. Spell what you wrote for me," he retorted.

I shouted right back, "What's the matter? You don't think I can spell Kevin?"

"I just want to make sure you do not spell it with your accent," he said jokingly.

"Very cute," I responded.

It was a funny, loving exchange between two young parents; a moment that I had dreamed of was now my reality. I was finally a mother.

Until that phone call, I had no idea what my son's name was. Keith could have picked anything for him, and I had no clue what he would come up with. I had been left calling our baby "baby" until the phone call. But, after I knew his name, I was excited when the nurse finally brought him in from the nursery, so I could spend time with him and feed him. He had a name now! He was not just "baby." Somehow, that made him more real and made my role as his mother more real. When she handed him to me, all wrapped up in a receiving blanket, I held him up and said his name aloud to him for the first time, "Kevin." My heart swelled up in my chest looking at the little miracle I had made with Keith. He was my boy. My Kevin. I was filled with joy at the sight of him.

Each minute that passed, my baby—Kevin!—went on inhaling and exhaling: a miracle! His hands were no bigger than quarters, his veins as thin as strands of hair. He stirred, he sighed. And then, there was Keith: the man who had wanted no children was now enjoying fatherhood as much as I was enjoying motherhood. I might not have been a wife in the eyes of society, but I was a mother, and my child had a loving father. Even though I was unmarried, my family would welcome the birth of Kevin. They loved me and respected me as an accomplished professional. Besides, my parents had been worried, as I was the last of the six sisters to have a child. Everyone would love Kevin. I watched the rise and fall of my baby's chest, so slight. I had to stand perfectly still.

I returned home very happy in my new role as a mother, but I soon became a little restless and moody, despite Claudia's best efforts to lighten my load. She loved Kevin passionately. I missed the presence of Keith who was now not only my common-law husband but also the father of my son. I felt isolated from my colleagues and eager to return to work, but Keith felt strongly that I needed to be home with the baby until I joined him in D.C. I worried about finances, as we spent a lot of money on telephone bills and plane tickets for the trips between Washington, D.C., and New York. On Fridays, Keith gave me some pocket money to help assuage my desire to return to work. "Now, you have your own money to spend. You do not need to go back to work."

One day, Claudia abruptly resigned. She would not discuss her decision; she chose only to apologize by saying, "I need to go, I need to leave." That same day, she packed all her belongings and left me alone with the baby. Later, I would learn that the lovely woman who had become my friend, the nanny of my newborn, carried a secret that was never shared with me. As a young adult, she, too, had had a baby out of wedlock; unfortunately, her child had died as an infant, only a couple of months old. Claudia's pain resurfaced while she cared for baby Kevin. Unable to deal with her inner turmoil, she left our employment, never to return into our lives.

Suddenly, my life had changed. I had gotten what I so desperately wanted—motherhood—but I was dealing with more than expected. *Sweet and sour.* With Keith in Washington, D.C., and the baby's nanny gone, I was unable to work. I adored Kevin, but here I was, a young mother with a few months old baby, all alone in Upstate New York, far away from family and deep in depression. It became evident that baby Kevin and I had to relocate to Washington, D.C., even sooner than expected. Before I officially resigned from the rehab center, however, Keith wanted to make sure that he was secure in his position first; we did not want to be faced with a situation where both of us were unemployed. I also had to obtain my Washington, D.C., license as a registered nurse, as required by the regulations of the District of Columbia. Furthermore, Keith had to hunt for a larger apartment: his one-room studio would not do.

In the meantime, I continued to care for Kevin on my own. One morning, after he had had a slight fever, I woke up to find baby Kevin covered with a rash that had spread over his entire little body. He was only slightly warm to the touch, but he was red as a strawberry. I called Keith who advised me to call the pediatrician immediately. I was able to obtain an emergency appointment with the on-call pediatrician. As I dressed, and then strapped my sick baby in his car seat, I wished I did not have to go through this experience alone. I was soon on my way to a doctor I had never met in a part of town I had never been, praying aloud to Mother Mary and Jesus and calling for help to every saint whose name

I could recall. As I drove and prayed, baby Kevin cried himself to sleep. When I finally arrived at the doctor's office, my son was diagnosed with roseola, a rash only seen in infants and very young children. I was given instructions on caring for my sick baby.

When Keith took a couple of days off to extend his weekend at home, I felt relieved at the prospect of an adult conversation; I had been spending entire days talking "baby talk" with little Kevin, my only companion. Moving to Washington, D.C., became an emergency and a major priority for Keith who could not stand to be separated from us any longer.

MAKE IT WORK FOR YOU!

Rule #12: Remember It Is All Peaks and Valleys

Reflection: Be That One in a Thousand!

The average sea turtle lays 100 eggs. It is the end of a long journey for her. After she lays her eggs and covers her nest, she returns to the ocean to begin her migration again, not knowing what will become of the eggs she has left behind. Scientists estimate that, on average, only 1 in 1,000 hatchlings survive to adulthood, but that one sea turtle in 1,000 is a miraculous creature who has learned to survive against the odds. She has traveled the world and come home to lay her eggs in a cycle that her kind has been repeating for eons. What an accomplishment! But, also, what a monumental loss.

- Journal it: think of the hardest experience you have been through. Take a few minutes to write about the experience. How did it impact you, and what did you do to get through it? How long did it take you to recover? Who helped you see your way out of the dark time? Now, remember the moment you felt some relief from the grief of the event. What happened to lift your spirits back up? What did you learn from the experience?

- It is important, as we are caught up in the day-to-day minutia of life, to take some time to celebrate. It doesn't have to be anything fancy (though, as you will see later in the book, I love a good party). Set aside some time each week to do something special that brings you joy. Go out with friends. Take a walk on the beach. Eat an ice cream cone. Smell the flowers. Pencil some "me time" into your schedule, and make experiencing joy and connection to the beauty in life a top priority.

Rule #13: Embrace Change

Reflection: All Around the World and Still Right at Home

The leatherback turtle is an epic world traveler. During their annual migrations, they swim up to 10,000 miles in search of jellyfish and to complete their pilgrimage to their nesting sites. Over the course of their journey, the leatherback traverses a variety of terrains, between Japan and Mexico, across the wide Pacific and back again. They make their environment work for them, whether it is the warm coastal waters off Baja, Mexico, or the deep, cold Pacific. Their journey is a constant adaptation to new environments, and they move at a comfortable pace.

- Think of a time when life threw an unexpected curveball your way. How did you handle the shock of the new situation? Did you cling tightly to the old situation or were you excited to see what unfolded? After the shock wore off and you accepted that change was going to occur, no matter your preference, what positive gains were you able to take from the new normal?

- Find an old photo of yourself from a time when you were happy. Take a good gander at who you were then. What were the things that brought you joy then? How has that changed? What has remained constant in sparking your delight? What brings you joy now? Now, look 10 years forward. Do you think the same pleasures will remain a part of your life, or will you find new ways to find happiness? Jot down a list of things you would like to try. Then, check them off one by one as you expand your experiences.

Rule #14: Preserve Relationships

Reflection: Symbiosis Means You Are Never Alone

At first glance, a sea turtle looks like a solitary creature, but closer scrutiny reveals that sea turtles are miniature eco-systems involved in a number of symbiotic relationships. The Yellow Tang fish give them a good cleaning in a mutually beneficial arrangement that gives the fish a meal of dead skin and algae. The turtle receives a spit shine as the result of its relationship to the Tang fish. A variety of hitchhikers such as barnacles and algae, small crustaceans, and the occasional sea cucumber hang on tight and keep the turtles company on their travels. There is even a variety of crab called the Columbus crab (planes minutus). These crabs find a cozy spot in the nook between a sea turtle's tail and its shell, and settle down, often with their mate; now, that is a good friend!

- Make a list of people you can go to for advice on either personal or professional matters. When is the last time you contacted them? If it has been more than six months, consider sending them an email or a message to let them know how you are doing and that they are important to you. Maybe plan a lunch date with some of them—not because you need anything but because you would like to spend time with them.

- Look in your community calendars for events that are coming up that give you an opportunity to meet new people and learn something new, whether it is an art talk or an author's reading. Find the time to fit one of these events into your calendar each month. Go in with no expectations and see what unfolds.

RULES TO LIVE BY

In this chapter, I settled into my new life in Washington, D.C., with my new baby and common-law husband—if you can call it "settling." I did not get to sit still very long. I had childcare to manage, a career to start building, power struggles at work, and a big surprise in a little box from Keith that the mailman delivered one day that changed my whole life.

Rule 15: Stay Attuned to Invisible Struggles

I have come to realize that everyone is really two people: there is the person we show to the outside world and the person we keep hidden to protect ourselves. It is a natural part of human nature to hide your vulnerabilities. With that in mind, it is important to remain attuned to the struggles and unspoken pain other people are experiencing. I had two separate babysitters with personal issues I was not aware were causing them grief. One had schizophrenia (see chapter seven, "Wedding Bell Blues"), the other had lost her own child (see chapter six, "Sweet & Sour"). It does not matter if you aware of what causes a person's pain. We all have issues that we deal with privately. The important thing is to be aware that we all hurt for many different reasons. Taking a sensitive approach when dealing with others is the wise way to relate to people.

You should also be sensitive to your own pain. It is important to keep your personal issues separate from your work life, but, if you are going through something, take care of yourself on your own time and find someone you can trust to confide in. I went through some significant health issues during my career and managed to keep those out of the workplace. My husband and close friends were there to support me when I needed someone (see chapter 11, "How Did We Do It?"). Bottom line, keep your emotions in check in the workplace (see chapter 13, "Every Beginning Has Its End").

But it is also important to remember you are not a robot. Take time out of your life to take care of yourself. Give yourself time to grieve when you experience a loss.

7

―――――

Wedding Bell Blues

Washington, D.C., was lovely and much cleaner than New York. We moved into an apartment in the northwest section of the District of Columbia where the trees cascaded on both sides of the street, like a beautiful picture frame. The buildings were much lower than the skyscrapers of Manhattan. I was in awe of the museums, the Kennedy Center, the Cherry Blossom Festival, and the beautiful detached single-family homes with well-manicured lawns reminded me of my nanny days with the Silvermans in New Jersey. It was such a pleasant place to live, and, yet, I had to manage the trials and tribulations of being a new mother in a new city with no friends or family connections. I missed my sisters and their children, my friends at Sinai and at the Burk Rehabilitation Center. I wanted to work, but reliable babysitting for our son remained an issue.

While I was trying to find reliable childcare, I used to take Kevin to a lady named Mrs. Soriano to watch him. I was driving a green Pacer back then; it looked like a bubble with big windows all around it. One day, after I parked in front of Mrs. Soriano's building, I accidentally locked the keys in the car, with the baby in the car seat. It was a hot summer, and I could not open the car! In a panic, I ran upstairs to Mrs. Soriano and let her know what had happened. She could not leave the other children she was watching to go be with Kevin, so she watched him through her window. I took a taxi, and ran to my apartment. It seemed to take forever, though it was probably only a few minutes' ride each way. I was frantic to get back to my baby and get him out of that hot car.

The taxi waited for me as I got the spare key and went back to open the car door. I leapt out of the taxi when we arrived and pulled Kevin out of the car as fast as I could. Thankfully, he was fine.

When I carried Kevin to Mrs. Soriano. I looked at her and I asked, "When is it going to be easier? When does it get better?"

She looked up at me and said, "It never gets better. The issues are different, but the challenges are always there." It was similar to what my mother said. When you have a child, you are always a mother. The circumstances of motherhood will be different as they grow older, but there is no such thing as "it gets better." Thank God, Kevin was all right that day. Being a mother comes with a good share of panic and fear.

With the assistance of my sister Paulette, I recruited older women from a church in New York City and moved them to Washington, D.C., to live in the apartment with us for childcare. Having been a nanny, knowing all that I brought to that position, I was having a hard time accepting mediocre services for Kevin. By this child's second birthday, I was on my third nanny. I, then, registered my two-year-old son at a daycare on Connecticut Avenue. Before long, the daycare lost a five-year-old girl at the National Zoo during an outing. That day, without a second thought, I removed Kevin from the school and stayed home to care for him until other arrangements could be made.

Kevin was a handful! That child had more energy than I could keep up with at times. Once, when he was about two years old, I was at the airport with him and turned to pick up a piece of luggage from the conveyor belt. When I turned back around, he was gone! The airport was full of commuters, people rushing this way and that, and, in that crowd, I could not find Kevin anywhere. Anything could have happened to him in a crowd of that many people. I started to panic and yelled out his name, but thankfully, in just a few moments of searching, I found him calmly standing behind a pole watching the luggage revolve on the conveyor belt.

He was always hiding from me in public places, and it tested my vigilance. Anytime we went clothes shopping, he would hide from me inside the racks of clothes at the store, and, no matter how much it upset me, he would stay there while I searched through all the racks until I found him. It was a relief when I had some help, because that child was unstoppable most of the time.

With tremendous joy, I helped my parents plan a visit to New York. They scheduled a short stay in Washington, D.C., to meet their grandson, and we kissed and hugged and laughed when they arrived the following Thursday. Kevin seemed a little moody, but, with all the excitement around him, this was no surprise.

The next day, however, the baby was crying nonstop. I held him in my arms, but no amount of affection, food, or drink could soothe him. His temperature was not abnormally high; however, he was getting warmer.

"He's in pain," my mother said. "When is the last time he had a bowel movement?"

I had no recollection of the last time he had had one. He was now thrashing with pain, so I called the pediatrician whose office was on Connecticut Avenue, only a few minutes from our apartment. Once I described the thrashing, the leg spasms, and the constant crying, the doctor advised that I take Kevin to the children's hospital immediately. My parents accompanied me to the emergency room, Kevin's grandma in the back seat, still trying—unsuccessfully—to stop the crying. He was very sick.

The ER nurse assigned us to a cubicle and, soon, doctors were all over my son. By the time he was taken to Radiology, he was in so much pain that I had to hold him down for an x-ray of the abdomen.

Then came the wait for the x-ray results.

This was before cell phones, and I had no way of getting in touch with Keith. After work on Fridays, he often met with friends for drinks before coming home. At least during this emergency, I was not alone: I was lucky to have my parents with me.

When the doctor returned to the cubicle, where we tried to keep Kevin as quiet as possible, he looked somber. "The x-ray revealed an intussusception.

We need to prep him for surgery immediately." The surgeon on call was already on his way.

Surgery! I did not remember studying intussusception in nursing school, nor did I remember such a diagnosis in the pediatric unit at the hospital during my clinical days. Later, I would learn that intussusception occurs when the small intestine intertwined in the large intestine, creating a bowel obstruction that can only be relieved by surgery. In that moment, however, I knew one thing: if he was to undergo surgery, Kevin's life was in danger. My imagination unbridled, I was now sobbing inconsolably, scared to death for my son and missing Keith's presence. I was in physical pain. My anxious parents, who did not speak a word of English, were at a disadvantage, but they tried their best to help me cope with this crisis.

Finally, after what seemed to be another long wait, the surgeon arrived. "Relax," he said. "I'm not going to operate on your son. The baby does not have intussusception." The internist had misread the x-ray. "It's a bowel inflammation," Dr. Mark explained. "It can be relieved with medication and, as a nurse, you should be able to care for him at home."

What a relief! After all the paperwork was processed, a nurse administered an intravenous medication, which brought Kevin relief soon thereafter; the doctor gave the green light for his discharge. My son was only a toddler and already had two scary emergencies. Unfortunately, inflammatory bowel syndrome is a chronic condition that flairs up and continues throughout adulthood. I could not help but to ask my mother, who had nine children, what to expect in the future years.

Her answer was not so reassuring. "It never ends. And once a mother, always a mother."

By the time we returned home, the medication had fully taken effect, and Kevin was back to being his little mischievous self. He was ready to enjoy his grandparents' visit until they returned to New York. Keith, on the other hand, was distraught. Once again, he was not present when his son had an emergency, but I did not blame him. We both understood our limitations as parents.

As much as I loved my son, being a stay-at-home parent was not an option I could be happy with. I felt listless without a career. Every Sunday, I unsuccessfully scanned the available positions in the "Help Wanted" section of the *Washington Post*, looking for employment in urology, until I decided to explore other nursing positions. I eventually scheduled an interview for an evening position as an assistant director of nursing at The Washington Home, a nursing home very close to our apartment. I had never been to a nursing home prior to this visit. Yet, my interview with the directors of nursing and human resources went so well that I was offered the position at the end of the interview.

I was not certain that working at a nursing home was the direction I wanted to take with my career. I was still hoping for a hospital position, preferably in urology. I did not immediately accept the offer, requesting time for my decision. I still had not made up my mind when, two weeks later, I was contacted by the human resources director who informed me that the administrator wanted to meet with me. I almost declined the meeting with the administrator, but Keith had been encouraging me to accept the position, which he considered an upwardly mobile move for my career. Because I trusted Keith's judgment, I agreed to go to the second interview. The administrator, Mr. Matlock, was so impressed with my professional experience and vivacious personality that he once again offered me the position. Only, this time, he increased the salary that had been quoted by Human Resources. I accepted the position during that second interview, even though it was not my first choice and the salary was less than what I was making in New York. I would buy time until I secured the right spot at an acute care hospital.

Because I had occupied multiple leadership positions in acute care, and at Burk Rehabilitation Center as an independent clinician in urology, I was confident that I could easily learn the nursing home's policies and procedures, regulations, and functions. I was also confident that I had the drive to excel in this new position. The Washington Home never had a minority director, and I was the first African-American assistant director ever hired in the 90-plus years history of this nursing home, and I had no choice but to blossom. In the third month of my employment, Mr. Matlock received a letter from the most difficult family of one of the residents, complimenting him on hiring me. Needless to say, he was very happy.

My life started to change for the better in Washington, D.C. I was happy that all three of us were under the same roof in a family unit. I made friends, and my driving skills improved. I even found a beautician and joined a tennis club. As to be expected, some days were more challenging than others, as I juggled life with a common-law husband and a young son, and trying to fit a game of tennis in my busy schedule—all before three o'clock in the afternoon, when I had to report for work. I was still looking for a reliable caretaker for Kevin. After my unpleasant experience with three live-in nannies and the missing-child episode at the daycare, I was referred to a woman who cared for children in her home: I would drop Kevin by two o'clock in the afternoon and collect him late in the evening on my way home from work. I was finally happy to have found someone that I could trust.

One early morning, however, I received a call from the babysitter's daughter asking me to make other arrangements for Kevin. The thought of losing yet another babysitter was stressful. Not again, I thought.

"What happened?" I asked.

Her mother had to be taken back to the hospital, she said. During the conversation, I learned that her mother was schizophrenic and had been in and out of the psychiatric hospital for many years. I wondered about the degree of the illness. Had my child been in danger with a woman with a serious mental condition? The thought alone was overwhelming. I also felt guilty: I worried that having to care for my toddler, my little "terrible two" son might have exacerbated the babysitter's symptoms and precipitated her rehospitalization.

Once again, I had to face the reality of juggling both work and Kevin. Keith and I discussed strategies, but the fact remained that we still had no one to care for our son. I had been so desperate to have a baby and now I felt trapped. I never expected that this little creature would have so much control over my life: he was so dependent on us for his survival. It was then I started to develop a different appreciation and understanding of motherhood. Being a nanny was much different than being a mother; this was a 24-hour, seven-days-a-week responsibility. I prayed to Mother Mary for guidance. In the end, I requested an emergency leave of absence at work from a position that I had held for less than a year. Luckily for me, I was well liked and was performing at such a high level of excellence that my request was granted, although only for two weeks.

Keith suggested that we send Kevin to his mother in Barbados. As painful as his suggestion was, I agreed out of desperation.

During the week, I was so preoccupied with work and playing tennis that I did not miss Kevin as much as I did on the weekends. I would cry from Friday evening to Monday morning, still searching for permanent childcare so that I could bring him back home to us.

My evenings at work could be very difficult. I was often faced with urgent clinical and administrative situations, and almost every evening had its own crisis. After working very late one night, I received an early morning call from Ms. Lola, my director of Nursing, requesting that I return to work immediately.

"There's a detective here," she said. "He's asking questions."

"A detective? For what?" I asked. My mind was already searching high and low for the purpose of this meeting with a detective. An old fear returned—one that I had not experienced in a while. I was transported back to the days when I lived under the threat of deportation. I took a deep breath: I was now a legal citizen of the United States. There was nothing to fear.

"I do not know," the director responded. "But you need to come."

My daily routine was shot. I quickly left for the nursing home.

I met with the detective whose questions concerned a male employee who had left work urgently the night before, during my shift. I recalled the circumstances for his departure, but my recollection was very different from the detective's assertion. To my knowledge, the employee had left because his teenage son had just been shot on a basketball court; I had offered my prayers and asked him to call us about the wellbeing of his son. According to the detective, this man was actually an "armed and dangerous" fugitive running from the law. A licensed practical nurse from another state, he carried a loaded gun in his boot, even while at work. I vividly recalled the dark brown boots, but never thought that they were a holster for his gun.

"His wife must have tipped him off," the detective said.

She had been contacted by the authorities, so she knew they were tailing him to the nursing home. Because of this employee, and similar incidents throughout the United States, new Federal laws were enacted to prevent offenders from working in nursing homes and personal care positions in private homes.

After a three-month stay, Kevin returned from his grandmother's home in Barbados.

He was now enrolled at a very distinguished preschool called All Saints All Day Child Care. He was the only black child in the school until I met Gloria, a new mother who was looking at the school for her son, William. We spoke on the street for 15 minutes and, in that short period of time, I was able to convince her that the school was the best place for her son, based on my extensive research and interaction with other parents and staff members. At the next parent reception, Gloria and I met Alice, her husband Ed, and their son Blair. Within a few weeks, the school now had three black children. The administration was very happy with their ability to now boast "diversity," and I was finally happy with childcare. Those three boys truly enjoyed their childhood as brothers, and their parents remained friends for life.

Gloria and I spent a lot of time together with our boys, not only on play dates but also on trips. We took William and Kevin with us to a convention Gloria was attending for work, I watched the boys while she was in meetings, and we all played together in between. We also traveled to Florida to pick oranges and to Hawaii for vacation, and I discovered, as I was doing these things with my son, that I was giving myself the kind of childhood I missed out on in Haiti, where fun was much less of a priority. So when Kevin learned to ski, I learned to ski as well. We both learned to ice skate and roller skate. As my son grew up happy, some part of me grew happier, too, having a chance to build moments I had missed out on in my own childhood.

When he was about five, Kevin started spiking fevers often. Each time I took him to the pediatricians at Kaiser Permanente, a health management organization (HMO), they would prescribe antibiotics for him, course after course, in the same way I was always on antibiotics when I was a teenager. And he would get so many ear infections! The antibiotics would not stop coming!

One day, after I returned from Kaiser with another prescription for more antibiotics, Keith went ballistic. "Give me the number," Keith said. "This needs to stop. He needs to figure out what's going on. He cannot keep putting the child on antibiotics." He called the pediatrician, had a serious conversation, and, at the next visit, Dr. Stark gave me a referral for an ear, nose, and throat doctor (ENT).

The ENT gave him antibiotics but also scheduled surgery for two weeks after our visit. The doctor found that Kevin's eustachian tube had a curve in it. They wanted to put an artificial tube in his ear to drain the wax and fluid. Once they did that, the doctor said, his own tube would straighten and the artificial tube would fall out.

The doctor had warned me, "You might see it on his pillow, or you might never see it. It might fall out and you won't find it."

Taking my five-year-old in for surgery was traumatic. He wanted nothing to do with the doctors and would not go to them when it was time to prep him for surgery, so I had to hold him as they gave him the anesthesia to put him to sleep for the procedure. His body was so small, and he looked dead. Even though I was a healthcare professional, it was terrifying to see him like that. I did not want to let him go. They took him from my arms and put him on the stretcher to go to the OR.

After they took him from my arms, I went one way, and my husband went the other way. I was crying. I do not know what Keith went to do. But we split in the moments after our son went in for the operation. It was too much to bear in that instant. Thankfully, the surgery was successful, but it took a lot out of us emotionally.

As he grew older, Kevin took on extracurricular activities—lots of them—and, because I was the only person in our family who could drive, it became my responsibility to take him to his different functions. When Kevin was in first grade, the principal of the school insisted that he try out for an audition for a play. Many students from his school went, and he got selected for the play, *Really Rosy*, at the Studio Theater. This added a lot to my stress, and, at times, pushed me to the limit, because it was something I had to squeeze into an already-packed schedule. I took Kevin to all his rehearsals, and, after rehearsals, when the play opened, I had to take him to performances.

During rehearsals, I sat in the car and did my office work. Then, he started performing: Friday nights, Saturday nights, and Sunday afternoons. As the only driver, I had to take him to all the shows, despite my workload. At times, the stress was too much, but it was worth it to spend time with Kevin, to see him happy and doing the things he loved to do with his friends.

Kevin also loved wrestling. I used to take him to his wrestling matches. It was more of a challenge to get work done there. Imagine the scene, at the stadium: the kids are wrestling, a bunch of people are screaming all around me, and I open my briefcase to do office work while everyone else is laughing and having a good time around me in the stands. They all looked at me like I was a crazy person. But I could not take time put down my work to enjoy the matches, because I was too busy with my obligations. At that time, it was the only way I could set aside time for him, so I gave him what I could.

When Mr. Matlock, the administrator of the nursing home, resigned, Jim, the assistant administrator, replaced him. Jim's first major action was to terminate the director of nursing, and I was promoted to replace her. I thought about my luck. I was always at the right place and at the right time. It was as though every step I took and every move I made had been mapped out just for me. I was now responsible for the complete nursing department on a 24-hour basis instead of just the evening shift, but I could be home in the evenings with Keith and Kevin, enjoying family life.

My tenure as director of nursing lasted 10 years, the longest director's tenure in the entire history of that nursing home. I became very well known by government officials and others in the healthcare business in the District of Columbia. Under my leadership, the nursing home enjoyed several years with zero deficiencies in the nursing department during annual inspections by the Department of Health. The new administrator modernized almost every department in the nursing home, and we earned everyone's trust and respect. The receptionist, Miss Madeline, often called me for insight, even when her concerns were not related to nursing. When asked to refer those questions to other directors, she responded, "I called you, because I know you have the answer." And she was right. I had the answers, because I was like a sponge, absorbing every tidbit of information, which I generously shared with others. I had knowledge. I had power, and I learned to use it to my advantage to become a force to be reckoned with. I read and familiarized myself with all the District of Columbia's long-term care laws and regulations. I was well versed in all the Federal codes of regulation and their interpretive guidelines as they pertained to the Centers for Medicare and Medicaid Services (CMS). I studied the Federal enforcement book for nursing homes, and I could recite the State Operating Manual used by the surveyors. I could challenge every deficiency long before Informal Dispute Resolution was created by CMS. I reviewed and revised all of the nursing department policies and procedures to ensure our compliance with all regulations.

To maximize my success in the nursing home industry, I had to take risks. I was constantly seeking out what I called forward risk. In a way, I was making myself available by positioning myself to be a value-added professional, not only to my peers at the nursing home where I worked but to other colleagues in the business of directly or indirectly caring for seniors. Because of my knowledge, power, and leadership skills, I was invited to join several committees. Participating in those committees helped me to grow in the nursing home business. I not only had a chance to meet other top professionals, but I also gained a reputation of being a hard worker. People knew that I would deliver when I was part of a group. I was asked to join the Mayor's Health Policy Council team to assist with rewriting the nursing and medical regulations, an assignment I gladly accepted.

It became clear to me after a few years in the business that directors of nursing were being used as scapegoats by the nursing home administrators each time a facility failed their annual survey from the Department of Health. Many times, nursing was not the sole culprit of a poor survey; however, the nursing director was almost always discharged from their duty. It appeared that this action was taken to show the government that the administration was making changes to improve quality when, in many instances, the person who should have been fired was the administrator. Unhappy with this observation, I wrote a letter to all the nursing directors, inviting them to join me for lunch at my nursing home. Over lunch, we discussed the need to meet monthly to develop a support system for each other. We shared notes, policies, and procedures, and we discussed concerns of management and staff. I became the founder and the first chairperson of the District of Columbia Directors of Nursing Committee in Long-Term Care.

By now, Keith had made a job change from the OAS to Intelsat (International Telecommunications Satellite Organization) as a systems analyst for a much higher salary. Kevin was attending Lafayette, the best public school in the District of Columbia, the elementary school in our Ward Three neighborhood. I joined the PTA to stay close to his development in school while meeting my own professional growth goals. I was very active and participated in as many of his school functions and class outings as I could fit in my busy schedule. I was reliving my childhood vicariously through my son. I did things with Kevin that my parents did not have the knowledge, the finances, nor the opportunity to do with me as a child. We collected pumpkins from a patch during a school outing. I stood on the side of the road with a proud smile on my face, watching him parade with his classmates at school events. We both dressed up on Halloween. I dressed him as Superman, Fat Albert, or Big Bird and went door to door with him to collect candy from our neighbors.

To say that life had changed for this poor girl from Haiti would be an understatement. While I was happy and proud of my accomplishments, I kept my eyes open for bigger and better things in my life. Like a turtle, I continued to stick my neck out.

In the healthcare industry in the '80s, black employees mostly belonged in the kitchen; they also served as nurses' aides, porters, and janitors, except for a handful of registered nurses who had managed to make it to the top. As the first African American in a leadership position at The Washington Home, I was a rarity. I felt that I had a banner to carry, which made me work even harder: I had to prove myself and shine on behalf of my fellow black workers. A reflection of the times, the nursing home was a nonprofit business managed by a group of volunteer board members who were 100 percent Caucasian. I was constantly challenged and, at times, harassed by others, particularly my peer directors. Several board members heavily questioned Jim, the administrator, when I was promoted to director of nursing, mainly because of the color of my skin. They often made comments about me that were clearly racial. I was aware of many such comments, because Jim and I worked well as a team; we were both driven and focused in implementing our goals for the nursing home. Understanding the culture, I had no choice but to strive to be the best that I could be, using obstacles to become an exemplary leader, partner, and mother. But, even as I became a valued employee, a hard worker with the skills to bring the nursing home deficiency-free inspection results, some still refused to accept me.

The nursing director's office was large and spacious, with a rectangular conference table and chairs. It also included my desk and another desk that was occupied by a male board member who had volunteered to "help with paperwork." In reality, he had been tasked to monitor the first African-American director and to report on whether I was bright enough to handle the job.

"Imagine reporting to work every day and having a board member sitting in your office watching your every move," I told Keith.

But I was a trooper—I have been all my life. Through prayer, I strive and shine in the presence of adversity. Within a year, trust was established, and this board member suddenly could no longer be bothered to volunteer his time to assist with paperwork. The position was eliminated.

The Washington Home building was very old. Its laundry room was located in the lower subbasement, in a space with no bathroom and no hopper for shaking the residents' linen before the diapers were placed in the washing machine. For this reason, the nursing staff had the responsibility to "pre-treat" all soiled diapers in a resident's bathroom before bagging and sending them to the laundry. This procedure, established long before I was hired, created a major friction between Allan, the laundry director, and I, because, on multiple occasions, the nursing staff failed to rinse the diapers. The laundry staff often washed unrinsed diapers still full of stool, which created a particularly unpleasant working environment, and, at times, the cleaned linen was delivered to the nursing units with dry feces.

I understood the problem and sympathized with the laundry staff who had to work in such unsanitary conditions and endure the unpleasant odor. I conducted multiple in-service educations on the procedure, took my staff to the laundry room to demonstrate the situation and why it was imperative for them to rinse the diapers in the residents' bathrooms, the same way they would have done at home caring for a baby. This topic was even addressed at all new nursing employee orientations. The nursing department operated nonstop, 24 hours a day, seven days a week, and 365 days a year.

Because I was managing a staff of over 200 nursing employees, it was an impossible task to monitor the behavior of each employee and ensure that every single diaper was rinsed before bagging. Again and again, my staff failed to follow the proper procedure, and Allan continued with his harassment. On occasions, he tried to embarrass me at department directors' meetings when laundry was discussed. I understood his level of frustration, but he failed to appreciate my dilemma and my inability to identify the non-compliant employees or nursing units. The administrator was aware of the tug-of-war but continued to preach collaboration as team members. The solution would have been to close the in-house laundry and use a contracted company for this service or to relocate the physical laundry department. Outsourcing the laundry service was cost prohibitive. Fortunately, a new facility was being built, and the old building would soon be razed. Resolving the soiled diaper issue was a few years away.

By regulation, in the absence of the administrator, the director of nursing was in charge of the facility. There came a time when I was acting as administrator in Jim's absence, and the laundry director filled a bag with soiled diapers, making sure the stool was visibly smeared on the clear plastic. Allan walked into my office and dropped the very large bag in the center of my office, which petrified the board member. The bag fell so hard that the noise was heard before the bag was even seen.

The director stated angrily, "Tell your staff to stop sending shit downstairs." He then turned his back and walked out.

Stunned, the board member looked at me with a very sad face. He softly said, "I am sorry."

I was mortified not only by the action of this white man, but by his audacity to behave in this manner, especially in front of the board member. Without a word, I picked up the bag of soiled diapers and placed it in an empty closet, making sure that it was locked to prevent any residents or staff from having access to it.

When he heard about the incident that night, Keith was livid, calling Allan's action insubordinate since I was the top authority in the building. He was urging me to act. This time, it was I who kept myself calm and collected.

"Allan, the laundry room director, is looking for a fight. I'm not about to lower myself to his level."

The mere fact that he had waited for the absence of the administrator to express his anger in such a humiliating fashion was clear bait for an argument. He expected a confrontation. But he had underestimated my integrity and intellect. I had a lot of self-control. As first lady, Michelle Obama, would say years later, "When they go low, we go high." Allan's lack of respect for me as a woman of color, and as the acting administrator, had put an end to any civil exchanges over dirty diapers: I was done.

The following day, I chaired the directors' morning meeting, and not once did I mention a word about the diaper incident—not to Allan individually or to the group. He had no clue as to what I did with the bag, and he must have wondered about my plan of action. For three days, we shared no words, and I managed to stay out of his way, except at morning meetings. But over those three days, things were brewing inside that closet where I kept the bag of soiled diapers.

Monday came, and Jim returned to work. We met immediately after the morning meeting, as was customary, to recap events that occurred in his absence. I gave a very comprehensive report to my boss but saved the best for last. Before sharing with him the diaper incident, I excused myself for a minute, went to my hiding closet, and grabbed the big bag full of soiled diapers, which now gave out an awful odor. Reenacting Allan's theatrical gesture, I barged into Jim's office, lifted the bag as high as the top of my head, and dropped it in the center of the room. The smell exploded, and Jim jumped from his seat as though I had just smeared the stool all over him. I then explained what had happened, and how I had dealt with the incident in his absence.

Jim was shocked. He simply said, "I am sorry, Solanges. I will take care of it."

The laundry director was employed by a contracting company that provided staffing for housekeeping and laundry services to the nursing home. I never asked Jim how he handled the situation. All I know is that Allan was removed from the facility, and the company's contract was eventually terminated.

It is very important as a leader to know when to act. For every action, there is a reaction. Being able to control one's behavior is key to growth as a leader. Our authority will constantly be challenged. The way we handle this challenge, however, is a major factor in how successful we can become. As a young professional, I learned to never allow anyone to get a reaction out of me that I would regret later. I am always reminded of Ernest Hemingway's quote: "Today is the only day in all the days that will ever be. But what will happen in all the other days that ever come can depend on what you do today." All it takes is one Allan in your life to destroy your future. This incident could have had a completely different ending if I had taken his bait. Reacting to his action was analogous to taking a risk without any thoughts of the potential consequences.

Keith had resigned from his systems analyst position at Intelsat and started a health clinic with a partner. He became an entrepreneur in his own right. We were both doing very well financially. We purchased our first home very close to the apartment building, because we were both very fond of the area and its accessibility to public transportation.

Kevin was now old enough to walk alone to the elementary school from the house. He enjoyed having his friends at the house for sleepovers and was trusted to spend the night over his friends' homes. He grew up to be a very friendly young man well-liked by everyone. My relationship with Keith continued to blossom. We had many friends, entertained a lot at our new home, and were often told that we were the perfect couple.

Even though Keith had made me the perfect common-law wife and to our son the perfect mother, I was not satisfied. As an ever-faithful Catholic who attended church every Sunday and celebrated fervently every religious holiday, there was still a part of my life that was unfulfilled. For a Christian, marriage was an important sacrament: I continued to pray to Mother Mary about my dream to someday be escorted by Keith to church for our wedding. Whenever the opportunity presented itself, I would remind him that we were not obeying the commandments and following the Church's doctrines and that I was living in sin by not being married in Christ. Keith had grown up in the church; he had been an altar boy for many years at St. Matthias church in Barbados. As an adult, however, he had taken the position that he had paid his dues to the church and had no reason to continue to attend. During one of my nagging moments about marriage, with a firm voice he said, "Solanges I do not need a man in a white robe to tell me how to run my life, nor my household."

Since my arrival in Washington, D.C., everyone assumed that we were married. When people referred to me as Keith Archer's wife, I never corrected them. At Kevin's school, I was "Mrs. Archer" (when I was not simply "Kevin's mom") to which I politely answered. My now-grown nieces, nephews, cousins, and friends all assumed that we were married. In any case, leaving Keith was never an option that I was willing to entertain, even though I was saddened by the fact that I was living in sin. I was at least smart enough to know that abandoning my home could have had a detrimental effect on my son—and me. Keith was a great man, and the most wonderful father to Kevin. I made a vow to myself never to discuss marriage again. Keith's position on marriage was his to live with. It might be impossible to get him to change his mind on the subject, but, maybe, I could figure out a way to get him back to church. Instead of fighting it, instead of praying to God for marriage, I prayed for forgiveness.

It was a very cold winter day in Washington, D.C., and I had a bad case of the flu, which kept me home from work. It was close to noon when the doorbell rang. At the front door was a deliveryman requesting a signature for a package. I accepted the box that was addressed to me. I looked at the return address: a very famous jewelry store on Fifth Avenue in New York City.

"Cartier! I did not order anything from Cartier," I said. Then, I called Keith. "A box was just delivered from the Cartier store in New York. Do you know anything about it?" Before he had a chance to answer, I said again, "I know that I did not order anything from Cartier."

"I did," he said. "Open it. It's for you."

While he was still on the phone, I tried to open the package. "I can't," I said. "I need a knife."

"I will wait," Keith said. "Go get one."

Because I was so weak with the flu, I walked slowly down the stairs to the kitchen. After I got the knife, opening this box was like trying to break someone out of Fort Knox. Having been burnt before by a small box, I refused to imagine what this box from Cartier contained. I would find out soon enough. When I finally got the little brown box opened, what was inside it was obviously a ring box. Without opening it, I went back to the bedroom. "I got it open," I said on the phone.

"Did you look at it?"

"No, I did not open the small box."

"Open it." I could imagine that teasing look on his face. I wish I could see it. "It's for you!"

It was a beautiful yellow gold ring with diamonds all around it. A real wedding band.

All I said was, "How beautiful."

He said, "You can set the date."

Tears were running down my cheeks. "For us to get married?"

"Yes, for us to get married."

There you have it: After fourteen years as lovers, then common-law parents, and then co-owners of our first home, we, the "perfect couple" (as our friends called us), were finally headed to the altar.

"Let's discuss it tonight," I said.

I felt grateful that my prayers of forgiveness to God had miraculously been granted. But, still groggy from the flu medications, I wanted to get back under the covers. Sleep would not come, however. I could not help but to think about what had just happened. It blew my mind. What kind of a wedding would we have? How would I explain to our 7-year-old son that Mommy and Daddy were getting married? What would such an announcement do to his young mind? "A wedding!" I exclaimed. "That is out of the question."

Had Keith expected to get the mail himself since he was usually home earlier than I was? Had I not been home to receive the package, would he have proposed differently? Had this all worked out to his advantage so that he did not have to follow the proposal traditions that he so hated? Was it a coincidence that I just happened to be home? Was it God's plan to make me sick so that the event happened the way it did? Why was my fate so designed?

"You can set the date." What kind of a proposal was that? After so many years of such an intense relationship, what a way to ask your lover to marry you! But Keith was who he was, and I was in it for the long haul. I had developed a profound appreciation for Keith and understood his psyche. I was so enthralled by this man and dedicated to maintaining our relationship that I was not fazed by any of his actions. Many women would have long ago abandoned the relationship, but, because of my faith, Jesus guided every step and every move I made by giving me the courage to hang on. I stayed for love and for my son, but also (in truth) for my own personal and professional growth. I realized that this intellectual and rational, kind and mild-tempered man, who was 10 years my senior, really loved me and wanted what was best for me. He had pledged to help me reach my potential, and he was doing just that. The love that existed between Keith and me was stronger than the challenges of life, and, together, we flourished. I would never have abandoned what we had built together: our own little family. I had the best partner any woman could ever dream of—he was a fantastic friend and an exemplary father.

That evening, my fever and chills worsened. When Keith arrived home, he worked hard to nurse my illness with Theraflu, hot tea, Tylenol, a humidifier, and a warm blanket. Dinner for me was a can of warm Campbell's chicken noodle soup and for Keith his favorite quick meal: onions, three different colored bell peppers sautéed with some seasoning, all mixed together with a can of salmon over white rice. Because of my flu, he made every effort to avoid any close contact with me for fear of catching my bug, so he slept in the guest room. And just like that, the day that I had been hoping, waiting, longing and praying for came and went in a flash, spoiled by illness. *Sweet and sour.* Throughout my life, I have never been fully immersed in full and complete happiness without something robbing me of the moment.

We decided to get married as soon as possible. A big wedding was no longer as important to me as it had been in my teenage years and earlier in our relationship, when all my friends were getting married, so we decided on a small wedding with no fanfare. Several of our friends who had had their dream weddings in their early 20s were no longer married. I, on the other hand, was still with Keith. We were finally going to bless our relationship before Christ, and I was mainly interested in receiving this very important sacrament of my faith. I had been baptized as a baby; I had received my first communion and then my confirmation. The sacrament of marriage was next in line to fulfill my religious faith. To me, this marriage would end a sinful situation and would also legitimize my son. These facts were more important to me than a long white dress, a veil, and a procession of guests.

It was November, and I was in California with the nursing home's medical director, presenting one of my papers at the Gerontological Society of America, an association of doctors, nurses and other professionals in the aging field. Both Keith and Kevin accompanied me on that trip. While browsing at a shopping center for designer clothing, Keith noticed a beautiful two-piece outfit in a display window; it was silk, in light beige and burgundy. "Let's get a closer look," he said. He liked it so much that he encouraged me to model the dress for him, and I knew right away that I would wear it for our wedding. We had big fun in the store and eventually purchased not only the dress from the window but another beautiful one-piece burgundy silk dress that we both liked.

All my siblings were married with children; therefore, we had lots of nieces and nephews. Since we were all struggling—some more than others—to support our families, we decided to celebrate Christmas together, turning the festivities into one big party. We took turns pulling names out of a hat for Secret Santa. It was a way to ensure that everyone got to enjoy Christmas and that each child received at least one gift. My siblings and I took turns hosting the event every year, and it just so happened that it was my turn to welcome everyone at our house. Keith and I decided to use this occasion for our wedding celebration.

The religious ceremony took place at the Immaculate Conception chapel of Saint Anne Catholic Church on the afternoon of Christmas Eve in the presence of Keith's friend Eddy, the best man, and my oldest sister Ritza, my matron of honor. Ritza wore the burgundy dress that Keith had bought in California.

In this little chapel were also my mother, father, and my sister Paulette. It was what Keith wanted once he finally gave in and sent me the ring and what I had grown to accept: a simple yet beautiful ceremony. We had written our own vows and, as usual, Keith helped me correct my grammar and spelling. I had also worked on my pronunciation. We pledged our love for each other at the altar, before God. Keith was opposed to a long white dress with a train and to a procession of people, but he was not opposed to a wedding cake. So, I had gotten a one-layer white wedding cake, and a set of his-and-hers wedding tumblers as souvenirs of our wedding. My sisters had prepared a wonderful Caribbean meal for lunch, and we had wedding cake for dessert.

It was a big day for me. I was finally married, and it filled an empty spot inside me I had been carrying for years. It also brought me closer to my own mother in a way. I understood, after saying my vows, how hard it must have been for her to stay with Ambroise all those years in a common-law marriage, outside of the grace of the church. Having my relationship with Keith sanctified by holy vows legitimized our relationship in a way it had not been before. We now had something sacred. We belong together, and I knew, that day, that my own mother had also gone through the same kind of struggle I had to walk down the aisle.

The night before the wedding, Kevin was sent to a sleepover at his friend Blair's house to shelter him from the family chit-chats on what was happening. Even my two best friends, Alice (Blair's mother) and Gloria (William's mother), had never found out that Keith and I had never been married. Other than family, I told no one that I was getting married, nor has this part of my history ever been shared. Only close family members were aware of the wedding having taken place earlier that day. By evening, the house was filled with family, young and old. Our Christmas tree reached the ceiling, and countless gifts lay on the floor. Children ran around, dancing to Christmas music, the oven was on, and yes, there was a whole lot of drinking going on.

Just before midnight, I emerged in a beautiful red dress with my Mrs. Santa's bonnet and distributed gifts to all our guests. There was no going away on a honeymoon for us newlyweds: we partied until the wee hours of the morning in our own home. It was about four o'clock in the morning when I climbed into the same old bed next to my husband, exhausted after our big wedding/

Christmas celebration. Keith had abandoned the party hours before, needing to escape from all the commotion. He enjoyed being alone and had no love for big crowds. I had not been a bit concerned when he disappeared from the party: I knew exactly where to find my husband—this precious gift from my angel of the sun.

MAKE IT WORK FOR YOU!

Rule #15: Stay Attuned to Invisible Struggles

Reflection: Where Does the Light Lead You?

It is a sad fact, but, as of this writing, six out of the seven sea turtle species are endangered, and the seventh is threatened. A turtle is at its most vulnerable to threats from predators as it hatches from its eggshell and makes its way from the nest to the ocean, and then, to a lesser degree, as it is growing to maturity. After it reaches adulthood, if not for the things mankind is doing to its natural environment, a turtle would only need to really worry about shark attacks. We think of the big things that are harming the sea turtle population, like oil spills and pollution, and hunting, but even the artificial lighting on a beach can throw a turtle off course and lead it to its death. It is another example of how the things we do not think twice about can cause great harm. Be mindful. Tread lightly.

- When you greet people in your day, ask them how they are doing, and really listen to their answers. Sometimes, all a person really needs to brighten their day is to feel they are being heard. Be someone who listens.

- Make a list of people you can contact if you are in a crisis. Reach out to them and let them know they are important to you, and ask how they are doing. Or, write them a note to let them know how important they are to you. Be there for the people who are there for you when you need them.

RULES TO LIVE BY

If I did not have enough on my plate already with my career and home life and making sure it all ran smoothly, I took some advice from my husband, and got another degree. It was a busy time, yes. But I had support, and I knew it was leading me to better things for myself and my family.

It was also a period in my life where I had to fight for justice, both in my workplace, where an administrator seemed to want my head on a platter, and at school, where a professor gave me a clear signal to stay in my place. I have never been one to sit still and be quiet.

And then I found a note on my pillow one night with a message to make a call to someone important—no matter how late. The next day, I was in for a meeting I would never forget.

Rule #16: Be Fearless and Fight for What is Right

Fear is a vital instinct. It warns us when we are in danger, but it is also important to understand the difference between fear that is reasonable and fear based on insecurity that holds us back. One thing to look out for is people who use their powers to bully others such as the administrator at the nursing home where I worked (see chapter eight, "The Fishing Expedition"). People who use their power to push you around will play on your insecurities, if you let them get under your skin. Do not allow yourself to be intimidated by anyone. You are just as important as anyone else in the world. Speak up. When I knew I had earned a better grade than what I was given by my professor, Dr. Smith, I fought the grade (see chapter eight, "The Fishing Expedition"). Even though I did not win that battle, I felt some satisfaction in having my voice heard. Do not be afraid to say what you need to in order to stand up for yourself. Sometimes, if you speak up and are bold, the person you are communicating your needs to will often come through for you in a big way. Push past your insecurities and have a can-do attitude; you will gain much more than you would staying scared and silent.

Rule #17: Maintain Your Reputation

Remember, it is not who you know, it is who knows you. There were many times throughout my career when my reputation helped me through adversity and opened doors for me that might have remained shut tight, if I had not worked to prove my dedication as an ethical leader in the healthcare industry. I was consistent in insisting on holding not only myself but also my staff to a set of high standards we all had to stretch to meet. Once you set high standards for yourself and for others, word spreads. People become aware that you are a solid professional. In Washington, D.C., where I built my business, careers were wrecked by negative coverage in the press and by political infighting. I was always mindful of the publicity my company received and made it a point to stay out of politics.

My company avoided one serious scandal, which could have created a lot of problems, because a social worker knew she could trust me to handle a delicate situation with one of my residents. As it turned out, there was a reasonable explanation, and we resolved the matter quickly and quietly (see chapter eight, "The Fishing Expedition").

Part of building a solid reputation is making time for others and never allowing yourself to fall into the trap of believing you are better than anyone else (see chapter 10, "A New Reality"). People will trust you if you prove yourself trustworthy, and one way of doing this is by letting others know you respect them. In a professional setting, respect is something you earn by showing your best side.

It is important that people respect you for your intellect, but they will also have a higher regard for you if you take care of your body and are mindful to make sure you are well-groomed and dressed. I learned a good deal about how to present myself from the time I spent modeling while I was in college in New York (see chapter five, "Nursing School"). Be proud of your appearance and make sure you dress for success. Be a role model to those you supervise and show some etiquette. Once I started encouraging my staff by teaching them how to dress professionally, morale improved drastically (see chapter nine, "Climbing the Mountains to a Dynasty").

8

The Fishing Expedition

I had plenty to keep me occupied, but Keith encouraged me to return to school.

His favorite line was, "If you think any hospital will hire you without a graduate degree, you have another thing coming."

My plate was already full. I was responsible for almost 200 seniors at the nursing home and over 200 staff members who cared for them. But, because Keith was so relentless about it, I enrolled at Georgetown University, in an evening master's degree Health Services Administration program. Since I was already working in a leadership capacity in nursing, this program was essential for my professional growth. In addition, it fit into my demanding schedule.

I balanced multiple facets of life simultaneously and learned to wear multiple hats, compartmentalizing to keep the different aspects of my life organized. At four o'clock in the afternoon, I removed my director-of-nursing hat to metamorphose into a student and wore my imaginary student hat. On my way home from school, I put on my mommy-and-wife hat. This was my routine for two years while I strove to obtain my graduate degree. I never forgot that I was, above all, a mother and a wife, both responsibilities I took even more seriously than career advancement. I did, however, sacrifice quality time with my little family in order to meet my educational goals, knowing I could count on Keith, who was my biggest cheerleader. He waited at the house for Kevin to return from his afterschool program so that they could work together on homework. He cooked dinner, did the laundry, cleaned the house, and, yes, pressed my clothes and polished my shoes. He even read all my assigned books to guarantee I received an A on my book reports by critiquing my papers and giving me feedback on my work. Keith was the angel that God had tasked with taking care of me. The more I progressed, the prouder Keith became.

Ambitious and driven, I always wanted more. Some of my nursing assistants drove Mercedes-Benzes and BMWs, while I drove an old beat-up green Pacer. I wanted a new car, but the only way to afford one was to work for it. Every Friday and Saturday, from 11 at night till seven in the morning, I worked in the intensive care unit at Georgetown University Hospital to save money for a new car. Still, I found the time to write and published several articles related to aging and the administration of health care services. I became a sought-after speaker.

Just as in my schoolgirl days in Haiti, good grades mattered to me tremendously. When I obtained an unfair D in one of my classes, I was determined to fight it. In my inimitable "Solanges's style," I challenged the grade all the way to the dean of the nursing division at Georgetown University.

I was the only black student in the program and, in my two years at the university, I only had one professor of color. I was an A and B student—curious and dedicated. Most of the teachers loved me, except for Dr. Smith who lived in New York. Once a week, she boarded the shuttle airplane from La Guardia Airport to the National Airport (renamed Ronald Reagan Airport) to teach an Ethics and Law class, and then flew back to New York the same evening. She tried to be cordial but wore a disdainful face in the classroom, and I knew right away that it would not take much to rub her the wrong way.

In the first week of the semester, some of my classmates brought copies of a nursing journal I had been published in, and asked me to autograph the article for them. Although the class session had not begun yet, I saw Dr. Smith frown. As the students gathered around me, impressed by the article, and in awe of me—a black woman who had "made it" as a director of nursing and was now attending Georgetown University—I could feel the weight of my professor's profound dislike. I could see it in her body language, in her downturned mouth. The students, that evening, were too interested in me, and their lack of focus on the class angered her. Even as Dr. Smith presented her prepared material, the students' conversations were not about ethics; she stopped on many occasions to ask students to focus on her lecture. She was not happy with their enthusiasm at my success. I sensed a dark fury was brewing inside this woman's head.

"She's jealous," Sandy, a brunette, whispered.

"Uh huh," Caroline said.

"And you're black," Suzy said. She always spoke her mind.

Dr. Smith never warmed up to me, even though I completed all my assignments with zeal. When Georgetown University published a brochure that prominently featured me among my white classmates, she was the only one who did not comment on it. In the early 1980s, a woman of color photographed in a Georgetown University publication to advertise a graduate program was rare— and more than Dr. Smith could handle. I was black, intelligent and driven, and those were my crimes.

Dr. Smith was not known as a tough grader, so, when I received a D in the class, I knew she was using her power to try to keep me in my place. I found it ironic: the professor with a specialized course dealing in principles and fairness violated both ethics and non-discriminatory policy in the way she graded my coursework. Having read my paper, the dean agreed that the D was an unfair grade. "It's not perfect," she said, "but, according to the rubric, you should get at least a B minus." By University policy, however, only the professor was authorized to change a grade, and Dr. Smith was unwilling to travel back to Washington, D.C., to do the paperwork. Fortunately, the grade would not affect my ability to graduate, so, in the end, I earned my master's. Having this unfair grade still irked me.

Keith was unrelenting in his quest to ensure I met my potential. He pushed me to study harder than I would have on my own, and, as a result of my diligent work, I successfully passed both the national and Washington, D.C., examinations and obtained my license as a nursing home administrator. Around the same time, Jim resigned from the nursing home, and a new administrator was hired.

During our very first meeting, Garrett, the new administrator, told me, "I was told that, if I am to exercise my authority as administrator, the first thing I ought to do is fire you. I was told that you've got your nose in every department, and that you'll undermine me. You seem to think *you* are the administrator."

I remained unfazed. By now, I was used to challenges. With a smile, I answered, "Why don't we work together? You can evaluate my performance, and then decide for yourself whether you need to get rid of me. Your personal assessment should be your guiding light, not what others have told you about me."

We worked together for a while, but, after three months, the incessant rumors in the building—and the racist comments—started affecting the work environment; I realized they could become destructive to the facility. Conflicts, real or perceived, have the potential to interfere with quality of care and, in turn, negatively impact nursing home residents. When I walked into a department directors' meeting with champagne and orange juice for mimosas, I was not being confrontational; I wanted to put an end to the triangular communication between directors and managers and the malicious misinformation that could eventually inflame the situation. I wanted to stop the gossip. I offered a toast to celebrate Garrett's successful completion of his probationary period. "Rumor has it that you're planning to get rid of me," I said. "I want the directors and managers to know that you and I have a great working relationship. Don't we, Garrett?"

Stopping the rumors was more important to me than even my position as director of nursing. I was a registered nurse with a master's degree from Georgetown University with experience in multiple facets in nursing and nursing management; I was armed with a license to practice as a nursing home administrator. I knew I was marketable, but I still struggled with separation anxiety, so I stayed in my director of nursing position, tolerating Garrett's attitude. I was well aware that most of the rumors about me originated from the administrator himself. He resented my leadership skills and my perceived authority in the building. He was jealous of my status in the community, as most of our employees and colleagues (in and outside of the facility) looked up to me and respected my opinion. I had knowledge and power, and I knew how to use them for personal and professional growth.

In the '40s and '50s, Haitian parents had no handheld cameras
to document their childrens lives. Usually, the first picture is
taken at a photo studio by a professional photographer for the
childs first communion. At this event, the child is dressed like a
mini bride and devotes her life to Christ.

Ambroise was no more than 5 feet tall with a Napoleon complex. My mother, a very tall woman, stood at 5'4".

My mom and her two sisters. All three contributed to our upbringing.

Ambroise and Francesca's children, minus Gerald who died before this picture was taken in 1979.

Gerald as a young lad.

Reginald as a teenager.

I returned to Haiti to say goodbye to my dad's firstborn who was diagnosed with stage four cancer, and I was introduced to my last sister, Gladys, born from my mother's housekeeper. She looked just like me.

Francesca's six girls.

My newly found cousin Josiane and her husband Jacques in Paris, France.

At the Silvermans, I felt like a princess, even though I was a nanny.

I traveled with the family and met actors and actresses like Lulu in the movie *To Sir, with Love* with Sidney Poitier.

On the road with the Silvermans.

Our wedding.

Christmas and wedding
reception combined.

Playing tennis,
our favorite pastime.

Valentine's Day celebration.

Cruising with my husband Keith.

Life with my husband
Keith and son Kevin.

Gloria and I met at the
boys' nursery school,
and we remain a
foursome to date.

Life with my son Kevin.

Father East blessing
our new home.

My son Kevin's law school
graduation. "He made mama
proud."

Enjoying life with my son
and his family.

At an AHCA convention, I became the first and only African American to have been elected vice president of this national association.

Me and Ana
at our first AHCA Gala.

At another AHCA convention, the board of the Coalition of Women unveiled the captioned picture, "The Face of Long-Term Care is Female." Yet, all the top positions were occupied by white males.

Me and Veronica at one of the Washington's Center for Aging's nursing homes' perfect survey celebrations.

Addressing my seniors and guests when I was called out for my big emergency phone call.

My two partners, Doc and Victor, who believed in my ability to build a solid business.

Very politically charged, defending quality care for the nursing home residents.

Joining my seniors on Capitol Hill. Fighting to keep Medicare coverage from being cut for nursing homes.

President and Executive Director for DCHCA.

On Capitol Hill with AHCA.

The only Haitian girl with her own $300 bill.

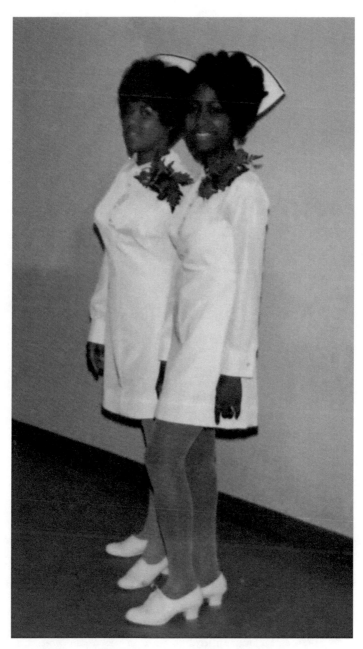

Erith and me at Capping Ceremony.

Forever a lifelong learner, I obtained my doctoral degree.

When the assistant administrator position became vacant, I should have been immediately promoted. I had proven myself fit for the position through many years of hard work. Despite my stellar qualifications, my degrees and licenses, and my familiarity with the nursing home staff and residents, my application was denied. As an intelligent and driven black woman, I constituted a threat for Garrett, who gave the position to a less qualified white candidate, who was a registered nurse but not licensed as a nursing home administrator in the District of Columbia. Although licensure was not a prerequisite for the position, it would have been considered an asset and a determining factor in the selection under any other circumstances. Jen had worked with the administrator at another facility—and she was "one of them": white.

Garrett was intent on finding a reason to fire me. Desperate, he befriended Sarah, the assistant director of nursing, who reported to me, hoping to get exclusive information or uncover some dirty laundry to justify his plan. I had known Sarah for years. When I was the assistant director of nursing for the evening shift, Sarah was head nurse on the day shift. When I became director, I promoted Sarah to assistant director. What Garrett did not know was that Sarah and I were more than colleagues. We were such good friends that Kevin called her Auntie Sarah. When Sarah purchased her first home, she lovingly referred to the swing set in her backyard as "Kevin's swing set," since she had no children of her own. In the end, she gifted the swing set to Kevin.

We vowed not to allow the administrator to break up our friendship. A loyal ally, Sarah revealed to me anything Garrett said or seemed to be planning in his effort to get rid of me. As the situation escalated, however, the administrator realized that Sarah was not going to turn on me. Instead, he hired an African-American consultant from his hometown of Philadelphia. Ms. Clara's task was to evaluate the nursing department, since Garrett himself was not a nurse. She spent a couple of weeks at the facility, where she reviewed policies and procedures, and interviewed families, residents, and staff. She analyzed past reports from the Department of Health, and even called the ombudsman who confirmed that the nursing department was experiencing a very low number of deficiencies. All nursing positions were filled, and no outside staffing agency was being used at the facility. There were no lawsuits against the facility, and families had no complaints, which were the usual reasons to terminate a director of nursing.

Prior to exiting the building, Ms. Clara met with me as part of her data gathering and was very gracious in providing me a verbal report of her review of the department. Her findings were benign, and she complimented my managerial skills. However, she never met with me in the presence of the administrator, nor did I receive a copy of the consultant's report, which would have allowed me to address any concerns. Despite the positive findings from the consultant, Garrett played one last card. He gave me the worst evaluation I had received in my 10 years of work at the Washington Nursing Home.

Although livid, I was ahead of his game: the administrator's intent had been clear to Keith and me from the start. I took the evaluation home to my husband and advisor, and, together, we devised a plan. Garrett could not know what it meant to be black in the United States of America in the '70s and '80s: we had dealt with discrimination and injustice for most of our lives. We were no strangers to challenges. We were intelligent, proud professionals who, unbeknownst to him, had been documenting his malicious actions and words, which could be damaging not only to my position but also to my professional reputation.

Sarah had warned me about this man's fishing expedition, and Keith and I were ready. This battle was not mine alone but Keith's as well. Because he saw himself as my defender, it was personal. No one was going to harm his wife. He seemed more affected by these developments than I was, even though I was the one who had to face Garrett daily and manage a department despite the tension. Keith worried about me. He called my office frequently, which confirmed that this issue was taking its toll on him. "The nerve of that man," he said about Garrett, "to attack my wife, my angel of the sun, her worth and integrity." He was furious and determined to get retribution. I vowed not to allow these events to affect my performance, nor the care delivery to my residents. The situation only made me stronger and more focused.

We contacted Dominic, a friend of ours, who was also a civil rights attorney, for advice on how to proceed. He encouraged us to send a simple letter to the members of the Executive Board of Directors at the nursing home. "One of the members is a colleague," Dominic said. "He'll get the message." He wrote the letter on my behalf, using our input. It took a few weeks to get the required information—all factual. "You do not want to appear subjective, biased, or emotional," he explained. It was also important that the letter be clear, so that the Board of Directors could make a decision based on facts. He promised that, if this strategy did not work to our satisfaction, he would formally file a case against both the home and against Garrett for harassment.

The board never met with me to discuss the letter. An attorney on the board was assigned by the chairman to handle the case. He and Dominic negotiated a settlement. Dominic made several recommendations: That the unfair evaluation be expunged from my personnel file and replaced with an unbiased re-evaluation that accurately represented my performance. That I continue to work at the facility without any reprisal, so long as I maintained the same level of performance. That I be compensated for failure to promote, since I had been well-qualified for the position I was denied. That I also receive a substantial compensation for punitive damages in light of the administrator's abuse of his power. Finally, he recommended that the board pay for his legal fees.

The board agreed to all of the recommendations. My honor, respect, and pride were restored.

While the settlement was being finalized, I was out of town, speaking at an annual convention held by the Gerontological Society of America. When I arrived home around midnight, I found a note on my pillow: I was to call Ms. Veronica, the director of the Office on Aging, right away, no matter how late. Her home number was also inscribed on the pad.

*   *   *

In the '70s, the city of Washington, D.C., had a large population of frail seniors in need of care. Because there were more patients than nursing home beds available, seniors were often transferred to places as far away as Boston; the lucky few remained closer to home, in Virginia or Maryland. Most of these seniors, however, crowded the city's general hospital and several private hospitals. Although these patients—many of them wards of the government— were ready for discharge, long-term residential care was not accessible. This situation created a major backlog at the hospitals and a shortage of acute care beds, which affected emergency ambulance services. Ambulances were often rerouted, because the emergency rooms were unable to transfer acute-care patients to hospital beds, as those beds were occupied by seniors awaiting admission to a nursing home.

The mayor was in hot water. Senior advocates from AARP wrote impassioned op-eds about the bed shortage in the newspapers, and the morning and evening news reported on the situation more frequently than the industry would have liked. The Office on Aging monitored these concerns and worked diligently to find a solution. The office housed the "Ombudsman Program," which dealt with complaints from families whose loved ones were transferred from the District of Columbia to nursing homes often too far away to allow for regular visits.

Then, a big breakthrough happened. A large but dilapidated nursing home complex stood vacant in the northeast section of the city. It was privately owned, and the owners, faced with cost-prohibitive renovations, followed the advice of their consultants and relocated to Maryland. The D.C. building, now vacant, could be the answer to the government's prayers, as it could potentially provide over 250 beds. The Office on Aging sought approval from the mayor to purchase the building. The need for nursing home beds was so dire that the mayor authorized the acquisition, despite the high cost. While the buildings were purchased in the low eighty-thousands, the renovations would cost several million dollars. The nursing home, the solution the city was longing for, was a complex of three connected buildings, each constructed in a different year. The very old facility, which covered almost four corners of a city block, was bandaged enough to meet some, but not all, federal and state regulations. The commercial kitchen, still under renovation, was in such disrepair that the cooks used a small kitchenette on the first-floor, which should have been reserved for special functions.

This purchase was the second government-owned nursing home in Washington, D.C. The first home, spacious as well, was in the southeast quadrant of the city, and was plagued with deficiencies, which explained its poor reputation. Newspapers and TV news anchors often decried the fact that the government did not have licensed personnel with sufficient knowledge and experience to manage the home. Learning from this, the Office on Aging decided to hire a contractor with experience in nursing home management to operate the newly acquired facility. Dick, the director, and Karen, the long-term care coordinator, launched a request for proposals, and later interviewed, then hired a company in Indianapolis to manage the Center for Aging nursing home. However, the District of Columbia Minority Business Opportunity Commission (or MBOC) required that any major contractor not certified as a minority company subcontract a percentage of their workload with licensed minority firms. Unfortunately, the minority contractors were ill-prepared and lacked experience to complete the task at hand. From the start, this nursing home was faced with many citations due to structural issues—the primary reason the previous owners had vacated the building.

This MBOC program was in its infancy. On the one hand, it opened doors to small minority business entrepreneurs who, otherwise, would never have had a chance to bid on lucrative contracts. On the other hand, many of these small minority contractors lacked the resources to complete large-scale projects and had difficulty coordinating services at a facility of this size. There was an urgent need for staff training to accommodate the incoming residents, but, unfortunately, there was no time to address the training issue. Seniors had to move out of the hospitals immediately. The transfers to the nursing home were not well planned; staff members did not know many of the policies and procedures and did not know how to operate as a team. It was a logistical nightmare.

The Indianapolis company was located too far away to effectively manage the myriad of problems that arose. Within a few years, this nursing home had a major case of resident abuse and a reputation of delivering substandard care, just as they had at the first government-owned nursing home located in the southeast region of the city. Surveyors from the Long-Term Care Administration in the district cited the facility with over 100 deficiencies. Federal surveyors added other deficiencies to the list and threatened to close the home if the district did not bring the facility into compliance within 90 days.

Ms. Veronica, the new director of the Office on Aging, who had been closely monitoring the events, called an emergency meeting in an attempt to save the nursing home. She and her trusted team worked hard on a plan to clear both State and Federal deficiencies, in an effort to keep the facility operating.

"Call Solanges," somebody told her.

It was midnight when I arrived home from my speaking engagement on the West Coast and found the note on my pillow. When I contacted Ms. Veronica, the director of the Office on Aging, she was still awake, anxiously awaiting my phone call. "I am told that you are the only person who can help me," she said.

We spoke for about an hour, and I listened to her concerns. I agreed to help.

The next morning, at eight o'clock, as soon as I arrived to work, the receptionist handed me a new message from the director of the Office on Aging. "She said to call her as soon as you arrived," Madeleine said.

"I can meet with you after work," I told Ms. Veronica when she tried to convince me to meet with her immediately. "I've been out of work for a whole week. I have some catching up to do."

Ms. Veronica was persistent. "How long do you need to do that?" she asked, still pressing on the urgency of the meeting.

We finally agreed to meet at her nursing home, at seven o'clock the next morning, for a couple of hours. I had never had the pleasure of meeting one-on-one with Ms. Veronica prior to this. I was, however, an admirer of this very eloquent woman. I had seen her deliver an impassioned speech at a function, never once looking at her notes. I had also watched her on television, testifying in front of the city council. Always very sharply dressed, usually in a red, she could speak for hours and, yet, remain sharp and accurate, commanding a beautiful and strong aura that demanded respect. So, the next day, I was excited to be in the presence of a woman I held in such high esteem. I could not believe that Ms. Veronica had asked *me* to consult on her facility. I was honored, and I wanted to create a good impression.

I received a copy of their deficiencies report. Having been in the long-term care profession for about 10 years now, I speed read through the reports and reviewed the facility's deficient practices. I decided to stay longer than I had intended for a nine o'clock meeting. Ms. Veronica had summoned the administrator, the director of nursing, all the managers, and other department directors to the boardroom for our meeting. The room was filled with somber people who feared for their jobs and were clearly intimidated by the presence of the director of the Office on Aging.

It was a time for me to showcase my knowledge and skills but, most importantly, demonstrate a desire to help this highly respected woman of the community and the aging residents in the facility. I identified the problems highlighted in the deficiency reports and offered ways to address them. I offered to return to the facility on another occasion to review their corrective action plans before the administrator sent them to the respective health care regulatory agencies.

It was eleven o'clock, and I was anxious to get to my own nursing home for work. As I exited the building, Ms. Veronica followed me.

"I want you here," she said.

I was stunned. "You want me here? As what?"

"Anything you want," she firmly and calmly said.

I thought about it for a moment. "Working under your current administrator would hinder me from turning this facility around," I said with a frown. "I would have to come in as an administrator and … "

"You got it!"

"What do you mean, *you got it*? Got what?" I asked.

"You can be the administrator," she responded.

I was in shock. I had had so many concerns about my current position. "Is this facility not managed privately under contract?" I was intrigued by the director's decision to change administrators before talking to the management company.

"Don't worry about that," she said. "I gave them the contract. I can take it away."

When I got into my car, she was still standing on the portico of the nursing home. I drove to work, excited. Such a big position—offered on the spot. A million thoughts went through my mind. Maybe I would not have to deal with Garrett any more. Maybe I would not have to be a director of nursing in a hostile and racist environment. Maybe I could become an administrator and make real changes that would lead to better lives for hundreds of elderly residents and their families.

When I arrived to work, even though I was already late, I sat in the car shaking in amazement. I had to collect myself for fear that others might read something in my behavior. But what would they read, anyway? I was bewildered but also apprehensive. I talked to myself out loud. "I've never been an administrator—not even in training. How can I take over a facility in a fragile glass bubble for my first position?" Then, I heard my inner voice: *Why not? You are an angel, after all, the angel of the sun. God has looked after you all these years. What makes you think that He would forsake you now that you need Him the most?* In a flash, I snapped out of my state of panic and my confidence returned.

Garrett's covert harassment and unpleasant attitude continued until the resolution of my harassment complaint. I still had to deal with him. The more unrelenting his torment, the stronger my self-control. His sarcasm did affect my spirit, but I remained poised and graceful in his presence. I refused to allow him any victory over me, and I certainly did not allow him to affect my work.

Dominic, our attorney, finally informed us of a settlement in the case—a major success. Pleased with the way the case was resolved, Keith and I agreed to the terms. One major condition of the settlement, quite important to the Board of Directors, was that both parties refrain from discussing the details of the case with other employees. Another condition required that we maintain confidentiality regarding the amount of the settlement. This was the largest amount of money we had ever had in our hands at one time. Keith and I wisely used it as a down payment on our first home.

I expected Garrett to make my work life even more miserable than it had been, now that he had not only lost the case but had also been reprimanded by the Board of Directors. Keith and I discussed the new administrator position I had been offered, and I decided to accept the offer, pending a meeting with the management company, and the termination of the administrator still running the facility at that time.

Within days, a corporate representative flew in from Indianapolis to meet me. He conducted the interview at a restaurant on Wisconsin Avenue, close to my office so that I could use my lunch hour and remain discreet. He explained the contract between his company and the government, along with the company's philosophy, goals, and values. We also discussed the regulatory issues of the nursing home and what leadership skills and management style I would use to bring the facility to compliance. He shared my concern: I had never worked as a nursing home administrator, not even as an assistant administrator.

I explained, however, that I was currently managing a nursing home. I spoke of the letters the administrator had received from families praising my management skills and of my ability to turn the evening shift into a better working environment for staff, and a more home-like environment for the residents. I reminded him that, since my appointment as director of nursing, I functioned as administrator in the absence of all the sitting administrators. Then, I said, very matter-of-factly, "After all, sir, I am a licensed nursing home administrator, which proves that I'm ready for the position."

He gave me a big smile and nodded. We, then, discussed salary and benefits, the company's bonus structure, and the supervision and training I would receive. It was important to the director of the Office on Aging that I start work immediately, due to the urgent needs of the facility. I insisted on providing the month notice required by my current employer. With an offer letter in hand, I resigned from my director of nursing position, giving Garrett the one-month notice as per the facility's employee handbook. Garrett, however, wanted to accept my resignation, effective immediately.

Given the pressure to start at my new facility, this offer to resign "effective immediately" should have been acceptable to me. I could have begun working within days of the offer, but it was not acceptable to me. I politely refused to abruptly leave as though I had been fired. I would not give Garrett the satisfaction he seemed to derive from the whispers and gossip it might provoke. I insisted that I needed time to say goodbye to my staff and to the residents' families with whom I had, for the past 10 years, developed a strong bond. Most importantly, I needed time to prepare the residents for my departure.

Those residents had become my extended family. They filled the void left by the family I had left in Haiti and in New York. I was not about to allow Garrett to push me out before I had properly informed everyone of my resignation, on my terms. After I called my husband, who agreed I should remain firm, I marched like an army sergeant to the personnel office and explained my position. The personnel director helped me convey my willingness to compromise with Garrett: I would work a full week before leaving the facility. I made it clear that refusing my request would be seen as retaliation and that I was willing to carry my concern to the Board of Directors. Garrett knew how determined I could be, so he relented. I set a departure date.

The next morning, I announced at the department directors' meeting that I was leaving. Given the animosity of the administrator towards me since his appointment, it was not a surprise to my colleagues that I had finally had enough. I, then, informed the nursing staff of my departure—first, the morning shift, then the evening shift. I returned at midnight to meet with the night-shift employees. All week, I notified families as we saw each other around the building. I made it a point to notify the residents that I knew might be affected by the separation. I also spent time with some of the residents I knew would not miss me but that I would dearly miss. Finally, I spent time with the residents who would miss me but who were unable to express themselves.

Working in nursing homes at any level requires a special kind of personality. The job can be very taxing. In general, nursing home employees are compassionate, understanding, and loving. They can become very attached to certain residents and mourn some resident's passing with the same intensity they would mourn the death of an immediate family member. Often, nursing home employees attend funerals of residents they bond with.

One resident was very close to my heart. Her name was Ms. Parnaby, and she was in her late 80s. She had been a registered nurse in her younger years, and, in her delusions, she was still practicing nursing. I had nicknamed her "supervisor," a title that she cherished as she walked alongside the nurses who distributed medication. I spent the week talking, laughing, and shedding many tears. Separation had always been a difficult emotion for me to handle, and this one was incredibly painful.

On my last day as director of nursing, my staff gave me the biggest, most unbelievable going away party in the employee cafeteria. How had this party been organized with such short notice? I did not know. I was just glad that I had not allowed a cruel man to deprive us of this moment. In retrospect, this was a battle worth fighting, for a successful finish. I had spent 10 memorable years at the facility. How could I have allowed this prejudiced, bigoted, insecure white man to rob me of great memories by walking away without saying farewell? I splurged on the homemade food and the dishes from Roy Rogers and Almond Pizzeria. There were soft drinks and, yes, there were even gifts. I kept those gifts for years and can still remember who gifted each item. It is with pride that I show my long-stem wine glasses and say, "These ones, oh! Yes, these were from Ms. McAlvin, one of my nursing assistants." Or I will say, "This vase was from Ms. Rio. She was a nursing assistant. We worked together decades ago."

My strong Catholic faith had guided me to this nursing home and, like a child obeying her parents, I had conformed. I believed in the Spirit that walked alongside me and that carried me through all my tribulations. I had entered that nursing home with the intention of working there for only three months, until I could secure a position in urology at an acute-care hospital. Ten years later, I was fully consumed in a new field. Keith took pleasure in teasing me, saying I had no conversational skills, except for nursing home jargon. I read only nursing home laws and regulations, nursing home policies and procedures, nursing home magazines, and anything else that pertained to nursing home life. I had become exemplary in my field, caring for frail and fragile seniors. It had become my passion. It had become my life. As a nurse, I enjoyed helping everyone, but helping seniors brought a kind of fulfillment like none other.

MAKE IT WORK FOR YOU!

Rule #16: Be Fearless and Fight for What is Right

Reflection: Nothing Gets in My Way

Sometimes, on their journey to the open ocean, baby sea turtles have to cross deep ditches in the sand to reach the water. They do not pause in their race to the ocean, they just move forward and leap out over the ditches in their efforts to reach their destination. And, if they tumble on the way and land on their back, they flip themselves back over and keep going. They do not pause to wipe off the sand from their bodies. They are too busy fighting to get to the water to care. Keep fighting to reach your goals, even if you get a little dirty. There will be time to spruce yourself up once you reach your destination.

- Identify the people in your life who make you feel intimidated when you have to confront them with an issue. Ask yourself what you are really afraid of. What is the worst that could happen if you spoke up and said how you are feeling? Find a mirror and practice speaking your mind to them. Let it all out to yourself. Use, "I feel … ," as a starting point and say how you feel when you are near them and why. Then, the next time you are face-to-face with one of them, look them in the eyes when they speak to you. If you are not ready to speak up, start by meeting their gaze. Remember, it is important to keep your emotions in check, and that includes not showing any fear.

- Find a cause that matters to you and get involved. Sometimes, a minimal time commitment can make a big difference. What do you care about in your community? In the world? Can you find an hour or two a month to put positive energy in the right direction?

Rule #17: Maintain Your Reputation

Reflection: I Have Got a Rep to Protect

The snapping turtle has a nasty reputation due to its impressive beak and savage defensive behavior, but here is its big secret—it mostly just wants to be left alone. It is actually fairly shy. In the water, it avoids humans and will swim away if people get close. But on land, when it is heading to and from its nesting site, a snapping turtle is at its most vulnerable and will gnash and clamp down with its jaws if molested. Despite its reputation for a harmful bite, a snapping turtle exerts far less pressure than a human when it clamps down. In this case, that nasty reputation is a lifesaver. Most people will not mess with a snapping turtle, because they are rumored to be so ferocious. Let us keep this a secret, though; we would not want to hurt its reputation.

- Think about how you want other people to see you. How does that conflict with how you behave? If you want to appear confident, fidgeting or biting your nails might not project that image to others. Identify areas where your behavior does not match up with what you want people to notice about you, and then focus on letting your better attributes take the spotlight. For example, if you want to appear confident, practice holding yourself tall and speaking clearly with strength. These things take time, so be patient with yourself.

- Get yourself to a beauty salon or a manicurist and spoil yourself. Find a stylist who will help you find a look that projects the image you want others to see. If it is time for a new wardrobe, and you cannot afford a whole closet full of new clothes, hit up a consignment store and find one or two items that are classy, fit well, and say you are something worth looking twice at.

RULES TO LIVE BY

I officially took over as administrator of a nursing home in this next chapter, and I had the challenge on my hands of turning this place around. I was intent on being proud of my hard work to correct this situation.

But there was more than just my pride at stake. The wellbeing and contentment of my residents was a major concern to me. Big changes were happening in my field that revolutionized the care my residents received, and I remained at the forefront of fostering that change. Once I saw the changes that happened in the first home we took over, I set my sights on a career path that would give me more autonomy and allow me to build a dynasty.

Rule #18: Be A Detective

When my company took over management of the Center for Aging nursing homes we ran, we were walking into situations where mismanagement was the modus operandi, and the problems seemed overwhelming. Often, the causes for the problems were not immediately apparent. I had to become a detective to find ways to get the homes in working order—and I had to act fast. It is important, no matter what industry you work in, to always keep yourself educated about changes in policy or operations. Better yet: make change where you can; write new policy; find better ways of operating. It is imperative to remain astute. When we took over the Johnson Home, my husband Keith spoke to everyone in the nursing home, in part to build relationships, but also to identify problems so we could solve them more easily (see chapter 11, "How Did We Do It?"). Pay attention to what is going on around you. In my company, we had a plan of attack for problems we identified:

1. Assess the problem.

2. Write a plan to solve the problem.

3. Implement the plan.

4. Evaluate the results and find solutions to any ongoing issues.

I found that developing a consistent management style was effective when dealing with issues that arose with my staff (see chapter nine, "Climbing the

Mountain to a Dynasty"). When you are consistent with how you practice management, people trust you, and they follow you (see chapter 10, "A New Reality"). It is also important that your employees feel empowered.

A big part of my role at my company was identifying weaknesses in my staff, reeducating them, and giving them the responsibility to manage their duties (see chapter nine, "Climbing the Mountain to a Dynasty").

Sometimes, you will run into problems that pop up out of nowhere and require damage control (see chapter 13, "Every Beginning Has Its End"). What do you do then? Go back to being a detective, assess the problem, and write a plan.

9

Climbing the Mountain to a Dynasty

When the Center for Aging nursing home administrator was terminated, I was instrumental in assuring that he, too, was given a week to properly say his goodbyes. I wanted the transition to be as smooth as possible. I spent that week in Ms. Veronica's office, going through every document brought to me from the nursing home. Once I officially became the administrator of record, I was prepared to tackle the biggest challenge yet of my professional life.

On Monday morning, I proudly hung my newly framed nursing home administrator license on the wall of the Center for Aging nursing home's lobby. Only then did I call my best friend Sarah, now the acting director of nursing at The Washington Home, my previous place of employment, to let her know about my new position.

The next day, she called me back with an anecdote:

At the department directors' and managers' meeting, when it was her time to speak, Sarah said, "I have an announcement to make." She paused to get everyone's attention. "As of yesterday, Solanges Vivens has been appointed administrator at the Center for Aging Nursing Home."

In shock, my harasser said, "Administrator! You mean *director* of nursing."

I could imagine Sarah's smirk.

"Oh no! She is the *administrator* there."

Garrett almost fainted.

We burst out laughing.

He who laughs last, laughs best, they say—I take great satisfaction in recounting this story. It still makes me chuckle to imagine the puckered look on his face when he received the news: I had become his peer.

I must have been the luckiest child on earth. My father was right: there was a special star in the sky the night before I was born. I have always been at the right place, at the right time, in the angel of the sun's warm embrace. I knew the angel would not leave my side as I prepared myself for the challenge ahead. God only knew what I was up against. I had no experience as a nursing home administrator. The facility was under a microscope, watched by the Long-Term Care Administration in D.C., the regional office of federal surveyors for nursing homes, the corporate office of the management company that had hired me, the director of the Office on Aging, the Ombudsman Program, AARP, and the mayor's office—not to forget the *Washington Post* and the morning and evening news. The scrutiny was intensely stressful.

I was not intimidated. I had learned a strong value system from my parents. I learned how to be tough from having to defend my individuality among my many brothers and sisters, my sophistication from living with the Silvermans and from my godmother's influence, my management style from working as a registered nurse at Mount Sinai Hospital, my assertiveness from working independently as a nurse clinician at Burk Rehabilitation Center in Upstate New York, my persistence at mastering all rules and regulations from studying at Georgetown University, and my leadership skills from serving as director of nursing in a hostile environment. I knew I could apply all those qualities to the task at hand and turn this facility around, even when the obstacles seemed insurmountable.

While making rounds my first evening at the facility, I was greeted by a licensed practical nurse.

She looked me in the eye and said, "We understand that you have class. But we do not need your class here. We need money."

With a straight face, I responded, "I understand. But money will come with class. You first have to be classy if you want money."

I then smiled, and continued making my rounds to meet the residents and staff.

I would not get frazzled, I promised myself.

And I did not. I had been working as an administrator for 90 days when I received a call from Ms. Paula, a colleague director from another nursing home.

She giggled. "I've just been paid."

"For what?" I asked, puzzled.

"I bet on you," she said. "I said, of course, you'd make it to 90 days."

Apparently, many people in the city had bet that, in light of my inexperience, I would not last long in my position. Some had bet on 30 days, some on 60. Others, like Ms. Paula, who knew my clinical and administrative skills, my strength, my character, and my leadership capabilities, believed that I would succeed: She had chosen the longest bet: 90 days.

"What many people fail to realize," I said, "is that I do not know how to spell the word failure. That word has yet to become a part of my professional vocabulary."

I was focused, ambitious, and driven. I functioned best in extremely difficult situations, which had made me a good intensive care nurse. From day one, I harnessed the adrenaline from stress to be successful. After six months, the man who had interviewed me for the job flew in from Indianapolis to congratulate me on turning the facility around. He gave me two gigantic gifts: the first was a major salary increase; the second was the suggestion that I form a company in order to bid on the management contract for the facility.

"Our contract expires next year," he explained, "and my company will not be bidding this time around. We're too far away to be successful in this city."

He was so impressed with my performance that he volunteered that I should form a company and bid on the contract. He offered to guide me in this new endeavor.

The Senior Beacon, a major senior citizens' magazine, published an article that recapped the history of the facility and all its progress under my leadership; it included a picture of me. Since the media usually reported on the failures and shortcomings of nursing homes, this article represented a victory for the concerned stockholders.

*   *   *

It was a struggle to get things in order. Our medical staff consisted of a consortium of three universities. These university physicians—men with big egos—shared the same space, vying for power in a remarkable battle for turf. This was compounded by three nurse practitioners who fought for autonomy to practice without much oversight. To turn the facility around, I quickly became the hunter, searched for prey, and thinned down the herd by taking out the weakest stragglers. My goal was to find any mismanagement in that facility and eliminate it while ensuring that residents received quality care.

I dismantled the consortium, which everyone thought impossible because of the universities' power and their political connections in the city. Data in hand, I articulated some of the problems and terminated two university contracts immediately; I renewed the other, and the medical team of the remaining university was entrusted with caring for the entire facility. Using my extensive knowledge in nursing, I, then, assessed the nursing department; I developed and implemented an action plan that only I, a nurse administrator, could have effectuated. My predecessor had not been a nurse. Without my kind of experience, he had been ill-equipped to handle those changes. In contrast, I used my assets of leadership and clinical knowledge as an advantage.

This nursing home had one director of nursing, three assistant directors of nursing, nine registered nurses (each assigned to one of the nine nursing units), and three licensed nurse practitioners. I recalled a passage from an economics book: "more is not always merrier." *So many top licensed professionals tripping over each other*, I thought, *and yet the facility has more than 100 deficiencies.* There were too many doctors and nurses—with absolutely no coordination of care among them. The nurse practitioners often discontinued the doctors' orders, rewriting orders so frequently that the nursing units could not keep up with the changes, and often administered the wrong treatment; the registered nurses relied so much on the nurse practitioners that they were no longer independent thinkers. Either by omission or commission, this situation created major deficiencies. So, in addition to canceling the consortium, I dismissed all three nurse practitioners, saving the facility a large amount of money. Besides the management and care issues, the facility also had a staggering deficit close to $2 million, which made it difficult to increase salaries.

Despite my demanding administrator duties, I continued to publish and accepted additional engagements as a speaker. I also became a nurse educator in order to help my nurses develop into the kind of leaders I envisioned. I created an educational plan and put it into practice: every Wednesday, I summoned the registered nurses from their units and into a classroom, where I taught the art of leadership. A nursing home, I pointed out, is a *nursing* home and not a *doctor's* home, because nurses are the care managers, not the doctors. The residents, I taught them, should be the nucleus, and the registered nurses the first layer that surrounds the nucleus. Everyone must come to the registered nurse leader in the unit first before the residents.

I empowered those nurses and, before long, they started to show leadership and take control of their nursing units. Within six months, changes at the facility were noticeable. The residents and their families were happy—and so were staff members when they received a raise after I terminated the unnecessary positions. My philosophy in the acute care setting had always been *happy staff, happy patients*, and happy patients healed faster. In addition, happy residents meant happy families, and happy families meant fewer lawsuits for the facility. The end result of this equation was happy stockholders. A win-win for all.

With that mentality, I tackled all my challenges big and small with successful outcomes. In the grand scheme of things, overstaffing, poor care coordination, low employee morale, and interpersonal conflicts were the slow-moving beasts I was able to eliminate quickly. However, I was faced with a more difficult and subjective issue: the facility had two camps—the whites and the blacks.

Teamwork was not practiced among the employees, and the groups kept themselves segregated from one another, even during lunch. Animosity and disrespect existed between them in a "he said, she said" culture. In an effort to discourage rampant gossip, I introduced my practice of circular management: whenever a conflict involved more than one person, I would bring all parties together in a circle to openly discuss the issue at hand; this would help keep all stories straight and also eliminate instances of finger-pointing and triangular communication.

Before circular management became the official modus operandi, the staff tried to interject me in the building's gossip.

One afternoon, a housekeeper walked into my office, requesting to speak with me. I politely offered her a seat, prepared to hear her concerns.

The conversation, however, started with the employee saying, "Someone told me that you said ... "

I quickly interrupted. "Stop. If you are here to repeat what another employee told you, I'll ask that you leave my office, and return with your colleague. I want you to tell me everything in front of him or her to make sure that there are no misunderstandings."

"I can't do that," she responded.

"In this case, my dear, I cannot help you. I don't want to get in trouble." I knew I sounded like a damsel in distress, one of those movie characters in fear for their lives. "You don't want to get me in trouble, do you?" I asked her.

"How? You are the administrator. How would you get in trouble?"

At that point, I explained the difference between circular management and triangular management until the employee understood the danger in repeating what others had said. I shared with her the findings of the "telephone experiment," which proved that a conversation could completely change meaning, from the originator of a statement, through a chain of misconstrued repetition, to the last recipient.

Before long, the gossip greatly subsided in the building, and trust developed as a result.

The staff was curious to see how I would tackle the race and class issues. Instead of addressing these issues head on, I implemented small steps with great results.

First, I focused on the dress code. A provision of the government contract provided staff members an allowance for their uniforms. However, in many cases, their appearance was still deplorable. An employee once reported to work in a Mickey Mouse T-shirt in lieu of his uniform, thinking that was acceptable. Putting my arm around the employee's shoulders, I discreetly whispered in his ear that he was out of uniform. "You need to clock out, go home, change into the facility's uniform, and then come back to work."

When an employee dressed appropriately, I made a big deal of it, loudly congratulating him or her on their professional appearance. I did it so often that some employees started dressing to the nines, fishing for compliments from me. I went so far as hosting a fashion show for the benefit of those employees who had to wear business attire, modeling what was and was not acceptable to wear to work.

One day, I complimented Chikita, a former restorative aide who now worked as a unit clerk and no longer needed to wear a uniform. I could see that she was very happy with her promotion: her makeup was flawless; she wore a sharp black pinstripe suit, a crisp white shirt, and black pumps.

As she walked past a group of employees in the cafeteria, I called out to her. "Wow! Chikita, you look so nice! You must have a boyfriend in the building."

She responded loudly, for everyone to hear, "Isn't that what you expect?"

At that moment, I said to myself, "*Yes*! It's working."

Dressing up became contagious: everyone was looking nice. Even those in uniform took pride in looking their best. As an incentive, I implemented a monthly "Best Dressed Award," and the plaque floated around from unit to unit. The desire for the plaque was so great that the units competed to win the award. I, myself, always managed to look younger than I was. I pulled back my long hair in a ponytail, secured by a bow. I had a different bow to match each "outfit of the day." To my surprise, one morning I realized that all the female employees, at every level of employment, had their hair pulled back in a ponytail, secured with a bow. I was flattered. This gesture was a sign of love and acceptance. Although I was very hard on my employees, they appreciated my leadership and the positive changes I was implementing.

Every Tuesday, I led the weekly department directors' meeting, similar to the one I was accustomed to at The Washington Home. On the second Wednesday of the month, I met with the directors and managers, and, on the third Wednesday, with the general staff, which also included directors and managers. These meetings were intended to foster better coordination and to diminish race and class issues, as there were further divisions between the higher- and lower-paid white and black staff. I managed to bring every employee onto the same playing field. We were steadily developing into the cohesive team I had envisioned.

I also took all instances of resignation very seriously, determined to find out the real reason behind each departure. At a voluntary termination meeting, a registered nurse explained that the facility did not pay enough. When employees needed extra money, they lingered in the unit past their appointed clock out time to force overtime without working when needed. With this knowledge, I immediately created a new policy: overtime had to be approved ahead of time by the employee's immediate supervisor, except in the case of last-minute call-outs when the nurses had to remain because a colleague called in sick. When I required both employee and supervisor to sign and date an overtime form, the overtime expenses decreased considerably. Before I came on board, overtime exceeded the budgeted amount. I increased the allotment to better manage the facility, instead of letting employees manage the payroll.

At another exit interview, I learned from a recreational therapist that employees often plotted questions to ask me at the monthly general staff meetings, because they were trying to figure out whether I was street smart or book smart.

"And what did you conclude?" I asked.

She replied they were unable to figure me out, because I seemed to have the answer to everything. The key, I told her, was to network with every member of the internal staff, at all levels, and with external colleagues who could advise me, and indirectly become active participants in my personal growth.

Because I was a mentor to many of my staff members, every word I said carried weight and value. At one point, many people were leaving, and we always held a farewell party. One day, at one of those parties, I grabbed the microphone and made a joke, "From now on, no more farewell parties; we'll only have parties for the new hires." I was kidding, but my employees took my words to heart.

Shortly after this, when Mr. Peterson, from Central Supplies, resigned, an employee came to me and said, "I came to ask you permission to have a party, because Mr. Peterson resigned."

I said, "Wait a minute ... Since when do you need my permission?"

"But you said no more parties, "the employee responded.

Of course, Mr. Peterson got his going away party, but it meant a lot to me that my employees put such importance on what I said to them. I realized, then, that I had built a strong, cohesive team and had earned their respect. Going forward, I made it a point to be more careful about what I said in jest.

It was November, and now, as a team, we were planning a Thanksgiving dinner party for the residents. At one of the general staff meetings, I announced that the employee cafeteria would be closed so we all could eat together as a family in the multipurpose room.

A male employee shouted from the back of the room, "Do you mean we have to eat with them? We've never eaten with the residents before."

So, I thought, *I did not have two camps. I had three.*

With a straight face, I responded, "As of today, there shall be no *them and us*; there shall only be *us*."

Prior to my arrival at the nursing home, staff never ate with residents. In fact, prior to about the mid-1980s, in most nursing homes in America, residents were treated very much as patients, separate from staff, with very few choices.

I was interested in a change in the long-term care model towards a Swedish philosophy called "normalization," later adopted in the United States as "culture change." This model embraced patients being treated as individuals, and the staff were encouraged to foster more independence in the resident population. I wanted family-style meals to become the norm—not just during holidays but year-round. "Normalization" later revolutionized long-term residential care and fostered radical changes in residents' health and overall happiness, which led to fewer behavioral outbursts and radically impacted the long-term healthcare industry globally. It was about the same as taking someone who was being treated like a lab specimen and giving them some dignity, and the difference it made in their lives was remarkable.

On Thanksgiving Day, volunteers helped the families bring the residents to the multipurpose room. As everyone ate together, it became a joyous occasion. We served Martinelli's Sparkling Apple Cider in fancy plastic glasses. This reminded the employee who "did not need class" that she was now working in a classy nursing home. The next morning, a resident in the skilled nursing unit refused to get out of bed. When a nurse asked her why, she said, "I went to a party downstairs yesterday and drank too much champagne. I have a hangover. I just can't get up this morning." I chuckled to myself at the thought of fake champagne and imaginary hangovers.

It had been a successful and classy Thanksgiving indeed. Soon, camaraderie took root and began to flourish. Eating a family-style Thanksgiving dinner became customary at the facility. If *nursing* was at the forefront of the term *nursing home*, then I wanted to be sure my team understood that the concept of *home* was just as important as the nursing; together, we were building a *home* for the residents, and it was our job to make it as rich as it could possibly be.

Because I had no prior experience as a nursing home administrator and was under such close scrutiny, I spent most of my waking hours at work. A receptionist noticed my constant presence at the facility, even late in the evening, after all the day-shift employees had left.

"Don't you have a home?" she asked.

I felt that the nursing home needed that level of attention to turn it around. I invested 16 hours almost every day and still managed to stop by the facility on

Sundays after Mass at the Shrine of the Immaculate Conception. The church was close to the facility, so I could meet with the staff that only worked on weekends.

Once a month, after dinner with Keith and Kevin, I returned to the facility to meet with the night-shift employees. Those meetings were important in helping turn the facility around, because I learned why these employees were unhappy. One issue involved the implementation of the weekend schedule. As a rule, any employee working the night shift enjoyed the weekend off, including Saturday and Sunday nights. Instead, the current schedule allowed for Friday and Saturday nights off, with employees returning to work on a Sunday—a thorn in their sides. The employees had been complaining for years, but no one had figured out how to undo this scheduling error until they had my eyes and ears.

I pledged to work at making life better for them.

And I did just that.

I worked with the night nursing assistants to find a way to provide enough coverage, so the nightshift employees could be off on Saturday and Sunday nights. The graveyard-shift employees became my biggest supporters; they would do anything for me. They had a special party for me one night, just to say thank you. *Happy night staff, happy residents.*

The northeast section of the city, where the Center for Aging nursing home was located, was riddled with prostitutes. I sometimes joked that I had done everything in my power to turn that facility around, "short of selling my body on 18th Street." It was true: I had given it my all.

My efforts paid off. Within a couple of years after I became the administrator, the Centers for Medicare and Medicaid rated the facility as the top nursing home in the District of Columbia.

*   *   *

Beginning in my teenage years, as a factory worker, I had worked for others and consistently given my all, whether as a nanny, a nursing assistant, a registered nurse, a director of nursing, or as an administrator. I remained loyal and committed to those who paid me a salary, and the prospect of one day owning my own nursing home business was a far-distant dream. It did, nevertheless, remain a goal, one Keith and I discussed at length after the offer extended to me by the management company's director. Together, we strategized the best way to start a corporation to take over management of the nursing home. We thought it might be best to join forces with an established company, rather than starting a new one without any history, as the government might be reluctant to award a multi-million-dollar contract to a newly formed corporation.

Thus, our search for an established company began. First, I met with three gentlemen—two of African-American descent, and another of Indian descent—who were owners of a health management company, with no nursing home component as part of their portfolio. I presented a proposal that would make me a partner; in return, I would bring to their company my nursing degrees, licenses, and experience, along with a multi-million-dollar contract. They nearly kicked me out of their office: they had worked very hard to create and maintain their business, they said, and my audacity flabbergasted them; how dare I ask for partnership before I proved my worth and value to their company? My promise of a contract was not enough. They offered me the opportunity to join their company as an employee and still bring the contract to their business. I respectfully understood their position but declined the offer and left their office disappointed but not defeated. I was focused, patient, and determined to work for myself. I was not about to sell myself short. I knew for a fact that my nursing and administrative credentials were a precious commodity that did not exist elsewhere in the city. Finding the right partner with the right fit was essential to my endeavor.

If not them, then who? I wondered.

I called my friend Myrtle, my former supervisor at Mount Sinai Hospital in New York. We met over coffee the following week to discuss joining forces for this new endeavor. Myrtle welcomed the idea, "a win-win," she said, as we had had a fruitful working relationship in the past. She was the sole owner of a long-term home health care agency, but, like the prior group, did not have the nursing home component in her portfolio. After the rejection of the three businessmen, Myrtle's enthusiasm created trust—the most important ingredient in forging an alliance. I saw us as the perfect duo: we were both professional nurses with management experience but, above all, we were friends. After an exciting and productive meeting, we agreed to draw a memorandum of understanding, and then form a company under the umbrella of Myrtle's home care agency.

"We might need more partners," Myrtle pointed out. "We're still missing some of the requirements."

*   *   *

As a leader, I believe that accessibility is imperative to those that we serve. Except when privacy was needed, I practiced an open-door policy at the Center, ready to welcome any staff, family member, or resident into my office for open communication. This policy provided unsatisfied family members an opportunity to vent their frustrations directly to the administrator instead of a lawyer, which decreased the potential for a lawsuit. Disgruntled employees were empowered to present their individual grievances, a release that became a deterrent for union activities.

My open-door policy became very beneficial to me in my quest to find a partner for my new company. One day, Victor, the owner and director of the rehabilitation company that provided therapy services at the nursing home, stopped by to my office for small talk.

He casually asked, "What is someone like you doing here?"

"What does that mean?" I responded in shock. Before he could add another word, I added, "Where do I belong?"

With all good intentions, he said, "Solanges, a top professional like you, with all your attributes and experience, should not be a facility administrator." He went on to explain that I could be a regional director for a major nursing home chain. "You could oversee several buildings, for a much higher salary."

I vehemently countered by telling Victor that I was exactly where I needed to be at this point in my life. I had my one-, three- and five-year goals.

"Please elaborate," he said.

I explained that, within three years, I planned to have my own management company and take over managing nursing homes throughout the United States. In five years, I would be the owner of my own nursing home.

He was stunned. "What if I told you that my partner and I share the same goals?" He paused. "Except, we do not have someone like you to complement our portfolio and make it happen."

This statement changed a casual conversation into a serious one, requiring a different level of attention. I closed the door to give Victor my full attention.

"I would like to arrange a dinner meeting where the three of us can talk," he said. Victor was a chiropractor, and his partner, "Doc," a geriatric physician. Together, they owned a rehabilitation company that provided services in Washington, D.C., and in several other states. Their portfolio included everything Myrtle and I needed.

I agreed to the dinner at an Italian restaurant in Bethesda, Maryland, on one condition: that both Myrtle and Keith be allowed to attend. At this casual meeting, the five of us shared our work histories and discussed the nursing home business. I emphasized to them the possibility of being awarded this multi-million-dollar contract if they were to join forces with Myrtle and me. We unanimously agreed to pursue the idea of working together.

Driving home, Keith and I discussed the company, who the players should be, and the percentage of shares per principal. My husband said, "I am not sure that I like this Doc guy. I think you should just add Victor to the team."

"I'm afraid we need him," I said. "I looked at the requirements for the contract. He brings a lot to the table."

Early the next morning, I received a call from Victor. Doc was requesting an urgent meeting, without Keith or Myrtle. That evening, we met at the same restaurant in Bethesda. Doc's agenda included one item: he was prepared to form the company; however, because he did not like Myrtle, he refused to work with her. *How predictable*, I thought. *My husband had warned me against Doc.* "I thought I had made it clear from the get-go that I was forming my own company with Myrtle," I said. "Excluding her is a definite dealbreaker."

After the meeting, I called Myrtle to share what had taken place the night before.

Very calmly, Myrtle responded, "Solanges, I will not stand in your way. This is a good opportunity for you, and I believe you should take it. Don't worry about me. I already have my business. Go ahead and form the company with them."

With Myrtle's blessing, I pursued the deal, because Victor and Doc might be the only chance at getting the contract.

As usual, Keith was right on point: Doc turned out to be difficult. He insisted that his personal lawyer represent all of us in forming the corporation. Keith vehemently opposed the idea and insisted that we should each have our own lawyer. After a lot of back and forth, I won this part of the debate, but the drama had just begun. Next came a series of meetings over ownership percentages. There were arguments between Doc and me, between the two lawyers, and, yes, Keith was in the middle of it all with his own strong opinions. Through it all, Victor was the perfect gentlemen, trying to keep the peace.

At what was to be our last round of negotiations, I was not surprised when Keith stood up in the middle of a heated argument. Without consulting me, he announced that he and his wife were leaving. He excused himself, confident that I would follow. My husband looked at me, and I stood up.

He, then, turned to Doc and said, "My wife is no longer interested in pursuing a business venture with you." He reached for my coat, put his hand on the small of my back, and guided me out the door.

Keith had always been my rock. I was his dear Caribbean woman, and he was my dear Caribbean man who had cleaned my nursing shoes, helped with my book reports, and found me new employment opportunities. Now, he was defending me against two white "partners" and two white lawyers who, he believed, did not have my best interests in mind. He was there to take care of me, and he was not about to allow anyone to disrespect his wife, a woman of color and a top professional. He knew what his wife was bringing to the table, and was not about to allow anyone to take advantage of her.

I was in North Carolina, at my friend Gloria's home for a well-deserved vacation when the landline rang. Gloria handed me the phone. "It's for you, my dear."

I assumed Keith was calling, but it was Doc on the line.

It had been exactly a month since my abrupt departure from the meeting. Surprised, I immediately assumed a business-like tone. "Doc, what a surprise! To what do I owe this call?"

"Honey … " he said.

And there it was: the word that Keith hated the most. He thought Doc calling me "honey" was condescending and inappropriate. I really did not care what he called me. I cared most about forming the nursing home management company.

He continued, "Vic and I decided your lawyer should represent all three of us."

I could not believe it. Why the change of heart? I politely explained that I would not be home until Sunday night, so the earliest that we could meet was the following week, after I had scheduled a meeting with the lawyer. After Doc agreed with the plan, I called Keith, who immediately contacted the lawyer to pick up the negotiations where we had left off. Time was of the essence, as the city was close to releasing its request for proposals.

At our next meeting, I educated the team on the current law: in the 1980s, under the administration of Mayor Barry, a percentage of any government contract won by a majority vendor was to be awarded to a minority company. If the majority contractor was already minority-certified, there was no requirement for minority contractor distribution. In light of this caveat, I insisted that I get 51 percent of the shares and that the company be registered as a woman-owned, minority-certified small business in the District of Columbia. Both Doc and Vic agreed with the terms.

Keith was a brilliant and well-educated man with a master's degree in finance. As a certified public accountant, he was very progressive in his thinking process—a clairvoyant man. At his suggestion, we used an acronym and avoided last names altogether; he wanted the company's name to survive the founders.

VMT LTC was formed in 1988 and incorporated as Vital Management Team in Long Term Care for the sole purpose of bidding on the government contract. We opened an office on M Street, in the northwest section of the city, hired an executive director for the company, and obtained our tax identification number, and insurance. I became chief executive officer of the company but continued to work as administrator at the Center for Aging nursing home, until we could submit the bid and, hopefully, win it.

There were lots of hoops to jump through and many obstacles along the way. At first, Ms. Maudine, the director of the MBOC (Minority Business Opportunity Committee) office refused the company's request for certification as minority-owned, out of fear that I was fronting for a white company. I was a woman of color, and I was not rich. So, how could I be a majority partner? She overlooked my multiple degrees and the extensive experience I noted in the application. The director was only trying to maintain the integrity of the program but, this time, she was wrong: I was, in fact, the majority owner of the business. Once again, Keith had to intervene by asking his friend Ron, a CPA, to attend a meeting at the MBOC building with me. With Ron's help, the company obtained its certification as a minority business in the city. I was that much closer to reaching my three-year goal. VMT LTC Management answered the government's call for proposals to manage the facility, and the wait began.

The government did not have the staff to timely effectuate contracts, so there was one delay after another. In the meantime, a series of one-page, short-term contracts were awarded to the current management company. Professionals in the industry constantly asked me about my future at the nursing home.

"I love my administrator position," I said. "I plan to remain, regardless of the management company in charge, as long as I remain appointed."

One day, at the end of a monthly gathering organized by the District of Columbia Healthcare Association (DCHCA) for all the nursing home administrators, one of my colleagues asked, "Solanges, who do you want to work for?"

"Myself," I replied, knowing full well that I had not only formed a company, but had bid on a project as well.

That response was real to me, yet laughable to my colleague who could not imagine that someday I may be working for myself.

I was under an unfathomable level of stress, but I continued to run the facility with very few deficiencies. We were not on the media's radar anymore, and, most importantly, there were no complaints from residents, families, or staff. This was especially important as we waited for the new contract to be awarded. What a tall order for a new administrator! I had always aimed for perfection, and reaching it had been particularly hard, given the infrastructure of the building. I had worked successfully in a government-owned facility, where everything required approval and functioned under many watchful eyes. A contract awarded to VMT LTC Management would mean fewer restrictions on my attempts at making the home shine. That would be the icing on the cake, for sure, after all my efforts at turning the facility around. I would take pride in improving this home and demonstrate even more forcefully that I was fit to be its administrator.

*   *   *

Prior to my arrival at the nursing home, the Office on Aging had hired an architectural firm to lead a major renovation project for this very old building, which was over 100 years old. On behalf of the government, the city's Department of Public Works had assigned Rufus, an engineer, to supervise the facility's renovation. Complicating the huge number of deficient practices to be brought to compliance, I was also managing a building slated to undergo a major multi-million-dollar renovation project.

My husband constantly reminded me, "Failure to prepare is preparing to fail." Thanks to Keith, this had become my mantra. Each time we kissed goodbye before I left the house for work, he said, "Don't forget, failure to prepare is preparing to fail." He had been saying this motivational phrase since the days he nagged me about getting my master's degree. It turned out that his advice was always on point.

As part of the master's degree curriculum, Georgetown University required that students complete an internship in a specialized area of healthcare management. I chose to develop skills in the design and decor of senior living quarters. During my tenure as director of nursing at The Washington Home, the board of directors planned to build a new nursing home on vacant land on the grounds of the current building. The plan was to demolish the current facility and erect the new one in its place. My involvement in this project was the catalyst for my internship choice. I spent several months at the architectural firm of Oudens & Knoop to meet the requirement. I also worked closely with an eco-psychiatrist, hired to assist the board of directors in designing their new building. My interaction with those distinguished professionals, in addition to having been a member of a team that had already developed a senior living facility from design to construction, gave me an edge over many other leading nurses in the city.

I ensured that the construction aspect of my history was clearly articulated in VMT LTC's bid to manage the nursing home, as I was certain I was uniquely qualified in D.C. at that time. With my knowledge and experience, I was the perfect person to lead this facility and its renovation project into a brighter future.

MAKE IT WORK FOR YOU!

Rule #18 Be a Detective

Reflection: Always on the Lookout

Baby sea turtles have it tough. They are little bite-sized nuggets of tasty protein for hungry predators like raccoons, crabs and birds. And, once they get in the water, there are a host of predators in the ocean craving some sweet, young turtle meat. The sea turtles that reach adulthood do so, in part, because they learn to keep their eyes moving and spot danger before it spots them, so they can avoid it. Be on the lookout.

- Try my method with your own issues:

  1. Assess a problem you are currently facing. How damaging is it? Does it need your intervention, or will it work itself out in time?

  2. Write a plan on how you will address the problem. Find a solution that works for you.

  3. Implement your plan.

  4. After implementation, give it a little time for the solution to stick, and then re-evaluate. Are there any related ongoing issues? Go back to step one and repeat until it is resolved.

- Practice looking for solutions instead of problems. Problems present themselves all the time, but it is the way we respond to them that makes a difference. The next time you run into a problem at work or school, ask yourself how it could be better managed. If it is outside of your purview (for example, an ongoing customer service issue with a vendor you deal with), take your solution to the person responsible for managing the issue. Be gracious but offer a new method to prevent a recurrence of the problem. Be polite. Thank them for taking the time to hear your concern and proposed solution. As you practice finding solutions, problems will become easier to manage, and solutions will come more easily to you.

RULES TO LIVE BY

When my new company won the contract, I became the first African American woman in Washington, D.C., to own a minority-certified nursing home business in the city. It felt like all eyes were on me sometimes. I was building a reputation in my industry and learning to manage unexpected issues, such as unionization efforts. We expanded our company and took on another division in home health care. And then the phone rang with an opportunity to expand our portfolio even further. Of course, I answered the call.

Rule #19: Manage What You Cannot Control | Be Ready for the Unexpected

Keith always said, "Failure to prepare is preparing to fail" (see chapter nine, "Climbing the Mountain to a Dynasty"). His wise words helped me head off a load of trouble over the years. It is important to be as self-sufficient as you can, but issues can happen despite our vigilance (see chapter 10, "A New Reality"). You can do a few things to get through the rough spots: stay positive, plan as much as possible, and seek a positive outcome. If you manage to find something positive during a terrible calamity, let it give you the strength to pull forward.

It is vitally important to know when to seek help. My friend Ana's life was tragically impacted by the terrorist attacks on September 11, 2001. It was nothing she could control or predict. The only consolation in some circumstances is to know you have a friend who will be there for you (see chapter 12, "Life & Loss"). It is okay to ask for help when the situation is so dire there is nothing left to manage. I know firsthand that this is much easier in theory than in practice. I was there when Ana needed me after 9/11. I did not hesitate to step up and let her lean on me. But, when my husband became ill, I had to learn very quickly how to swallow my pride and let people know I needed them (see chapter 13, "Every Beginning Has Its End"). It was then that I learned I never have to feel helpless. If I ever find myself in a situation of despair that I cannot handle on my own, all I have to do is ask for help. There is no shame in asking. I learned to use my resources.

10

A New Reality

After many months of suspense, the contract to manage the facility was finally awarded to Vital Management Team, Inc. Since I was the administrator at the same facility that my company was now managing, I became self-employed: the first African-American to own a minority-certified nursing home business in the city.

At the next meeting of the District of Columbia Health Care Association, it was with glee, and a lot of pride, that I announced my company had been awarded the government contract. It took a good minute before the first person gained enough courage to congratulate me; the whole room was in a state of shock. They could not believe it. No one knew I had formed a company, placed a bid, and been awarded the contract. It had been the best-kept secret in town. After the meeting, I made it a point to approach the colleague who had pestered me at almost every monthly meeting about my future at the facility. "Do you remember asking me who I wanted to work for?" I asked. "I responded: myself. Now you know that I was telling the truth. I am working for me. I am the owner and CEO of the company, and I'm staying on at the facility as its administrator." I spoke with eloquence, knowing that I wore a smirk reminiscent of my husband's.

It was time to show how high I could go, after so many of my colleagues had gone so low. When I was named administrator, I was not well-accepted by this association, especially by the white administrators—and there were many. I did not expect otherwise: one such administrator was best friends with the man I had replaced, and my arrival did not sit well with her, nor with his friends within the association. "We need to stop those directors of nursing from becoming administrators," she had said sarcastically at one of the meetings. "Before we know it, they will take over all the administrator positions in the city." This remark, of course, was directed at me. But it also constituted a threat to other directors of nursing with the same ambition of becoming administrators. District licensing regulations stipulate there must be at least one practicing licensed nursing home administrator on the licensing board. If this comment reflected the attitude of current administrators, director of nursing applicants could be blocked from becoming licensed out of spite.

Several years later, Garrett, now an administrator at an offshore nursing home in the Virgin Islands, was visiting from a U.S. territory. He mentioned in a DCHCA meeting that he was in the United States to recruit a nursing director. Seated at the head table, one board member shouted, "Why don't you take Solanges?" This was mainly to belittle me, even though I was chief executive officer/owner of my own company and the seated administrator at the Center for Aging nursing home. I simply humphed. While others were busy being sarcastic and nasty, I was busy improving the facility, quietly growing my business, and enriching myself both professionally and financially. I paid them no mind and refused to let them steal my hard-earned joy.

Because the nursing home was a government-owned facility, the contract required that we hold an annual open house—a grand affair, often attended by the mayor, most of their cabinet, members of the council members, and members of the aging community. The event was always festive: a feel-good event for the government, and a party for stockholders, residents, family, and staff. At one of those great, and fun, open houses, an employee approached me discretely and asked me to report immediately to the reception area for a phone call. I refused to abandon my guests and directed the employee to take a message or ask one of my directors to field the call for me.

I was seated at the head table when the employee returned once again and whispered in my ear, "I am sorry, ma'am. The caller will only speak to you."

Victor, my supportive business partner, and the most caring member of my board, had observed the back and forth I was having with the employee, our quiet exchange, and my annoyed expression. When I left the room abruptly, he followed me to the lobby, where the receptionist confirmed, "I am sorry, ma'am; this person insists on talking to you." She connected me to a phone in the hallway. Victor, sensing trouble, followed. He watched and listened closely as I conversed with the caller.

"This is the administrator," I said, lifting the receiver to my ear. "How may I help you?"

The voice on the other end of the receiver answered, "I am a social worker at the hospital, and I have one of your residents with me. She says she was raped at your nursing home last night by a man wearing a white lab coat. I wanted to notify you, because, as per hospital protocol, I have to notify the police immediately—along with the Ombudsman Program and Adult Protective Services."

My heart felt like it had been pulled out of my chest. I imagined the pain the patient was experiencing and the atrocity of her situation. I was also worried about my own situation. I had a facility full of guests and members of the media. The police investigating a rape case in the middle of it all? I could only imagine the magnitude of the horror that would create. "Would you tell me the name of the resident?" I asked. "Before you call the police, please allow me to review her chart to see who cared for her last night."

"Her name is Ms. Jambiyas," said the social worker.

"Oh, I know her," I said. "She lives on the second floor. Can I have a few minutes to run to the unit quickly?" I was begging her for time. "Please, give me a phone number to reach you. I will call you right back."

Victor pulled out a pen and paper to write the number as I repeated it aloud. When I hung up the phone, before I could utter a word, Victor said, "My God! Your face looks like you have just seen a ghost."

"It is worse than that, Victor," I replied. I pleaded with him to return to the function and not to say a word to anyone. I, then, asked the receptionist to page the director of nursing to the second floor STAT. I ran upstairs, praying to Mother Mary to help me get through this nightmare. The director of nursing and I rushed to the nursing unit where Ms. Jambiyas lived. We grabbed the chart, and flipped through to the nurse's notes, and then to the doctor's orders.

"She had a fever the night before due to a bowel impaction," I pointed out.

The physician had ordered that Ms. Jambiyas be manually disimpacted, and the procedure was performed by a male registered nurse.

"This explains the allegations," the director of nursing said. "She probably believed that she was being raped."

We were both relieved by the findings. The director of nursing quickly called the social worker at the hospital, and faxed the pertinent pages from Ms. Jambiyas's medical chart. The hospital would later confirm that there were no signs of molestation. Disaster aborted.

Still shaking, I returned to the festivities. The speaking portion of the program had ended, but the reception was still in progress with many people eating, drinking, sharing ideas, and commenting on the keynote address and on the progress made by the facility. I was bewildered by what had just happened. Again, my guardian angel had been at my side, and, again, I had dodged a bullet. Prior to contacting the police, the hospital's social worker had no obligation to contact me directly. Had she not placed a call, the consequences could have been catastrophic, especially if the media picked up on the story. It might have become a total fiasco. The situation could have been blown out of proportion before the exam results were in, vindicating my nurse, and the damage would have been devastating to the nursing home, the nurse who had performed the procedure on Ms. Jambiyas, and to me, personally, as the face of VMT.

The social worker called me, because I had earned a stellar reputation in the social work community. This was the result of relationship building. Networking is a powerful management tool, and I was lucky to have recognized its value early on in my career. Our director of social services at the facility sponsored an annual luncheon in celebration of Social Work Week. She usually invited social workers from various nursing homes and hospitals. I attended the event religiously, often as the keynote speaker. I personally welcomed guests to the facility. I spoke eloquently on a topic of interest in their field and was amicable with everyone, even though I did not know anyone's name. The secret of networking is that, by sharing oneself, we multiply what we receive in return: blessings. It was a true blessing that the hospital's social worker called me that evening, and she gave me that courtesy because she knew me.

I felt protected by my guardian angel, and, through my faith in God, I managed to survive another adversity.

The facility was steadily reaching the potential I had envisioned for it. I was becoming more of an expert at averting disasters almost daily. In my quest for perfection, I expected the best from my directors and managers, who, in turn, set high expectations for their staff. At the facility, everyone worked long hours. I knew that the employees were trying their best to meet my standards. Pressure was high: construction had started, and, to make room for renovations, nursing units were systematically closing a few at a time. Some residents were shuttled to other units internally, while others were transferred out to other nursing homes. Walls were erected to segregate staff, residents, and visitors from the construction areas. When asbestos was discovered in areas of the building, I hired an environmental hygienist, and the level of asbestos in the building was measured and posted daily.

I thought that I was handling these circumstances rather well—with determination, caution, and frequent evaluation. I realized some employees were becoming angry while others appeared upset at the continual interference brought on by construction. I continued to schedule regular staff meetings, and maintained my open-door policy, listening wholeheartedly to a fair amount of complaints from employees and family members. Aside from the inconvenience brought on by construction, there seemed to be no major issues. Or so I thought … until, one day, to my surprise, a union was picketing on the sidewalk of the nursing home, chanting that the employees wanted to unionize.

I had worked in a unionized environment before, at Mount Sinai Hospital in New York, but not at an upper-management level. I had also attended union meetings as an assistant head nurse when my actions had been challenged by the union on behalf of a nursing assistant I had disciplined. Now, as the CEO of VMT and administrator of the nursing home, I was clearly being targeted by this union, and the slightest failure to properly manage interactions with them could be costly to VMT. With an already never-ending to-do list, I knew that the union activity was more than I could reasonably handle by myself. It became imperative that I obtain the assistance of a labor lawyer, and our board agreed to hire Littler & Mendelsohn, a legal firm that had defeated a union campaign when I was director of nursing at the Washington home.

These new union organizers had launched a smear campaign against me personally. For several months, while the firm was in legal negotiations, union members picketed in front of the building, carrying banners and placards of a picture of me in a fur coat. Other photos showed my Mercedes Benz, and the men and women chanted that I had stolen a dollar from each employee's paycheck to buy expensive furs and cars. It was misleading. I had worked hard and had earned everything honestly. Ninety percent of the picketers were not even employed by the nursing home. In fact, most of my employees were visibly upset with the union organizers' tactics. They came to my office in droves, apologizing for the actions of the union and expressing dismay at the few disgruntled employees who had joined the protest. They knew that the union picketers were shouting false slogans. "We would never think such things about you," they said. "We know that your Caribbean pride would not allow you to steal from us."

When the union ballots were counted, the result was that our employees voted no to unionization—a great victory for our newly formed corporation, although at a cost of more than $40,000. Once again, with glee, I stood tall: I could not be defeated. I had won my first union victory as a chief executive officer.

The nursing home was surveyed by the District of Columbia and federal inspectors, independent of the city, and, finally, joint surveys were conducted by both district and federal inspectors. In general, joint surveys are the most difficult for any nursing home, because federal surveyors rigorously assess and critique the state's processes in implementing federal regulations. In lieu of a state inspection, our facility was subjected to a city survey, since the District of Columbia is not considered a state. The federal government pays for inspections in the thousands of nursing homes in the United States, the Virgin Islands, and Puerto Rico, which all receive Medicare and Medicaid funds. Essentially, joint and independent surveys are the Federal government's means of evaluating the services states provide on their behalf.

One of the most important goals of a nursing home is to pass muster during these annual assessments. Surveys are very stressful for nursing home administrators, as unsatisfactory findings can lead to dire consequences, such as civil money penalties whereby the facility is expected to pay a daily fine until a deficient practice has been corrected, and becomes compliant with federal and/or city regulations. It can mean a freeze on admissions. It can be the catalyst for the dismissal of a director of nursing, the arrest of an administrator, negative media coverage, and the termination of a management company's contract. It can also mean the hiring of temporary management to take over operations of a facility or, in the very worst cases, the permanent closure of a nursing home. I was vigilant at assuring a well-run facility, free of drama.

VMT spent more than 20 years operating this facility on behalf of the government. During that time, the nursing home experienced dozens of inspections. My goal was to take a facility with a history of over 100 deficiencies and lead it to a deficiency-free status. I managed to meet that goal on more than one occasion, and our nursing home was recognized by the federal government as being the best-run nursing home in the city. To celebrate this victory, we paid for a large ad in the *Washington Post*, expressing our gratitude toward the staff and congratulating them for their hard work. I must admit that I was enjoying the public recognition. I had managed the facility so efficiently that many government officials were now admitting their loved ones to our facility—a sure sign we had built a strong reputation for stellar care. On numerous occasions, the mayor held cabinet meetings at the nursing home. The facility's financial situation had changed dramatically as well. No longer managing a staggering deficit, we had begun to operate at a profit.

Surrounded by happy residents, families, and staff, I was now ready—and eager—to harvest higher-hanging fruit in my quest for perfection. I was never satisfied; I never had enough. I still believed that satisfaction is a precursor to complacency, which leads to a lack of drive, and manifests into obstacles to growth and development. If my son, Kevin, brought home a report card with an A, I complained that he could have obtained an A+, had he applied himself harder. I feel very strongly that maximum success should be the end goal of every endeavor. This conviction has been key in my journey from rags to riches.

My company had inherited a dispute that existed at the facility under the prior management. It was a $4-million discrepancy that Medicaid was asking the facility to reimburse. The management company's position was that Medicaid had failed to pay for care provided to its beneficiaries. The company asserted that these unpaid monies were partly the reason the facility had been operating under such a deficit. Determined to get to the bottom of this, I hired an outside CPA firm to conduct an audit of billing records and other documents. I requested they present their findings to the government and the board of directors at VMT. The research revealed that, in fact, Medicaid was negligent in reimbursing the facility. It was a moot point, since Medicaid was a government agency, and the nursing home was owned by the government. The successful resolution of the discrepancy ended a long-standing dispute and marked, once again, a successful chapter in VMT's management history. This was a big win for the facility. The revenue belonged to the nursing home, not to the contractor managing the business, so the unexpected influx of funds was directed toward the renovation of the building. The money was also instrumental in increasing employee salaries, which allowed us to remain competitive in recruiting the most-qualified candidates for open positions.

Because of this kind of success, for about 20 years, the contract to manage the facility was repeatedly awarded to VMT. Other companies in the city were curious to know how we continuously won the contract. Well, the government trusted the company, because we had consistently delivered quality care to our residents; we were also fiscally accountable, and very knowledgeable about regulations. Competitors, who desired to bid on the contract, called me first to see if VMT was bidding, to avoid wasting their money and energy. During a contract discussion, one nursing home management vendor commented, "The city would be stupid to take this contract away from VMT." Even a competitor was able to appreciate the quality of my company's work—and so did the government. VMT managed the facility for many years under different mayoral administrations, which was very unusual. I continued to oversee management at the nursing home while simultaneously supervising the executive director at VMT's corporate office. My partners were mainly investors that attended board meetings and provided both moral support and intellectual capital, especially during the union activity at the facility. They were instrumental in advising me on financial, insurance, and legal issues. Without interference, I was able to freely develop the company's goals and implement, manage, and continually re-evaluate the business to my rigid specifications.

In 1990, a federal regulation—the Omnibus Budget Reconciliation Act—mandated the certification of all nursing assistants working in nursing homes in the United States. To become a certified nursing assistant, one had to attend a licensed state school, complete a preparatory course, and take a state examination for certification. Considering this new regulation and the complications it would create for the nursing assistants on our staff, I decided to expand our company. I acutely understood the cost of a missed opportunity, so I immediately opened a nursing school to train nursing assistants and prepare them for the licensing exam. I was the first in the city to create a school with the sole purpose of meeting this federal mandate. Once my own employees were trained and certified, admission to the school was opened to any qualified applicant. Before long, the school grew to become an accredited education center, offering programs for practical nurses, pharmacy technicians, massage therapists, and home health aides—all in addition to the nursing assistant program.

Since I constantly challenged myself with new ventures, I added one more division to the company: VMT opened a Medicare- and Medicaid-certified home care agency that grew to provide healthcare services to over 300 homebound clients. Being successful is a choice; the key to becoming successful is learning to live outside your comfort zone. Fear of the unknown can be paralyzing, but I never let it hold me back from trying. I have always been a risk taker and have never been afraid to be a turtle and stick my neck out. I worked very hard and maintained a can-do attitude. While everything seemed to be going well for me, my partners, on the other hand, were not so lucky. Doc was forced by the federal government to close his businesses (which, thankfully, did not impact VMT's reputation since he never practiced medicine at VMT); on the other hand, Vic sold his rehabilitation company to a healthcare vendor like VMT, which prohibited him from holding shares in a competitive business. Keith and I bought out both partners and became the sole owners of VMT and our two new business ventures: the VMT Education Center, and the VMT Home Care Agency.

Once he had earned his undergraduate degree at Syracuse University, my son became a professional model in New York City. After a while, however, he returned home to attend George Washington University for his master's degree in business administration (MBA). During his graduate studies, he worked at

VMT to put into practice what he was learning in school. He was proud to work under his mother: the naïve French-speaking, Haitian teenage girl who had entered the United States of America without any knowledge of the English language but had managed to build her own empire through determination and hard work.

I had successfully turned my world around to become a force to be reckoned with. From secretary, I became the treasurer, vice-president, and then president of the same District of Columbia Healthcare Association that had been reluctant to welcome me as a new administrative peer when I took over as administrator at the Center for Aging nursing home. I still was not finished building our company, and a new challenge presented itself in no time.

Prior to purchasing the Center for Aging nursing home that VMT was managing, the government had, in their portfolio, another nursing home that eventually closed, a general hospital, and a psychiatric hospital. When dually diagnosed, mentally ill and developmentally disabled individuals no longer needed acute psychiatric interventions at the hospital. The federal government mandated that the mayor transfer these individuals to a more appropriate, home-like environment. In the northwest quadrant of the city, there was the Johnson building that had been seized by the Office of Housing and Urban Development (HUD) and remained unoccupied for about three years. HUD donated this building to the city as a gesture of goodwill to house chronically and mentally ill individuals from the psychiatric hospital. This gift from the federal government was a small, yet important token to the city, particularly considering all the disadvantages associated with being a district, as opposed to a state. This was a large building, with the capacity to house over 240 people. It was used to house transfer patients from the psychiatric hospital and to admit physically and chronically and mentally ill people from the community. All these patients were indigent and in desperate need of institutional care. In the past, about 150 seniors with chronic illness had been transferred from the psychiatric hospital to this building.

In the United States, safety codes are very strict for nursing homes, more than for any other type of healthcare facility. It has been said that nursing homes follow regulations that are stricter than those of nuclear power plants. It took a considerable amount of time to get the building cosmetically ready to meet some, but not all, of the federal and city regulations, in addition to meeting certification requirements for Medicaid, the one and only payer source for the patients populating the new building. Originally, this large edifice had not been designed to be a nursing home, which presented unique challenges. In addition, the facility was plagued with many issues, some more complex than others. The mayor wisely hired a management company to operate the building, as opposed to relying on self-management.

Every startup faces its load of challenges, some more difficult than others. The degree of difficulty is measured by the level of preparation dedicated to the project. The HUD-gifted building became a classic example that failure to prepare was preparing to fail. A well-developed plan should have been implemented in order to successfully transfer so many seniors with chronic illness to the new facility. Because of the fragility of this population, it was of the utmost importance to ensure as smooth of a transition as possible. Very early in the process, however, many of my colleagues and I became aware of the trials, tribulations, and obstacles to be overcome by the staff of this newly formed team. As they struggled with their new tasks, I was asked on numerous occasions to assist in preparations for the brutal city and federal surveys. The press was already reporting negative news, yet again, on another failing government-owned nursing home.

As I had done in the past for other nursing homes who had reached out to me for assistance, I reviewed their policies and procedures, read over past inspection reports and walked around the building to point out areas where the facility was deficient—areas that could be corrected before the official assessments occurred. As I reviewed the facility, I became more aware of the challenges faced by the management company. I shared my perspective—but the current management company already had more trouble than they could juggle. Many of the staff had stopped reporting to work; several vendors refused to deliver goods and services, because they were not being paid; and employees' paychecks were being refused at banks for insufficient funds. To make matters worse, the management company soon wrote a letter to the mayor, terminating their contract with the government, effective immediately. They abandoned the facility with employees' taxes and health benefits left unpaid.

It became a major crisis for the city.

One sunny day in the mid-1990s, at about ten o'clock in the morning, I received a call from the director of the city's department of human services, asking me to report to his office by two o'clock in the afternoon to discuss management of the Johnson nursing home. At that time, VMT, on behalf of the government, had already been managing the Center for Aging nursing home for several years. Under my leadership, that facility was totally off the radar of the media, and was operating in the black, both fiscally and managerially.

"Mr. Hawk," I said, "how do you expect me to report to your office at two o'clock when it is already ten?"

"I don't know," he replied. "I am told that you are the only one who can help me with this nursing home crisis we have with the government. I will see you at two, okay?"

I had no choice but to say, "Yes, sir," not even sure where his office was located.

In a matter of hours, I was able to assemble a solid team, consisting of VMT's executive director, who had a legal background, our accountant, who was a CPA, the company's attorney, and, of course, my beloved Keith who believed in me and stood by my side from the inception of the company and through all our tribulations. After Doc and Victor left VMT, my husband Keith had closed his own business to join my venture. Together, we all walked in to Mr. Hawk's office. He was surprised by the number—and caliber—of people that I was able to assemble in such a short amount of time. After the introductions, he said with a wide smile, "Anyone in this city who can assemble a team of this many professionals in such a short time belongs in my office."

At first, there was small talk, and even some laughter, until Mr. Hawk abruptly stopped to look straight at me. Very seriously, he asked, "Why have I never met you before?" He spoke directly to me, "Where have you been? I thought I knew everybody with a healthcare business in this city."

I adopted my husband's smirk, and answered, "I do my work, sir. I mind my own business, and I stay where I belong." My husband, who had always been my counselor, and my conscience, had taught me not to get caught up in city politics. That advice had served me well and made me "one of the clean ones"—an endorsement that had been given by the chairman of the Control Board at a hearing.

We discussed the issues facing the home, and Mr. Hawk promised to get a contract to VMT to take over management on behalf of the government. This contract would add a second nursing home to our company's portfolio. Our help was urgently needed. It was November, Thanksgiving week, and the employees of the disgraced nursing home had not been paid. The management company had completely abandoned the home, and, for the short period before the arrival of a new management company, the employees were legally under government payroll. Disappointed and angry, the employees had invaded the office of the city's administrator, and that of the comptroller/finance director, demanding to speak with the mayor and to be compensated for their work. Once again, the media was having a field day with this employee protest, both in print and on air.

During this time of unrest at the facility, VMT actively negotiated with the government's contracting office. VMT was making demands that were unusual, but necessary, in order to take control of the facility, and start the rehabilitative process of bringing the home under compliance, and resolving the employees' rightful complaints. One of the requests was that VMT be allowed to bill Medicaid and other payers directly. Additionally, they requested all receivables come directly to the facility to allow us to manage the crisis as efficiently as possible. Because of the nature of the nursing home business, I explained, the facility could not depend on a check from the city's treasury to stay afloat—we needed to expedite the payee process. As part of the contract, VMT also requested that the government advance enough funds to pay every employee, in order to bring back employees who had quit out of frustration. We also demanded funds to pay some vendors, as an enticement for them to return, or to continue to deliver, their goods and services.

The goal was simple: If employees knew that they would be paid in advance, they would be more likely to return to work. They had no money for transportation, no money for maintaining their uniforms, and, in some cases, no money for food. A paycheck was not only needed to get them back to work, but it also showed good faith and trust that the new management would make their wellbeing a priority. The government agreed to advance money to VMT as a loan to the nursing home until the Medicaid checks started being disbursed to support the facility. This loan was eventually repaid to the government from the Johnson nursing home revenue.

During these negotiations, the Control Board requested that I appear for a fiscal oversight hearing prior to the contract award being finalized. My team attended the hearing, and I testified in front of the board—about the company, about the steps we had taken that had turned the first government home from one with over 100 deficiencies, and with close to a $2-million deficit, into a profitable five-star facility. I pledged to the Control Board, the residents, families, and staff of the facility that we would do everything possible to improve the quality of care and to repair the lackluster reputation of the facility. Based on some of the questions, I could tell that members were interested in determining whether I had ties to the inner circle of the government. They learned that I was not known by any of the major players in power. They were satisfied that I was an independent practitioner who had received high marks from the Office on Aging for successfully managing the other government nursing home. In the end, a one-year contract was awarded to VMT to take over the daily operations of the facility in turmoil.

The company that I had formed, and of which I was now the sole shareholder, was about to become an even bigger empire.

All eyes were once again on VMT—and, therefore, on me. *She did it before. Can she do it again?* This was the question in the city. As the administrator at the Center for Aging nursing home, I was well-aware that, by law, I could not simultaneously be the administrator of the Johnson nursing home. Although Keith was smart and analytical, he was not a licensed nursing home administrator, and, therefore, not qualified to serve as the administrator of record for the new nursing home. Therefore, we maintained the current administrator, mainly because of her license. As a team, Keith worked with me to provide oversight at the new home, making sure that he had his eyes and ears on the ground, reviewing, observing, questioning, meeting with vendors, and analyzing all the facility's needs.

I worked in my administrator's capacity at the first home, and then spent my evenings at the new facility. My first order of business at the Johnson Home was to meet with the directors, then the managers, and, finally, I called a general staff meeting. The meetings were informative, but, at times, overwhelming, and even painful, as the staff discussed their ordeals. Some had not been paid for over a month; the prior management company had skipped out on their taxes, and their health insurance had been cancelled. One employee cried during an open meeting, stating that her blood pressure was dangerously high but she had no money to buy medication. In fact, this employee died a few months after sharing this information. I was told by staff, and subsequently observed, that the facility was infested with rodents. I also learned that the employees had filed a lawsuit against the government. While the facility was under VMT management, this case was settled out of court, and the employees were awarded restitution by the government.

Because of the turmoil, the new facility was placed on fast track by the federal government, which meant that we were surveyed, and resurveyed in excess of the regular annual inspections. We had our hands full, because the facility had a host of deficiencies. It had been cited by both District and federal governments. These deficits needed to be addressed quickly, in addition to the day-to-day issues we faced managing operation of a new venture. VMT had a quagmire mapped out for us—a map that we did not draw but was ours to navigate now that we were the new contractor.

The ideal nursing home administrator needs a strong clinical base, solid management experience, and a comprehension of the industry's lingo. In addition, they must be analytical when managing clinical issues and, in general, possess a broad knowledge of the healthcare system. A nursing home administrator does not necessarily have to be a nurse. Anyone with a degree in social work or any of the healthcare therapies tends to be at an advantage over, let us say, a beautician, a secretary, or even a finance guru, that also carries a nursing home administrator license. The Johnson facility's licensed nursing home administrator was a finance major and was at a great disadvantage, since she was not a nurse, and she had zero clinical knowledge. She was a new licensee with minimal experience. Some of the issues this administrator had to deal with included multiple surveys, a general lack of funds, and an inability to control staffing shortages for the nursing home. She had no idea, on any given day, how many employees were to report to work to care for the residents—and who those employees were. When asked by VMT, this administrator could not produce the number of employees assigned to any given department; provided with a name, she could not even verify an individual's employment status. The lack of upper-corporate management support became obvious as I interacted with this administrator. She had been doing the best she could with no help at all from above. As the sitting administrator, she was legitimately afraid to make decisions—even to sign paychecks. She was afraid of her own shadow. I sympathized with her, and I made it a point to work closely with her and to support her whereas others may have made the decision to immediately replace her.

Because we were able to get an advance on funds from the District, VMT was able to pay and recruit back many of the employees who had quit. We convinced the vendors that were owed money to return, and those who stayed were recognized for not abandoning the facility. One such company was the Nationwide Pharmacy Center; they continued to deliver medications to the seniors, even though they were owed thousands of dollars.

I resigned from my administrator position at our first home and hired a licensed nursing home administrator as my replacement so I could better supervise both administrators and offer them the support they needed. I was now better able to provide oversight at both facilities.

The staff at the Center for Aging nursing home did not want me to leave. However, they understood that it was best for both facilities that I resign. They were reassured of my continued attention, and of my dedicated support, to the facility. The staff gave me a magnificent farewell celebration. It was attended by members of the city council, and many other city officials, such as members of the Office on Aging. I was graced by a recitation of Maya Angelou's poem, "Phenomenal Woman." There were staff performances, and, yes, a lot of speeches and gifts from family members, staff, and even participants in the senior day program that VMT also managed for the government.

My husband and I took no vacations. We stayed focused and on task. I had no free time for myself, for my husband, nor for my son. Once again, I figuratively lived at those two facilities. We were sacrificing intimacy, as we became coworkers more than lovers, and our son, a young adult, was thriving, capable of handling school and personal recreation with friends independent of his parents. We were determined, and we chose, to be successful. No sacrifice was too big in our quest to build a minority company we could be proud of, a shining example in Washington, D.C.

MAKE IT WORK FOR YOU!

Rule #19: Manage What You Cannot Control | Be Ready for the Unexpected

Reflection: It Is All on My Back, but Mama Has Got My Back, Too

Turtles are fairly self-sufficient. They carry their homes on their backs and gather what they need from their surroundings. Until recently, scientists believed they were also deaf and could not communicate with one another, because they lack vocal cords. But Richard Vogt, a herpetologist, has discovered that giant South American river turtles call out to their hatchlings once they reach the water to help guide them to migrating colonies where they will be safer than on their own. According to Vogt's research, before they are even hatched, the babies start communicating with each other from inside their shells. This is a great lesson: while we can all shoulder a heavy load on our backs, it is good to know someone can help you find your way when you do not know which direction to head.

- Look at your bank account. Do you have enough money to cover you if an emergency pops up? If you have not planned for the unplanned, it is time to open an emergency savings account with enough money in it to support you for six months, minimum. Squirrel away as much as you can, even if it is only a couple of dollars a month. While you are at it, start planning for retirement. Set aside a little money at a time, and do not touch it.

- Make sure you are vigilant about your healthcare. Plan an annual checkup, PAP smear, and breast exam and schedule a dental exam. It is easy to wait until you get sick to manage your healthcare, but identifying health issues early can help you stay healthier longer by heading off conditions before they become chronic.

- Set up a living will and a care plan for yourself in case you unexpectedly become incapacitated. Identify someone who can act as your proxy if you ever have a situation where you cannot make your own medical decisions. Most primary care physicians or social workers can help you get the paperwork in order for a living will and a medical advance directive.

RULES TO LIVE BY

Rule #20: Find Ways to Measure Success

I remember the feeling of exhilaration the first time I bought myself a Mercedes. I had earned it! No more beat-up Green Pacer for me. I was driving in style (see chapter eight, "The Fishing Expedition"). It was similar to the feeling I felt when I signed closing papers on our big family home (see chapter 12, "Life & Loss"). Both of those occasions marked a measure of success for me; they told me I was getting somewhere. But status symbols and luxury items, while nice, are not the only measure of success. It is important to find ways to measure success in your professional life as well.

I had four basic goals in mind when my company took over management of the Johnson Nursing Home:

1. Create a home-like, cozy environment for the residents.

2. Improve staff morale (see chapter 11, "How Did We Do It?").

3. Win back the trust of the vendors who had canceled contracts with the nursing home.

4. Beautify the environment.

Once those four goals were met, we went to work on raising funds for equipment and leisure activities for the residents to improve their quality of life. None of these measures were for my own benefit, though I derived some vicarious joy from seeing the changes take effect. Happy residents, staff, clients, and vendors equals success. Happiness has a way of spreading like a virus. Make sure you are doing your very best to satisfy the people you come into contact with in your professional life—at every level; this is key to becoming successful.

11

How Did We Do It?

A s a company, we knew our first task at the new facility was to work on making sure the residents felt more at home before we could solve the more complicated issues. The beauty parlor received a coat of paint, new mirrors, new combs, and new brushes. It immediately became a place where residents could get pampered, exchange gossip, and meet new friends who reminded them of the connections they had had outside of the nursing home's walls. The modernization of the beauty parlor was a low-hanging fruit issue we checked off our very long to-do list, and it was an important one, because the comfort of the seniors in the home had to come first.

My next plan of action was also a priority: it was imperative I get back into the good graces of the exterminator, the first company to abandon the facility for nonpayment. Life in the city came with its share of mice, rats, raccoons, squirrels, and other creatures, even in private homes. Seniors, in particular, struggled to keep their environments free of rodents, especially when they lived alone. Rodents in a nursing home are very common. Any time a new resident is admitted, a nursing home runs the chance of introducing roaches, bedbugs, lice, and other insects. The Johnson Home was overrun with vermin, and we desperately needed to remediate the pest problem right away. Once the contractor returned, the rodents disappeared, and a checkmark was added to the list of problems we needed to solve.

Another low-hanging fruit was the cleanliness of the building. We discovered that the facility had only three buffing machines to clean the entire building.

Two of these machines had been sent out for repair, however, and had not been recovered due to a lack of funds, so only one machine could be used to clean the eight nursing units and all the public areas. No wonder the floors looked unkempt! Once the two machines—now functional—were returned, we purchased an additional two machines. The floors sparkled. The interior walls received a fresh coat of paint, and all the carpeting was disinfected and shampooed. The building looked good and smelled good.

Those were the most obvious issues we resolved to give a tangible appearance of improvement to the building. Once those goals were met, we set out to uncover deeper problems. The obvious problems were evident and easier to solve. However, the real issues at the facility needed to be researched, and handled effectively, in order to rehabilitate this nursing home once and for all. We declared war against bandage management.

My dear husband, the new president of VMT, whose offices were now located at the Johnson nursing home, became my researcher. He walked the building multiple times a day, speaking with everyone he encountered to gather information. He interviewed vendors, mingled with families, and talked to contractors working in the building. At the end of each day, he wrote a report that we reviewed together as we strategized over dinner. It was through this process, and the use of analytical skills, that bigger problems were unearthed.

VMT knew that, per contract, the previous management company depended on a monthly check from the government to manage the facility. What we did not know, until we entered the nursing home, was the admission and billing processes: the staff billed the payer source for care delivered at the facility; the payer source, however, issued reimbursement to the District of Columbia Treasury Department—not the facility. Instead of getting paid directly by the payer source, the home had been receiving a set amount of money from the District Treasury Department. In many instances, the government's check was late to arrive, delaying payroll, which upset the staff. Based on VMT's findings, in addition to the monthly check being late, the contracted amount was insufficient to cover the expenses of the facility. For this reason, banks were denying employees' checks for insufficient funds. That was our aha moment. Once the problem was identified, we needed to figure out a plan of action to recover the deficit the facility was rightfully due and relied on to operate efficiently.

Based on Keith's assessment and analysis, the previous management company—and its staff—knew that the amount of the check issued to the facility every month was insufficient. Not only was the allowance set in stone, it was not based on diligence and oversight, so no great effort was made to collect. The previous management company made sure they received their own—very generous—contract fee, but did not strive to ensure that the employees were paid, and that the facility was properly maintained. The welfare of the staff and residents had not been a priority. If money was a major problem, VMT would find a solution. This Johnson Home was owned by the government, as the Center for Aging nursing home had been—the same government that paid all nursing homes—yet the facility was struggling in terms of Medicaid reimbursements, which were the primary source of remittance for the indigent residents under our care.

The other discovery we made was even more shocking: the facility was not Medicare-certified. The irony! The director of the Long-Term Care Administration, which regulated this nursing home, had mandated that all District nursing homes be Medicare-certified; yet, long after the deadline, this government-owned facility was the only one without proper certification. VMT immediately completed the long application form. Within months, we were admitting residents with needs for skilled service and began to collect Medicare dollars to complement the Medicaid revenue.

In the 1990s, nursing homes were reimbursed retroactively, based on expenses. The more a facility spent, the higher the reimbursement rate the following year. Because this new home did not have enough funds to manage its businesses, the reimbursement rate did not vary, creating a vicious cycle that could only be remediated by changing the billing and payment practices.

At my first open staff meeting, I pledged that I would do everything in my power to make sure that their paychecks never bounced. Keeping that promise was important to me, so getting an immediate flow of funds to the facility became my number-one priority. I assembled a team to review the billing history for every resident at the facility, including those residents who might have received care prior to VMT's takeover of the facility, but whose services had not been billed. We started with the oldest files and we submitted invoices for their care—day in and day out.

Just as VMT had been able to recover four million dollars from Medicaid at the Center for Aging nursing home, we were soon able to recoup a big sum of money for the Johnson facility. Medicaid and other payers disbursed a pile of checks for services rendered that had remained unbilled and uncollected for a long time. The money allowed us to stay afloat. Millions of retroactive dollars poured into the building—money that was legitimately owed to the facility. Because of proper billing and an improved cash flow, the reimbursement rate of the facility started to increase. We increased the salaries of current employees and offered a better salary to applicants, which allowed us to compete for a higher caliber of staff—individuals that could truly turn the facility around. We terminated all low-performing employees and hired new staff that received a competitive salary.

Happy staff, happy residents. We worked aggressively at improving staff morale. The frequency of the surveys decreased drastically, to the point that even the surveyors were joyful. We received praise from the residents' families and, of course, the government was satisfied with their selection of a contractor that was able to shield them from all the negative media they had faced under the previous management company. VMT enjoyed high marks from all parties, just as we had received accolades for managing the Center for Aging nursing home.

The facility still faced structural issues requiring major renovation, and no government funds were immediately available—nor appropriated—for such a large renovation project. Understanding the situation, the mayor appropriated funds to assist with the facility's renovation during the following fiscal year. Unfortunately, when he lost the November election and had to give up his seat as mayor, the facility lost a champion who would have helped us implement the project quickly. The renovation was delayed indefinitely. The following year, Council Member Allen, who chaired the committee on health, made sure the renovation dollars were secured, but, because government budgets are developed far in advance of the fiscal year during which they are implemented, the building had to wait for funds to become available to start the renovations.

At a nursing home that struggled with finding the funds desperately needed for daily operations, I had to figure out means of bringing "fun" money to the facility to boost morale and of improving the lives of the seniors living in the Johnson Home. Residents needed more recreational activities, including more frequent community outings. There was a lack of funding for leisurely events.

I decided to seek some private funding, as I had done at the Center for Aging nursing home. We established a residents' community advisory board (known as RCAB). It was comprised of the president of the residents' council, the president of the family council, and members of the community. An employee of the recreation department staffed the RCAB on a voluntary basis, and I served as ex-officio on the RCAB board. The primary function of RCAB was to raise funds to meet resident's quality of life. In other words, the board members needed to bring in FUNDS so that the residents could have FUN.

When managing a nursing home, allowing it to remain a strictly Medicaid facility with no private-sector dollars to compensate for the shortfalls of Medicaid and no short-term Medicare rehabilitation services dollars to fill-in the financial gap can be a recipe for disaster. The life in such a facility is of minimal quality and can bring despair, considering that very few of the residents will ever return home or to the outside community. Most of those residents had been transferred from a psychiatric hospital and, having lived in that institution for a long time—sometimes, years—they had no home to return to, and, in many cases, no family to welcome them back into the community.

In addition, this facility was the place where most, if not all, of the city's homeless population was admitted, whenever long-term, around-the-clock nursing home care was required. Returning to the street was not an option. For most of these residents, it was their last home, and, for many, the best home they ever had. I wanted the men and women under our care to live a full life while in the nursing home. From the moment I walked through the doors of The Washington Home, my very first nursing home, and was greeted by seniors in wheelchairs, I associated them with my mother and father who were also growing old, and I resolved to treat them as though they were family. I promised myself to elevate their quality of life to the best of my ability—a responsibility that I held in prayer to Mother Mary. Through RCAB's fundraising events, including a black-tie function, we were able to raise enough money to purchase a wheelchair-accessible bus for the facility. We had a big ribbon-cutting ceremony when the bus was delivered. It was a happy day and marked the beginning of big changes for the residents.

Before acquiring the bus, the residents were not able to go shopping in the community, so the staff would bring in vendors, creating a mall in the residents' dining room where the residents could shop. Once they had their own transportation, the residents were able to leave the building. Each event was tantamount to going on a cruise—many of the residents had not left the home for years. The residents' favorite trip was to the mall, so that they could shop at Walmart, some in their motorized mobility scooters or in manual wheelchairs, assisted by staff members. There was no doubt that our company was making a difference in the lives of these residents. It was evident in their wide smiles.

While both nursing homes were flourishing and the corporation was recognized as one of the top 100 employers in the city, my personal life was in tatters. My time with Keith was focused mainly on discussing and worrying about the work that we now shared. I publicly played the role of the successful woman very well, but there was a dark side to this success—stress. I was a CEO in charge of two demanding nursing homes with more than 500 residents I felt responsible for; I was also responsible for hundreds of home care agency clients, and of a nursing school with a large number of students—a total staff between all of them of about 800 employees. The load had begun to feel unmanageable. It was finally taking its toll.

I got through my days on adrenaline. When I woke up in the morning, I could feel it begin to course through my body, and it often felt like I was running from one obligation or meeting to the next all day long with no time to rest until I got into bed. At night, when my head finally hit the pillow, I had collapse and sleep until morning when the whole rat race began all over again, and the adrenaline kicked in, spurring me though my day.

I often lashed out at my husband in anger and frustration, but Keith remained unfazed. He took all my tantrums with a grain of salt and was much more understanding than I could have expected. He continued to remain my rock, and he never fought back. One day, when he thought that I was at my lowest point, he held me by my shoulders, looking me in the eyes with exaggerated pity—his smirk not too far away. "Hold it a minute, Solanges! What happened? You are angry, cutting me right and left with words. Did you swallow a … razor blade?" We both laughed at his words. He hugged me and held me tight against his chest. He kissed me and reassured me that everything was going to be fine. I had a good cry on his shoulders and felt better, even if it was just for that moment. He had a special way of keeping me grounded, maybe because of the 10-year age difference between us.

I had nightmares, marked by episodes during which I was very hot, and then suddenly freezing. An electric fan sat on a chair in front of my bed to cool me down if I had a hot flash. A thick blanket lay on the bed in case I got cold, and it was often thrown over Keith in the course of the night. He had made it clear to me one day that he was putting up with me only because he loved me but that he had just about enough of my manic behavior. I developed a stomach ulcer that tested positive for h. pylori bacteria, which had to be treated with a strong course of triple antibiotics. I was in and out of my primary care physician's office. He had done all that he could to help me. As a last resort, I was referred to a physician who specialized in obstetrics and gynecology. In my late 30s, *I was much too young to be menopausal. Could it be the stress from work manifesting itself in such erratic behaviors?* I worried.

At one of my gynecological visits, I was seen by a licensed nurse practitioner who had spent a great deal of time reviewing my health record. She knew that I was a well-educated healthcare professional in my own rights and was also acutely aware that I had a lot on my plate: I was too close to my own situation to be rational. "I'm going to take a leap, even though it is forbidden in the healthcare system," she said. "However, I trust my judgment and feel that my suggestion is in your best interest." She sat me down and proceeded with the words that would be the catalyst of a cure to my illness. "I am going to refer you to an endocrinologist," she said.

Before she was given a chance to finish her sentence, the razor blade was out. "Endocrinologist! I'm not looking to get pregnant. Why would I need an endocrinologist?" Of course, I knew I was being irrational. Endocrinologists treat more than problematic pregnancies. Their primary function is to regulate hormonal imbalances in a wide array of conditions like thyroid disorders or diabetes.

"Shush," she said, touching her lips with her index finger. "Just listen." She continued. "I have a plan for you. We have a great specialist that I want you to see. I am not authorized to make this referral alone, but I am doing it for you, because I believe he can help you, Solanges. Please, go see him as soon as possible. I am also going to refer you to see a psychologist. I believe that you are under a lot of stress and pressure at work. Having someone to talk to outside of your workplace could be beneficial."

When I arrived home and told my husband about the nurse's recommendations, Keith was livid. "If the word ever got out that you were being treated by a psychologist, it would be the end of your career. Do you realize what that would mean to the business?" He took the referral from my hand and shredded it into pieces. In all the years we had lived together, I had never seen Keith so adamant about anything. He was my guardian angel, my advisor, and, at times, even my conscience. "Go see the endocrinologist, and we will take it from there," he said to end the discussion about my health, which was of great concern for him.

I was exhibiting other troubling signs and symptoms of stress. I developed carpal tunnel syndrome in my right wrist, experienced tachycardia with some trans-ischemic attacks (TIAs), and became a frequent emergency room visitor. All these health concerns led to multiple doctor's appointments, which exacerbated my stress, as I worked late hours to make up for time spent away from the facilities. I developed migraines and was eventually diagnosed with fibromyalgia.

The endocrinologist was a middle-aged Jewish doctor who made me comfortable. Dr. Cohen wore his yamaka (or kippah), which reminded me of some of my colleagues in New York. While a nurse at Mount Sinai hospital, I had the opportunity to practice alongside many doctors of the Jewish faith. I became emotional as I described my symptoms. He was kind and reassured me that I would be fine once my problem was diagnosed and a treatment plan developed. We talked in his office for quite a long time, and then I was given a sonogram, which he performed himself.

When I returned to his office, Dr. Cohen said, "I know you are fairly young, however, after examining you, I feel strongly that you are menopausal—and very advanced in the process." When I started to cry, he explained that crying was symptomatic of the menopausal syndrome experienced by many women.

"My mother was 50 when she had her ninth child. How can I be menopausal at such a young age?" I asked him, still in tears.

"I am going to put you on a medication that will diminish, and maybe even stop your symptoms."

After he prescribed Premarin, my symptoms gradually disappeared. I was once again the person that my husband had fallen in love with many years before. With the disappearance of my manic-like behaviors, my married life stabilized. I became happier in my personal life, and the business continued to flourish. I remained on that medication for a couple of decades, until research done by the Women's Health Initiative revealed a correlation between breast cancer and the extensive use of Premarin. Without consulting my physician, I abruptly discontinued the use of this medication, and, to my pleasant surprise, none of my symptoms recurred. As a nurse, I would not recommend anyone stop taking their medications without the oversight of their healthcare provider. In this case, I was lucky. However, the discontinuation of some medications can lead to sever side effects, including death.

MAKE IT WORK FOR YOU!

Rule #20: Find Ways to Measure Success

Reflection: Around the World and Back Again

Who really knows what a turtle is thinking? They do what they do for reasons we do not really understand. But there must be some satisfaction in reaching land after months at sea, and thousands of miles of travel. Female sea turtles must have a great sense of relief when they drop their eggs into the nest and head back towards the water. It is hard to say what makes a turtle successful, but they keep doing what they have been doing since dinosaurs lived on the planet, so it must be working for them. If it works, maybe it is best not to question why.

- Ask yourself what success means to you—not to anyone else. Find what it is that will fulfill your definition of success. Is it a big home in a nice neighborhood or a condo in the city? Is it a college education or learning a trade? Is it the balance in your bank account or a happy home life? Whatever the answer, write it down, and, from time to time, check and see if you are working towards meeting your definition. And, do not worry, you can always redefine what matters most to you.

- Make a list of goals. Divide them into long-term and short-term goals. What do you want to achieve in the next day? Week? Month? Year? Do you have a five-year plan? A 10-year plan? What are you waiting for? Start small, but dream big. Write down your plans and get going on checking them off as you accomplish them.

RULES TO LIVE BY

I found myself finally at ease with the trappings of success. I had a fabulous home, often filled with friends, a marriage that was also a business partnership, which was happy and thriving, and my business was running as smoothly as could be expected. I was making waves in professional organizations. There was a whirlwind trip for me and my husband, and then, just as it all seemed to be going my way, the world around me went crazy, and one of my dearest friends found herself facing a loss I could not fathom.

Rule #21: Be Patient and Humble

It takes patience to build an empire. They say Rome was not built in a day. Neither is a career—or a successful corporation. It takes years of hard work, planning, patience, and humility to see results. It is sometimes hard to have the foresight to recognize that you are building when you are in the middle of a construction zone, but realizing that everything is a process is key to reaching your goals. Brick by brick, you will get there.

Like the turtle, I move slowly, but I always get where I am going eventually. Sometimes, even in personal matters, you just have to allow things to happen and trust it will all work out to your benefit. I wanted to marry Keith desperately, because marriage is a foundational tenet of my faith, and because I loved him, but I could not be arrogant or pushy (see chapter seven, "Wedding Bell Blues"). I knew it was not the end of the relationship simply because I did not yet have a ring on my finger. I knew that my love for him was strong and that he was the most important jewel I needed. I was patient, and I stayed with him and showed him I would be a good wife. And, when he was ready to commit, he proposed. It took a while, but it happened when I least expected it. Marrying him was the reward for learning to be patient, and it was well worth the wait.

12

———

Life & Loss

One day, out of the blue, I told Keith that I had the 20-year itch. To his surprise, Mr. Know-It-All could not fathom what his wife was thinking. With a straight face, and with no hesitation, I said, "I want a bigger house."

"What does a bigger house have to do with a 20-year itch?" he asked.

"I know how you are set in your old ways: you are comfortable where you are, and, most likely, you're going to say no to my wanting to move. So, I'm letting you know that either I get a bigger house—or you go."

Without any emotion, he replied, "Go where?"

"I don't know." I shrugged. "Since you won't move with me, I will have to move alone!"

"Here you go again, with your assumptions! How do you know that I won't move?"

At that moment, I leaped into his arms, screaming in joy. I kissed him all over the face and neck. "You will?" I was elated—all smiles, like a kid in a candy store.

Then, Keith said, "I will move, as long as I have a say in the choice of the house."

He told me where he would agree to move, and where he would absolutely not live. Keith did not drive, so it was important that all forms of public transportation be accessible to him. Once he had agreed to move to keep me happy, he became involved in selecting a realtor and set limits as to what he would and would not do.

During the search for my dream house, I reached out to Sheila, an old friend, and one of my idols in the nursing profession. She was administrator of the nursing department at George Washington University hospital when I was director of nursing.

Sheila had resigned from her position at the hospital and had become a licensed realtor during her transition years. She took me house-hunting for hours every weekend. When Sheila thought she had found a house that met our criteria, she encouraged me to look at the house after work, which I did many evenings. Keith joined us on occasions, but he was never pleased. For 18 months, he humphed at all the options—until Keith found our dream home himself.

Our community distributed a monthly paper, the *Northwest Current,* which included neighborhood news and an extensive Classifieds section. One of the issues of the newspaper advertised a house for sale on the cover that looked like it might be perfect. After reading the house's description, Keith called me at work.

"I found your house," he said. Not *our* house, but *your* house, because, after all, the only reason he was even contemplating the move was because this was what I wanted. Pleasing me had always been his number-one priority.

"You did?"

"Yes. Please call Sheila to see if we can tour the house after work."

Before I could dial Sheila's number, I received a message from the receptionist: I was to call Sheila immediately. Sheila believed that she had finally found our dream home. And she had! She and Keith had laid eyes on the same house on the cover of the same newspaper. All three of us met at the address, accompanied by our son Kevin.

The walk-through of this house was just what we had been wishing, praying, and hoping to find. It was the perfect home for us. It included an independent studio apartment on the lower level, which would provide Kevin the privacy he needed as a young adult. Kevin was excited. "Buy it now, guys. Buy it today, so that I can move in tomorrow."

Ever since Kevin had returned home from his undergraduate studies at Syracuse University in Upstate New York, he had been craving independence, pushing us to rent an apartment for him on Georgia Avenue. We adamantly refused to let him move out of the house. In the city, the life of a young black man had no value: the police stopped and jailed young black males for minor offenses and, at times, for no offenses at all. Plainclothes detectives had once questioned Kevin just because he sat in his car in the alley behind our house, waiting for a friend to arrive. Another time, at a Popeye's Louisiana Fried Chicken, Kevin and three friends were harassed by the police because they "fit the description" of a group of young black males who had just robbed a bank. Keith and I lived in constant fear for the life of our only child. When Kevin was out with his friends, Keith waited for him to return home safely before he turned in for the night, regardless of the hour.

The city was infested with drug lords, and the murder rate was the highest in the United States. The District of Columbia had been nicknamed "The Murder Capital." Young athletes including Len Bias and others were found dead of illegal drug overdoses. Daily, on television, parents like us shared the pain of mothers and fathers having to bury their sons or daughters—the precious lives of these teenagers and young adults cut short by senseless murders, police brutality, or illegal drug overdoses. There was no way we could let him live alone in the city. It was totally out of the question. We promised him we would look for a new house with an apartment that would provide him his privacy but also keep him close to us.

The house had six floors and never-ending staircases. It was beautiful. As a bonus, it also came with a swimming pool. Although this was not a prerequisite for our dream house, we agreed to purchase the house, in part, because it would keep Kevin happy and close to us.

We agreed to buy at full price, because it was worth the extra money to ensure Kevin was happy in a location we felt he could be safe in. We closed on the house the last week of December, and Kevin started to move his belongings in as soon as we took possession of the keys. For three months, he lived alone in the house. The neighbors on that peaceful street worried about the young black men and women coming and going in and out of the house.

We were the first Black family in this section of Forest Hills, and we were greeted with suspicion from the beginning. When the neighbors complained, I visited them after work to reassure them that my son was only there alone temporarily; I explained that my husband and I would be moving in once the renovations to the main house were complete. Indeed, three months after closing, we joined Kevin in our dream home.

Because of Kevin, the home was already labeled "the party house." One Sunday morning, very early, the doorbell rang. A neighbor stood at our front door, requesting that the music be turned off.

"What music?" I asked, still half-asleep. "We are not playing any music!"

The neighbor, obviously upset, shouted, "What music? From last night! You are the only people around here who play this kind of music! I didn't sleep a wink last night because of that stuff blasting in my ears."

It took me a good minute to realize that she was referring to my son's urban music. The night before, Kevin had had a pool party with his kind of go-go music playing through the speakers buried up on the hill, in the grass above the pool. "I am so sorry, I will see to it that he turns off the music after his parties," I said as I closed the door. I could not help but wonder whether the neighbors disliked all parties or just ours.

Keith and I enjoyed having friends and family over to our big, beautiful home as well. There were barbecue get-togethers in the summer, birthday celebrations, and New Year's Eve parties. We once hosted an employee pool party. In fact, we used every opportunity to throw a party. We always invited the neighbors, who never attended, but, instead, looked for reasons to complain. The neighborhood's private, exclusive, and quiet life was suddenly disrupted by this new black family. One Fourth of July weekend, Keith and I were in Canada attending a jazz festival with our friends Carl and Sheila. When we returned home, as we were getting out of a taxi, before we even had a chance to reach our front door, three neighbors approached. One of them described how drunk the partygoers had been on the Fourth of July. "One girl," another neighbor said, "vomited on my lawn." He was visibly very upset by the incident.

They disliked Kevin the most, but also showed animosity toward Keith and myself. A neighbor entered our backyard to complain about the floodlight in the back of the house, requesting that we change its direction. He also handed us the specific type of bulb he believed we should use to decrease the glare, which was interrupting his wife's sleep. I politely offered him a stepladder. He climbed up, turned the direction of the light, and proceeded to change the light bulb. I thanked him. After all, the size and the type of bulb made no difference to me, nor did the trajectory of the light, so long as we met the legal requirements to provide enough lighting in the yard for pool safety. As he climbed down the ladder, he pedantically said, "I am not sure that you are aware of the kind of neighborhood you moved into." I gave the appearance of some deer with bright eyes and a bushy tail, eyes wide open, attentively listening to him, ranting and raving about how great Forest Hills was. "The white house at the corner was where Dwight Eisenhower once lived."

Before he could name another celebrity or a well-known figure who had once graced the neighborhood, I interrupted him. "You know, one day someone like you will say to a new neighbor: 'You see this red brick house on the hill? The Archers lived there.'" And, without another word, I guided him to the gate and closed it behind him.

But I knew it was not the end of it.

This family went even further with their complaints, writing us a letter requesting that our weekday parties end at 10 o'clock in the evening and our weekend parties by midnight—which they already did, as we were well aware of this pretty standard noise ordinance. In the event we failed to follow those rules, they warned, the police would be called. The letter was received but was never acknowledged, and the parties continued. This neighbor never called the police; his family eventually retired to Upstate New York. The rest of the neighbors embraced our family once they realized that we were there to stay, and the harassment ended.

It probably helped that Kevin eventually grew out of giving parties, became a professional model, and moved to New York City to pursue a career in modeling. A man of Caribbean upbringing, Keith never liked the idea of his son being a model; he used every opportunity to convince him to pursue studies in physical therapy instead. His hope was that modeling was just a phase—a passing interest born from the vanity of everyone telling Kevin he was a handsome young man, who looked just like a model. My husband discussed the topic with our son at every opportunity, without crossing the line into nagging, until he finally managed to convince Kevin to return home after a couple of years in New York and pursue a master's degree.

I arrived home from work one evening to find a note from Keith, asking me to free my calendar: an advertisement for a trip to London and Paris was also laid out on my desk. I read the details of the ad at least twice, searching high and low for clues as to why he wanted to take me on this trip. It was the first time he had ever taken the initiative to even suggest a trip. We had traveled before but always at my suggestion. As I waited for Keith to come home, I thought about a time, early in our relationship, when we were just starting to date. To celebrate Keith's birthday, I had invited a very good friend of his and his wife to a restaurant. I arranged for the waiters to bring a cake, and sing "Happy Birthday" to him. I was embarrassed when he said with a little bit of sarcasm, "You are confused, my dear. Today is not my birthday." With my limited comprehension of the English language and his British accent, I had understood his birthday to be on August 20. It was on August 28.

Being a very private person, he was uneasy with that level of attention focused on him. He made me promise that I would never put him through that kind of embarrassment again, even with the right birthdate, and I had kept that promise. I had never given him a birthday party, not at a restaurant—not even at our home. He, on the other hand, had arranged surprise parties for me on numerous occasions, including a classy black-tie affair at our home. He would arranged for my girlfriends Sarah and Irma to take me shopping at an outlet mall that was more than an hour away from the house. He had asked me in the morning to prepare some hors d'oeuvres for a business meeting he would be having at the house while I was on my shopping trip, and, like the good wife that I was, I had beautifully plated and refrigerated all the hors d'oeuvres.

My friends picked me up that day. We were out shopping for more than five hours. On the way back, within a mile of my house, Irma—who was driving Sarah's car—suddenly stopped at a gas station to make a call. (This was before everyone carried a cell phone.) I started to argue with her, as we were all very tired and anxious to get home at the end of a long day.

"Why are you stopping here?" I asked angrily. "We're almost at my house."

"I have to call Michael," she said, referring to her husband. "I need to let him know we are close, so that he can be ready to leave when I get there. I am tired, and I don't want to have to wait for him at your house to fetch me." She, then, jumped out of the car, and went straight to the phone booth.

Sarah was quiet the whole time, and I decided to follow suit, still burning inside.

When we arrived at the house, I led the way, keys in hand. As the door opened, the lights came on, and voices screamed in unison. "Happy Birthday!" I could not believe Keith had done all of that for me. All the furniture in both the living room and the adjoining dining room had been removed, and, in the midst of the brouhaha, I noticed the hors d'oeuvres that I had prepared in the morning sitting out for our guests. The rest of the food was catered, and he had hired a bartender. The women were dressed in beautiful, long gowns, and the men in tuxedos. When I finally recuperated from the shock, I rushed to my bedroom to change. I reappeared moments later in a stunning ivory spaghetti strap, sequin and rhinestone-covered gown, which featured a plunging heart-shaped open back. The beautiful gown had been waiting for me in the dressing room: true to character, he had even gone so far as to select what he wanted me to wear at the party. I could only smile at Keith's thoughtfulness. Sarah and Irma's husbands had also brought their gowns to my house, and they changed quickly as well.

I returned my attention to the travel pamphlets. How clever, I thought. Keith's 65th birthday will fall in the middle of this European trip. For the first time, I had discussed plans to celebrate the occasion. Had he planned this trip at the end of August to avoid a birthday party? To be far away from his friends on his birthday? In any case … a trip to Europe! What a great way to celebrate a milestone. I would take that over a party any day.

We flew to Manhattan where a black limousine took us to the pier so that we could board the Queen Elizabeth (the QE2) from the Cunard, one of the most luxurious cruise ship lines at that time. We crossed the Atlantic Ocean in six days. Every evening, we attended a black-tie dinner and danced our nights away to the tunes of an Antiguan band. We joked and flirted with each other as though we were two young lovers on our honeymoon. We bought every picture taken of us by the cruise photographer.

In England, we visited Owen—and his wife Helen—a childhood friend of Keith's from Barbados. To celebrate Keith's birthday, they prepared a real Barbadian-style, home-cooked dinner, which consisted of cou-cou (corn meal and okra), flying fish, and black cake, and, yes, we sang "Happy Birthday." Keith was all smiles. He celebrated his 65th birthday just like our wedding: the way he wanted it—in private, not with a large group of people. We were both happy.

An avid tennis player, and a lover of the game, Keith planned for us to spend a day at Wimbledon. We took pictures and spoke with some professional players and coaches. The following day, we boarded our first-class cabin on the Eurostar train to Paris, France, where we were to visit my cousin Josiane.

*   *   *

Early in the year 2000, I had received a letter from a woman in France, who claimed to have found me on the internet while researching her family genealogy. Her name was Josiane Vivens, and she believed we were related. Enclosed in her letter was her picture, and that of her husband Jacques. Looking at the picture, it was clear to me that this woman was as white as I was black, so I was a bit surprised she thought we were relatives. In the envelope, she also provided me with the family tree she had created based on her research, and her letter opened the door to a real adventure in family and friendship.

As the years went by, Josiane and I continued to communicate via the internet, phone, and letters, and exchanged numerous pictures, until Josiane traveled to America to visit her newly discovered family.

Unbeknownst to Josiane, I had contacted several other family members, inviting them to our home in Washington, D.C., for a welcoming party. Josiane and her husband Jacque arrived with gifts for all the people they were hoping to meet. My present was a bottle of French wine labeled with the name Vivens from a Vivens winery in Bordeaux, France, and this history of the family's connection with wine became another interesting bit of knowledge. According to Josiane's genealogical research, we were descendants of three French brothers. One of the brothers, an engineer, was sent to Haiti during the French possession of Haiti to build roads and bridges. While in Haiti, he married a black woman, and they started the family into which I was born. Josiane was the descendant of one of the other two brothers who had remained in France and was somehow connected to the winery that still bore our name.

Love and goodwill were shared between everyone who attended the party. Keith and I kept in contact with her, and our transatlantic voyage included a visit to their lovely home on the outskirts of Paris. We stayed with them for a few days. We dined on home-cooked French cuisine, and Jacque took Keith under his wing to teach him how to play golf.

*   *   *

I was very active, locally, as a member and officer of the District of Columbia Health Care Association (DCHCA), and, nationally, as a member of the American Healthcare Association (AHCA).

From its inception, 100 percent of AHCA officers were white men with enough money to travel for meetings to different states. At every open election, women ran for office, but the good old boys always found a way to win the seats. The road to leadership was long and tedious: one had to serve at a state level, then at the regional level, before becoming eligible to run for national office. My best friend Ana, who was also a nursing home administrator, and I often traveled together to attend the annual national convention. We were always amazed at the lack of women's representation at the board level. In order to increase our influence, we joined the Coalition of Women in Long-Term Care (COWL), the subset of a national association created by women members to prepare other women to hold leadership positions. We became very active in the association, reaching executive board-level positions.

In September, after our lovely, romantic trip in Europe, I traveled to Memphis, Tennessee, to attend a COWL conference. I was alone this time, as Ana was unable to join me. Early one morning, as I was getting ready in my hotel room for a session at the conference, some unexpected and tragic news was announced on the television: an airplane had hit one of the towers at the World Trade Center in New York City. I froze for a moment, staring at the screen in disbelief, and, just a moment later, I witnessed another airplane hit the second. The voice of the news anchor had an emotional edge as he announced that the United States had been attacked. I immediately called Keith who asked me to get on the next airplane home.

When I reported to the meeting room, everyone was discussing the events of what would become known as 9/11. Some of the attendees were glued in front of the television while others were on their phones, calling their loved ones at home. Given the circumstances, the conference was canceled, as the members' priority shifted to finding ways to get home as safely and quickly as possible.

Before long, it was reported that another airplane, on its way to California, had hit the Pentagon in Washington, D.C. I immediately called Keith back, trembling at the idea of an attack so close to home while I was so far away from my husband, my son, and the two nursing homes under my direction. I felt guilty for not being there to take charge of the situation and helpless to do anything to assist. By that point, all airplanes were grounded, and the only way to get home was to rent a car.

It was only the beginning of what would turn into a horrific tragedy that affected us on a deeply personal level. "I'm sorry, Solanges," Keith said. "Ana's husband, Ian, was on the airplane that hit the Pentagon. He was on his way to his California office. He died on impact."

It was September 11, and Ana's birthday was September 13—just a couple of days after his tragic death.

When I called my best friend, she was sobbing on the phone. "Ian is gone. We lost your second husband!"

It was a terrible loss. Ian and I had been so fond of each other, he used to call me his "second wife." He used to say, "After Ana, the only call that I'll always answer is a call from Solanges." It was urgent that I get home to my family, my best friend, and my business. A colleague at the meeting who lived in

Maryland reluctantly agreed to drive back with me, and then continue alone to his house. It took us 14 hours, each of us taking turns, driving two hours at a time. When I reached D.C., Keith was relieved. I visited Ana right away. We lived within walking distance of each other.

Keith and I were both there for Ana. We visited her every day, and her house was always filled with family and friends who wanted to extend their condolences and help in any way possible. But all she wanted was her Ian, and none of us could satisfy that desire. Keith and I selected a day before the funeral to cook a Caribbean meal for all of Ana's guests. We had a big spread of food on her dining room table, enough to feed everyone who came to pay their respects and offer their condolences.

Ana and I were both Catholic, and we both worshiped at the Blessed Sacrament church. I had become a member of the church after I moved to the city, and my son's first communion ceremony was performed at that church. I often volunteered weekly, preparing sandwiches for the poor in the church's kitchen. Yet, I never felt accepted by the congregation. One Sunday morning, I sat in a pew, waiting for Mass. Before I could kneel to say my prayers, a very old white lady seated in the pew directly behind me kneeled to make sure that her lips were close to my ear. She whispered. "Can't you tell where you don't belong?"

I turned my head, made eye contact with her, and sighed to make sure that she knew that I had clearly heard her question. Then, I kneeled, said my prayers, and walked out of the church before mass began. I never returned to Blessed Sacrament after that day—not until Ian's funeral. I was honored to read a prayer as a tribute to my good friend. By that time, unfortunately, Father Duffy, the priest in charge, still had made no effort at desegregating the church. Unsuspecting minorities often joined, Ana commented later, only to eventually abandon the church—for reasons, I assumed, were similar to those that had pushed me away.

I remained a support for my friend Ana throughout her bereavement period— and throughout the lifetime of our friendship. I could only imagine her pain at the loss of Ian; I could not help but wonder, if it were me, how would I ever get over Keith's death?

MAKE IT WORK FOR YOU!

Rule #21: Be Patient and Humble

Reflection: "The race is not always to the swift." —Aesop

That land cousin of the turtle, the tortoise, knows a thing or two about being patient and humble. In Aesop's well-known fable, the poor tortoise was bullied by the hare for his slow, plodding movements. "You'll never get anywhere, moving as slowly as you do," the hare mocked him.

"Oh, yeah, I will. I get where I need to, and I could beat you in a race," the tortoise responded.

The hare thought that was a laugh and accepted the challenge. The day of the race came, and the hare was fast off his mark and halfway down the track when he looked back and saw the tortoise moving slowly and steadily—but mostly slowly. Seeing how far ahead he was, the hare took an opportunity to lay down on the side of the track and take a nap. But he underestimated the tortoise, and slept too long. When the hare woke from his nap, he saw that the tortoise was almost to the finish line, so he dashed as quickly as he could to beat the tortoise in the race.

But as fast as he was, the hare just could not overtake the slow, steady tortoise that crossed the line, triumphant.

- Find an empty jar. Each day for a year, write down one positive thing you have done to enrich your life, even if it is small, and drop it in the jar. At the end of the year, look over all you've accomplished. It's quite a lot, is it not? Sometimes, we need to wait to see the results of small efforts.

- Identify some triggers that test your patience and ask yourself what the fuss is about. Why are you so anxious? Find a way to practice patience when you know it poses a challenge. Some people get triggered by long waits in heavy traffic or lines at the store. If that is the case with you, the next time you feel impatient waiting to move forward, practice some deep breathing and look at the people around you. They are all waiting too. If you are in line, strike up a conversation. It will make time pass more quickly. If dealing with a certain person triggers you, try to look at things from their point of view. They likely are not trying to test you. They have just got their own invisible pain.

RULES TO LIVE BY

This chapter was the hardest chapter in the book to relive for me. My family suffered a terrible loss that forced us all to put work to the side while we coped with it. I found my business in jeopardy; my reputation was threatened; everything I had worked so hard to build seemed like it was about to crumble. But it made me rethink what matters in life, and, if it all seemed like I was losing, it just pushed me back into fighting mode to turn it back around.

Rule #22: Prioritize

I had to learn to juggle a mountain of obligations in order to become an entrepreneur in my industry. Climbing to the top of my field required me to fill a lot of different roles: wife, mother, chairwoman, owner, CEO, etc. ... And, in each of those roles, I had to learn to prioritize tasks in order to manage my load. Otherwise, I would have become overwhelmed. When we revamped the Johnson nursing home, we started with what I considered the low-hanging fruit: the items that were of importance but that we knew would also have the most immediate impact on the quality of life of our residents and the morale of our staff and vendors (see chapter 11, "How Did We Do It?").

Knowing what your priorities are will make it easier to make decisions when you reach crisis points along your journey to success. There were times when I was furthering my education in pursuit of a career that I had to put quality time with my loved ones aside, because I knew that an education would lead to a better job and a better quality of life for my family. I was passionate about my career once I got into my field and found I was making a difference in people's lives and in my industry. But, when my husband fell ill, I knew that focusing on his wellbeing and comfort had to be my priority, even if it meant putting my career on hold for a short time (see chapter 13, "Every Beginning Has Its End").

13

Every Beginning Has Its End

Even though we had had a grand adventure to celebrate Keith's 65th birthday, had taken the QE2 to Europe, and danced our nights away, something troubling was happening to him that threatened our wedded bliss. For six months, Keith had been gradually losing weight. By December of 2001, it had become a point of concern, and, despite frequent visits to his primary care physician at Kaiser Permanente, he continued to thin down. For the first time in our years together as friends, lovers, and spouses, Keith was sick, and, because he had always been healthy and fit—the man exercised religiously and played tennis indoors in the winter for the love of the game and for the sake of fitness—this illness rattled me. No one could figure out why he was wasting away—by almost 50 pounds at this point—and becoming weaker and weaker by the day. We were a family in crisis.

The week before Christmas, I finally convinced him to see a specialist, an acquaintance of mine who worked in gastroenterology, to rule out cancer, since his primary care doctor was unable to arrive at a diagnosis, let alone develop a plan of care and treatment. I contacted Dr. Hall out of the desperation of my love for my husband; I was convinced he would be able to help Keith. It was difficult for me to request the appointment, because Dr. Hall had made unwanted sexual advances towards me on numerous occasions. However, I knew he was the best gastroenterologist available; it was worth my discomfort to try to find a solution to Keith's health issues. During my tenure as director of nursing at the nursing home, when Dr. Hall visited his patients, he could not keep his hands to himself. I had never mentioned anything to Keith. Like many women in this situation—long before the Me Too movement—I kept silent. Who would believe me? I certainly was not going to talk about it in the middle of a serious health crisis. Without hesitation, he accepted the case and admitted my husband, for which I was very grateful. After several tests and procedures, cancer was ruled out—but we still had no diagnosis. The weight loss continued.

Again, without waiting for my husband's approval, I took matters into my own hands. I became compulsive. It was my turn to be his voice, his guardian angel, and, for the first time, his advocate. I reached out to the Mayo Clinic, prepared to fly my husband anywhere for diagnosis and treatment. Finally, I was referred to a specialist at John Hopkins University Hospital. On the phone, I explained Keith's symptoms and begged the physician, Dr. Parker, to examine him. The more he tried to push me away (his schedule did not allow for one more patient), the more I pushed back. "You don't understand, doctor," I firmly said. "You must see him today. We need your help." I was desperate, crying on the phone but still careful not to let Keith hear the worry in my voice.

He gave in to my insistence. "How about tomorrow?"

"Great," I answered in gratitude. "What time, doctor?"

The next morning, I drove my husband to Baltimore, Maryland, over an hour from our home, and he was immediately admitted to the hospital. After 10 long days, he still did not receive a definite diagnosis even from John Hopkins. "Maybe hyper-vitaminosis," the doctor said after he learned Keith faithfully took various herbal supplements; *maybe* he had too many vitamins in his system. His vitamins and electrolytes were normalized before he was discharged to me, his wife, now his nurse, for tender loving care and observation at home. Our friend, Sheila, left her husband Carl in Montreal, Canada, and came to stay with us with the intention of cooking some delicious Caribbean meals to help fatten Keith up. Having Sheila in the house with Keith while I was at work was a great help, and a source of support to both of us. He had been emaciated, but started to look healthier after following Sheila's three-meals-a-day regimen. He gained back a lot of the weight and made plans to return to work but still retire in June, as planned.

On a Sunday morning, the first week of May 2002, Keith woke up with a dry cough. At breakfast, he commented that it was too bad: he had just recuperated from an unknown illness. "This, too, shall pass," I reassured him, but I soon became concerned when the cough worsened, and Keith refused to return to Kaiser. In anger, he asked me to sue both Kaiser and John Hopkins for failure to diagnose and treat him. I could tell he was scared. During his illness, two of his friends, who had been diagnosed with cancer, had died, and Keith feared he would be the third. Although he tried to remain strong for my benefit, I could tell he was losing faith in the possibility of a recovery. I was careful to keep him from seeing how scared I was, which was not easy. I was terrified.

The cough worsened, and, as Keith became weaker by the day, it was clear that he was not getting better. In fact, he had gotten so weak within just a matter of days, that he now required my assistance to shower and dress. At first, he refused to see any more doctors since no one had been able to find out what was wrong with him, but, when the continuous coughing hindered his ability to eat and drink, he reluctantly agreed to let me call his physician at John Hopkins.

"But, first, get a yellow pad and a pen," he said in a labored voice. Here was this man, so weak he could barely talk, asking me to get pen and paper—just as he had done when he was instructing me how to spell our son's name. "I do not want you to call my family, or anyone else. I do not want anyone to see me like this. What I do want, is for you to file suit against Kaiser—for failure to diagnose and treat me." It was as if he had come to accept that he would not survive this unknown demon that was taking over his body but sparing his mind. He was as cognitively sharp as before the illness.

I was trying to be strong for him, but it felt as if I was constantly on the verge of tears. He had always been there for me, and, even at this very low point of his life, he was preparing me for what was to come, slowly moving me towards acceptance of what he felt could be the end.

"Keith, we are losing time. Please, let me call the doctor." Before he could respond, I leaned over, gave him a kiss, and said, "I love you. I need to get us help, because I cannot do this on my own. I cannot let you die, honey. If I don't get help, you will die, right here, in the house." I ran up the steps to my office to make the call, not wanting to aggravate him with my assessment to the doctor. I was sobbing as I attempted to talk, and the doctor repeatedly said, "Take a deep breath, Mrs. Archer," trying to calm me down so that he could understand me.

"Do not bring him to me," he said. "I am too far away. And do not put him in your car," he advised. "Call 911, and have paramedics take him to a hospital immediately."

I helped Keith get dressed as quickly as we could manage. After the paramedics transferred him from the bed to the stretcher and placed him in the ambulance, they worked on him for more than a half hour. I sat with Kevin in his car, ready to follow them to the hospital, but the vehicle was not budging from the end of our driveway. I knocked on the back door of the ambulance. "Why is it taking so long?" The paramedics informed me that Keith needed to be stabilized before they could move him. As a nurse, I understood this reply to my concern. My husband's condition was perilous. He was much sicker than I had realized.

Keith was immediately admitted to the Intensive Care Unit of the hospital nearest to our home. Several different specialists examined him; he was given every blood test possible and too many MRIs to count. But still, no diagnosis. What was eating away my dearest husband? After a week at the hospital, all the tests were negative. It was puzzling and extremely frustrating, especially because I worked in the medical field.

After calling a family meeting, a pulmonologist requested permission to biopsy Keith's lung under anesthesia. My husband agreed. By then, he was too tired: all he wanted was an answer, a treatment, and, hopefully, a cure. The following morning, an anesthesiologist explained the danger of administering anesthesia in Keith's weakened condition, but we were all eager to identify the mystery illness that had taken possession of his body. It was worth the risk to find out what was making him so sick.

When the stretcher arrived, Keith kissed both Kevin and me. "I love you both." In that moment, the three of us were one—Keith on the bed, his wife, and son, each on one side of his frail body—feeling each other's breath and the movement of our chests as we hugged for what must have seemed an eternity to the attendant waiting to whisk him away to the operating room—and yet, to me, it felt like fraction of a moment. At that point, every second with Keith seemed to pass too quickly.

The two men were able to hide their tears, but I was inconsolable. I asked Keith for permission to call his family about his condition. "No," he said. "They were aware that I had gotten better, and that's all they need to know." Once he had recuperated from his prior bout of illness, he called his two sisters, Marita in Manitoba, Canada, whom he had not seen in many years, and Nola in Barbados, to let them know he was doing better.

We had visited Nola the year before when we had traveled to assess the construction of our retirement home on the island. Keith and I had walked the beach, holding hands, and we talked about death and dying. "You know," Keith had said, "when we get really, really old, we should not walk the beach but, instead, walk into the ocean, holding hands just like this, and then keep walking. Never look back. Being old and sick in a hospital is just not for me." I had been reassured at the time by the thought of being with Keith until my last days. Now, I was filled with uncertainty and afraid at the thought of living out my life without him.

When he was whisked away from us, Kevin and I left the room to meditate silently in the hospital's chapel. I prayed to Mother Mary until we left the hospital. At home, we awaited a call from the doctor. The call came, but the doctor advised us against returning to Keith's room, as he was connected to a respirator and unconscious.

Unable to rest, I was on the phone, crying, sharing my pain with others. Unlike my husband who kept a distant relationship with his relatives, I was—and am still—very close with my sisters and brothers, and, for that matter, with my nieces and nephews, and all my extended family. I needed their comfort in my loneliness and uncertainty if I was going to survive this terrible time.

Night came, and then it was morning, and I was still awake, dressed and ready, waiting for Kevin to take me to the hospital. He had forbidden me to drive; every day, he took me to the hospital, spent some time with his father, and then headed to the office. Later in the afternoon, Kevin would come back to take me home. My professional life, I knew, was in shambles—I had barely been in the office in the past six months. Nothing was as important to me as attending to my husband's illness. I could not think about anything but Keith's welfare. Even though he could not acknowledge us, Kevin and I believed that he knew we were there with him.

On the fourth day after the pulmonary biopsy, the house phone rang very early in the morning. It was Dr. Sharma, his pulmonologist at the hospital, "Solanges, you know that I have been very optimistic—" and, before he could finish, I started to scream. "No, no, no!"

Kevin jumped up the steps to be at my side. I was still on the phone, and the physician continued, "Keith had a terrible night. You and your son should come to the hospital as soon as you can. We worked on him all night, and I am now pessimistic about his recovery."

While Kevin got ready, I called my brother Jean Claude, whose wife, Mona, was a nurse, and asked them to join us at the hospital. Kevin drove us, and, for one last time, we were together as a family. As soon as I saw Keith, I knew we had reached the end of our journey together. He was covered with medical equipment and tubes. In addition to the respirator, he was being medicated with several IVs; other tubes just kept his veins open. I noticed two new catheters, which he did not have at our last visit. He was such a dignified man; I knew that he would not want anyone to see him in this condition, but I also could not leave him alone. I needed to be with him. My guardian angel was ready to leave this earth. "Why, but why?" I kept asking him, but I received no answer.

The doctor told us that Keith had "coded" twice during the night; his kidneys were shutting down, along with his other vital organs. He said that Keith was still alive only because of the respirator.

He advised us to allow him to die naturally and with dignity, so I made a call to Father East, asking him to rush to my husband's bedside to administer his last rites—a very important sacrament for devoted Catholics. I am Catholic—I believe in Jesus Christ and have a faithful relationship with my Blessed Mother Mary. I was, at the time, a member of the lecture's ministry at Nativity, Father East's church, and he knew me well. Within the hour, he arrived in the room with a prayer card of Jesus' radiating sacred heart. He placed it next to Keith's head as he prayed over him, anointed him with oil, and sanctified him in preparation for his journey to heaven without us.

My brother Jean Claude and his wife Mona prayed with the priest, Kevin, and me, and, after Father East left, we all talked to Keith, some silently, and others out loud, all with tears flowing. Crying inconsolably, I reassured him that I was going to be fine; I knew full well that he would continue to look after me, even though we would be physically apart until we met again in the afterlife. "You promised me that we were going to grow old together. Remember? What ever happened to that promise?" I asked him, as though he could hear me. "I know you did not want anyone to visit you in the hospital, and, as a good wife, I listened to you up to the end." With a trembling giggle, I said, "But I am going to give you the biggest going away party. You can't stop me now! I can imagine that little smirk on your face, though. I love you, Keith."

I had been in healthcare for many years, often advising families on death and dying. I had opened the first in-patient hospice in the city. I had acquired a professional understanding of the different levels of grief, and knew how to provide comfort to my staff and my patient's families in the face of great loss, yet, I was unprepared for this moment—for my own turn to grieve. There was no comfort to be found. My husband was only sixty-five years old. Why him? I found myself lost, not knowing what I would do without Keith in my life. I was losing my greatest advisor and champion. I looked at Kevin, who still carried a look of utter disbelief. "Son, are you ready? We need to let Daddy go. It is the best thing at this point. We both know what he always said: he never wanted to be kept alive by a machine."

Kevin silently walked out of the room to the hospital hallway. It must have been overwhelming to him. Both of his parents were in crisis, and he was powerless to change anything. I called the nurse into the room, and, after the nurse disconnected the respirator, Jean Claude, Mona, and I stayed with Keith until he took his last natural breath.

I left my brother and his wife at the hospital, and Jean Claude offered to call the rest of the family with the news of Keith's passing. The drive home with Kevin was silent.

The house was quiet, too, until one o'clock in the afternoon, just a couple of hours after we returned home, when a call came from the pulmonologist. "Solanges, my condolences," he said. "I tried to return to the unit before you left. Unfortunately, I missed you. Can you talk?" I sat down as he continued. "As you know, our pathology department ran various tests on your husband's lung tissues and the results were all inconclusive. We sent some of Keith's specimens to the Mayo Clinic, in the hopes of getting a diagnosis, and a possible treatment for your husband. We just got the result. There was nothing we could have done. Unfortunately, he died of a rare disease, with no etiology, and no treatment. This illness is seen mostly in Caribbean males, and we have no idea how it was contracted. It is called polymyositis. It causes swelling and weakens the lung's tissues, thus the dry cough and difficulty breathing. I am so sorry for your loss."

"At least, I know what took him away from me. Thank you, doctor." As I hung up the receiver, I thought about the grip of Death and about second chances.

Soon after we had bought our new home, I had stumbled upon an article in the *Washington Post,* about a family who was in a disagreement with Kaiser Permanente over treatment for their daughter, a teenage girl, who had lived most of her life in D.C. On her way to her out-of-state boarding school, she had been in a car accident. She survived but required extensive rehabilitation therapy, which led to a dispute over coverage.

I was shaken by an intriguing realization: this young girl had lived in the house that we had just purchased, and the coincidence was not lost on me when, a few months later, Kevin, too, was in a serious car accident. After hitting a guardrail, his Land Rover turned over several times. The truck was totaled. However, Kevin, along with his three friends, walked away without a scratch. It was as if Mother Mary had held the four young men safely away from the Land Rover as it somersaulted, only to put them back in again once the accident was over. Because, as far-fetched as it may sound, only a miracle saved those boys. Having seen the damaged truck, even the tow truck driver could not believe that the boys had been in the vehicle. "No way! No way those guys were in that truck!" he shouted to my husband and me when we arrived on scene.

Was there a mysterious presence about the house—one that miraculously protected young lives but was unwilling to save Keith? Was his death, in a way, a debt paid for saving the lives of the youths? Was there any correlation between his death and the survival of those two accident victims? In my sorrow, I found a brief moment of peace: maybe my husband had made the ultimate sacrifice—dying in place of others. I recalled that Father East had come and blessed the house before we moved in. Father walked from room to room with holy water and said a prayer as he walked in each room. Had faith played a role in Keith's mysterious death? I was trying to make sense of all those thoughts, but to no avail. There was no logic to explain the *why* that tormented me.

Finally, I came back to my senses. I could not just sit there, daydreaming and reminiscing, or trying to make sense of the unexplainable: I had a funeral to plan. In my denial during the past few months, I had made no burial arrangements, even though I had a very sick husband. I often recommended preplanning to our residents' families, and, yet, I had not taken the advice for myself. He was so young, though—and he had been so healthy, dancing the night away on a cruise just a few months before, and now he was gone. My husband had promised me we would grow old together. As a couple, we believed in the vows made to each other—that we would always be loyal and faithful until death do us part. Never in a million years could I have fathomed that my Keith would have died so young. Making funeral arrangements was not part of our plan, but God had written down the day he would be gone from this earth, and no amount of love could have changed his destiny.

I called the director of social services at one of my nursing homes for assistance, and, the next day, the funeral parlor claimed Keith's body from the hospital. My best friend Ana hurried to my side the moment she learned of Keith's passing. We sat next to each other—taking in the fact that we had both become widows at such a young age and within just a few months of each other. I had spent my 55th birthday at the hospital, at my husband's bedside. He had died four days after my birthday—just like Ana's husband had died a couple of days before her birthday—and was to be buried just a few days later.

Ana stayed close to me, just as I had done for her during her bereavement period. With her help, and that of my family, I contacted Keith's relatives and all of our friends, many of whom did not know he had been sick. These calls were difficult to make, but I made them nonetheless. Many expressed their regrets at not being able to attend the funeral. To the family members who simply could not afford the travel expenses, I promised financial assistance. Carl and Sheila,

Keith's closest friends, soon arrived from Canada. They wrote the obituary for the newspaper. They selected the prayers and songs for the service, the pallbearers, and the clothes that Keith would wear the last time we saw him. "What about his favorite tie?" Carl asked.

"He loved to wear his navy-blue suit, his white shirt, and red tie," I giggled. "I can just see him coming from work just about now, looking so dapper, happy to see the two of you here." There were moments of joy, remembering his favorite jokes—and his little smirk.

Kevin's friends all came to the house, young men and young women remembering "Uncle," as they so affectionately called him. He had been a surrogate father to those who did not have a father in their lives, and a fun uncle to those with a healthy father-child relationship. They all missed him, as he had spent time with a lot of them. Kevin secluded himself to his bedroom, his head in his hands, looking down at the floor. Even his girlfriend, who spent time with him at the house, could not soothe his sadness.

I had promised to give my Keith the biggest going away party I could pull off— and I did. Over 700 people attended the funeral of this kind and unassuming man. In addition to family, personal friends, and tennis partners, I counted several government officials, and numerous employees and colleagues—many of the attendees unexpected. At the repast, the Hilton Hotel had to open an adjoining room for the sit-down meal.

During Carl's eulogy for his best friend, Keith, I reached over to Kevin and whispered, "I am going up after Carl."

He whispered back, "Please, don't. You can't do it, Mom. You know you can't. Please, don't!" But I jumped up as soon as Carl stepped off the pulpit, before Kevin could reach out and stop me. Everyone in the church froze as I headed towards the microphone; they did not expect me to have the strength to speak.

I talked about how much my husband meant to me, about all he had done, with me and for me. "This man helped me to get my first checkbook, and he taught me how to write a check. He cleaned my nursing uniforms, and he polished my shoes. He selected the dress he wanted me to wear whenever we attended a party. He cooked for me. He was just a great man. I'm lucky to have met him and to have lived with him for 30 years."

When I was finished, I turned my back to the congregation and faced the altar for a public conversation with God. "God," I said, "you took Keith from me because you needed him. I beg you: Do not forget me. I am still on this earth. Remember me, Lord. I need you to be with me. I never once want to feel alone because Keith is gone. I know you will be by my side." I started sobbing as the congregation wept. Sharing my private thoughts about my husband had been very emotional—uttering my request to God out loud, even more so.

My husband's spirit was with God. I had his body cremated, and his ashes were split into two beautiful black and grey mosaic urns. I kept one in my bedroom. I carried the other urn to Barbados, where I gave him an even greater going-away party. We buried the urn next to his mother in his family gravesite.

As a teenager, and in his young adult years, Keith had been the Magic Johnson of Barbados. His basketball team—coincidentally named the Lakers—traveled to different Caribbean islands for fierce competitions. Under his leadership as the team's captain, the Lakers brought home many trophies. Keith was a celebrity player, and his mom had saved all the newspaper clippings about her son. Because of his mother's pride, Kevin and I were able to read about his youth several years later when we all visited her as a family. While Keith was still alive, a Barbados newspaper published an article about him and his brother Raoul. "Fifty years ago," the paper read, "the Archer brothers scored over 100 points together, in one game."

Within a few months of my husband's passing, I returned to Barbados to receive a posthumous trophy on his behalf. I was interviewed on live television about Keith's life in the United States. It was very difficult to talk about him in past tense. In many ways, it still felt like he was in my present. "I've always been grateful to have had such a wonderful, confident, and giving man in my life," I said.

I still miss him a lot. Even writing about him makes me melancholy all these years later. I was encouraged to get back to work immediately after his death, but I could not get out of bed to execute the simple task of getting ready for the day. I often sat in his walk-in closet, crying as I held onto his clothes and breathed in his smell. The lyrics of the song "How Do I Live?" by Leann Rimes—a song that caused me to choke up, long before my husband's illness and passing—took on a new meaning. I sang and I cried, looking for an answer. How would I survive without my Keith? What kind of life would I have without him?

I also wondered about our retirement home, still under construction in Barbados. We had planned to live there together. I was not Barbadian; I did not want to retire there alone. I loved him so much that I would have happily ended my life to be with him and continue through eternity together. I was in darkness. "Oh, God, where are the sunny days that warmed the 30 years of our relationship?" Would the angel of the sun once again brighten my days? What about Kevin? How would he survive losing his dad?

Per Caribbean custom, a widow is expected to wear only black, for at least a year following the death of her spouse—a visible sign of mourning. But I was no longer just Haitian; I was a Haitian, African-American woman who had been living abroad for many years. I refused to follow the tradition, even though my mother advised me to respect it. Since wearing black was not one of my religious doctrines, I had no obligation to comply; the custom was not a pain reliever. Black dress or not, I still hurt. I was angry to have my life interrupted at the age of 55. Why did Keith have to go and leave me all alone? I wanted to know. For a long time after his death, I could not talk about him without crying. I dreaded the daily delivery of the mail, as I was flooded with sympathy cards, each card accentuating the pain in my heart as I read it. As painful as it was reading these cards, however, and as morbid as it may sound, I held on to them for many years. They remained a tangible artifact of a life that was no more.

I was still struggling with tumultuous emotions when the time came for me to face the reality of returning to work. I finally felt strong enough to face the world—or so I thought! Each time a well-meaning friend or acquaintance wished me condolences on my husband's passing, the pain resurfaced, and, again, the tears trickled down my cheeks. I choked up as I recounted his last days. Tasks that were routine—getting up in the morning, getting dressed, getting in my car, heading to the office—were nearly impossible. Because Keith did not drive, I was accustomed to dropping him off at the corporate office and picking him up later. I had to remind myself to go directly to the nursing homes and to come right home without the daily extra stops along the way. My car rides became unbearable. We had attended many meetings together; I now had to sit through them alone. I felt his absence more and more, and I missed his company immensely. My now 25-year-old son tried to fill the void as best he could, but, as kind and attentive as he was, he just was not my Keith.

I had been away from the business for approximately six months. Even when I had been in the office, I had been mentally and emotionally absent—focused on managing my husband's illness, eventual death, and the planning of an unexpected funeral. Upon my return, and to my surprise, I discovered that the school had grown rapidly, from an average of 100 students to several hundred students. In the absence of both Keith and me, the staff had wanted to show us how well they could manage our family-owned business. They worked very hard at recruiting students to grow the school and leased space in an office building some distance from the main campus. Unfortunately, it turned out that this brand new building had the most expensive rent in the city. While the cost of the leased space was manageable, the sudden growth was alarming, and we struggled to keep up with the new demands that came with all the extra students.

In addition to Kevin and me, our corporate office included a chief financial officer, an executive director, a newly hired director of marketing, and a handful of other staff. This team was responsible for the management of the employees at the school and at the home-care agency. Staffing for those two divisions was in the hundreds. The school's large staff was enough to manage an average of 100 students, but it was insufficient for several hundred, which was the core of what became a major problem.

The chaos that ensued helped me cope with Keith's death. I became so busy, trying to bring order to the company, that I only felt his absence in the late evenings, when I arrived home exhausted. Once my body hit the bed, I covered my head and cried myself to sleep—and it became a ritual every night. During the day, I worked long hours, providing close supervision, not only at the two nursing homes but also at the home care agency and the school. My husband, the corporation's president, had been the one overseeing the business aspects of the three branches of VMT, and the void he left when he died was difficult to fill, not only my personal life, but also in managing our business affairs.

Through diligence, I soon realized the employees had been so busy growing the student body that school protocols had not been followed. No one had been monitoring the affairs of the school in Keith's absence, and teachers had not been reporting to class regularly. At times, there had not been enough teachers to accompany students to clinical practice, and unruly students had been submitting false information. When I inspected the school, I found that records were not being collected according to policy, and submitted files were not subject to scrutiny.

With Keith gone, Kevin, the vice-president, had been in charge. Unfortunately, he, too, had been coping with his father's illness, and now his death. As a new leader, he was supposed to learn the regulations of our business under his father's direction and that, too, was disrupted. He, like the rest of the staff, was excited about the growth, not realizing the associated dangers of rapid expansion.

The school, and our students, failed to meet a pass-rate criteria the Board of Nursing in the District of Columbia had developed. In response, the board acted against the school by suspending our practical nursing program.

This professional chaos was almost as painful as Keith's recent death: because I had taken two nursing homes in disarray and turned them into five-star facilities, in this city, my name was synonymous with quality; I would not lose my reputation. I made it clear to the staff.

Once Kevin and I were back in the office on a full-time basis, we worked around the clock, seven days a week to secure order amid a chaotic situation. We realized, however, that a lot more needed to be done to regain trust and the good name of the corporation.

I decided to challenge the nursing board in court. A large percentage of the other practical nursing programs in the city were operating below the required pass rate; therefore, there were no other qualified schools with a practical nursing program that had the capacity to absorb our students. Although new admissions to the practical nursing program at the VMT Education Center continued to be suspended, the program remained open for currently enrolled students through graduation. The angel of the sun continued to shine and, once again, I had another chance to salvage an institution in trouble—except this time it was my own.

Throughout my lifetime, I have refused to accept nor associate myself with the word FAILURE. I was not losing the school, only one of its programs; yet, for me, the situation was unacceptable. I declared war against the District of Columbia's Board of Nursing—particularly since the chairperson was a competitor, the director of the publicly owned District of Columbia Government Nursing School. That school also had a practical nursing program and was also operating under a conditional approval for not meeting the nursing board's criteria.

When the chairperson failed to recuse herself in the dealings with VMT's program closure decision, the conflict of interest was evident. In addition, the board had not presented a firm rationale as to why the program should be closed. It had also failed to allow VMT enough time to bring the school back to compliance. It was a fight that I was ready to take on. The concerns of the Board of Nursing were valid, that much I could concede. Had I been a member of the board, I would have recommended suspension of new student admissions until order was restored and the pass-rate of the school had improved. However, I vehemently disagreed with their decision to shut down the program completely, and I was determined to win this fight.

MAKE IT WORK FOR YOU!

Rule #22: Prioritize

Reflection: Me, My Belly, and the Ride

Turtles do not have very complicated agendas. Get something to eat, move a little towards the next stop, get some rest, repeat. Throw in some occasional excitement, like mating season, and laying eggs, repeat. But, if there is one thing a turtle knows, it is that they have to make their own wellbeing their top priority. Get something to eat, move a little towards the next stop, get some rest, repeat.

- Before you take care of anyone else in your life, make sure you are prioritizing your own needs and self-care above anyone else's. You can only be good to other people if you take care of yourself first. Get something to eat. Move a little towards the next stop. Get some rest and repeat. If you cannot fit those in right now, make yourself your top priority ASAP.

- When you are planning your day and writing out your agenda, prioritize the list of things to do by importance. This way, you can take care of the most important tasks first.

RULES TO LIVE BY

It took me a while to grieve the loss of my husband. I still find myself missing him. But I knew I had to move on as best I could. My friend, Ana, and I looked out for each other during this period in our lives, and found ways to inject some joy into our lives. I was in for a big battle in my business life, and I needed help to win it. I have found that, when a problem seems like it is overwhelming, solutions often show up just in time. An introduction can lead to a remarkable friendship with the right person to help you through turmoil. When it seems things are darkest, the littlest bit of sunshine makes a big difference.

Rule 23: Always be Aware of Opportunity

Throughout much of my career, I was lucky. Opportunities just happened. Sometimes they were accidental (see chapter 14, "When It Rains, It Pours"). But I also kept an eye out for opportunity and took advantage of it when I could. Understanding what was available to me made it possible for me to become the first African-American woman to own a minority-certified nursing home business in Washington, D.C.

Learn to keep your eyes and ears open for needs in areas you can fill. They are often profitable and personally satisfying. Understanding the need for trained nursing assistants led me to open a school to train nursing assistants for the certification exam (see chapter 10, "A New Reality"). This led to better opportunities for many young men and women in the industry, and, because vacancies were filled, it led to better care for residents.

14

When It Rains, It Pours

After the death of our husbands, the bond between Ana and I solidified. We were sealed together by our shared trauma. The relationship was therapeutic for both of us, and a flourishing social life helped us recover from our painful losses. Slowly, over months, we healed together. Having been touched so closely by death, we realized that nothing is promised in life, and so we were determined to have a good time while we still could. In the city, Ana was often invited to major functions. I was with her at most of these events, including the "Fight Night After Party," better known as "Knock Out Abuse," an annual function organized for the elite, high society, who's who of the District of Columbia. On other occasions, we put on our fur coats at FedEx Fields Stadium, before a Redskins football game, with a group of friends who catered their tailgating parties with caviar, champagne, waiters and a bonfire.

Ana sometimes hosted grand functions herself, for her hospital's executive members, and for politicians in the community. A year or so after Keith died, Ana asked me to assist her in hosting an important cocktail reception. Even though we did not work for the same organization, I accepted. The gathering was held at a prestigious hotel in the downtown Northwest section of the city, and the room, dimly lit by grand chandeliers, was alive with laughter and conversation—the sounds of contemporary jazz played in the background. There were side tables with chairs, and tall cocktail tables for those who wished to remain standing. In the center of the room was a very wide oval table with an assortment of hors d'oeuvres and extravagant flower arrangements of tiger lilies, orchids and peonies. There were two well-stocked bars, one to the north and the other to the south end of the room. The men were in suits and ties, and the women in splendid cocktail attire. It was a festive atmosphere.

At a distance, I noticed the silhouette of a man who reminded me of Keith. He was dressed just like my late husband—khaki pants, white shirt, a navy-blue double-breasted blazer, and what looked like Keith's favorite red tie. At first glance, this tall, slim figure could belong to no one else but Keith. I thought for a moment: was it my imagination—or wishful thinking? Was that Keith? Of course, it could not be. "Ana," I said, my tone expressing interest, curiosity, and somewhat disbelief. "Who is that guy?"

"He's our general counsel," she said. "By the way, he is single," she added with a grin on her face. "Do you want me to take you to meet him?"

"I'll walk toward him," I said, "then you come and introduce us."

"Better yet," Ana said. "I'll send my secretary. They know each other well."

I was dressed in a short, Garrett, black Neiman Marcus skirt suit, accented with red accessories, and red high-heeled shoes. Taking my sweet time, I walked around the buffet table, added some hors d'oeuvres to a small plate, and sipped a glass of red wine. I made my way closer to where this man was standing. By that time, he was joined by Ana's secretary, who greeted me as I approached. She, then, introduced me to Clifford, the hospital's general counsel. I was in awe—so much about him reminded me of Keith. Just like my late husband, he was tall, dark, and handsome.

But he was not Keith, and I was disappointed. What had I expected? That Keith would come back? Yes. I wished it had been him. My mind was playing tricks on me.

After our introduction at the reception, I had the opportunity to meet Clifford on different occasions. We managed to keep bumping into each other at one function or another throughout the city; we were once at the same hospital association dinner, and, on a few occasions, we attended the same political events. We had both been health care professionals for over 20 years, but we had never crossed paths before. Now, every time we met, he acknowledged me as "Ana's friend, right?" I responded yes but never gave him my name. He was not Keith—and I could not forgive him for that.

One of our more memorable encounters occurred as I waited behind a car to enter the garage of my corporate office building. At the entrance sat an old BMW, and the driver was having difficulties opening the gate, impeding my access to the building. The management company had just issued new codes to all the tenants, and I figured that the driver must be entering an old code, since the gate did not open. Impatient to get to a meeting, I moved my car closer to the BMW; I intended to enter my own code, allowing the car in front of me safe passage, and then immediately follow, so both cars could enter the garage in one swift motion. As I approached the car, I noticed that the driver was Ana's general counsel, Clifford. Without exchanging words, I hastily entered the code. "Thank you," he said simply.

There was no time for conversation, as I had already activated the code. I jumped in the car and proceeded to my assigned parking space. Clifford parked in the designated area for visitors. I took the garage elevator, on my way up to my office. The door opened on the first floor—and Clifford entered. My heart was beating faster. Why was I so excited to see him? He thanked me for opening the garage door for him, and apologized for having the wrong code. When the elevator stopped on the second floor, I said, "This is my office," pointing to a door. "Stop on your way out, and I will be happy to take you down."

I was at my desk when the secretary came in. "There is a gentleman in the waiting room asking to see you."

I knew who it was. "Are you ready to go down?" I asked, when I reached the reception area.

"I just stopped to thank you. They gave me the new code—you do not have to take me down." He kissed as the French do—one small peck on each cheek. "Thank you, again, for being so nice." He left, and I returned to my office in haste, eager to call Ana to rehash what had just happened.

Since the hospital reception, when Clifford and I had met for the first time, Ana had been pushing me to meet with him one-on-one, so we could get to know each other. She was convinced that, if we got a chance to get together in a more personal, more private setting, we might like each other. Ana was eager to play matchmaker. She reminded me of my husband who had been obsessed at making sure opportunity did not pass me by when he saw it.

It was now Ana's turn to ensure that she got to personally introduce her two friends. Her quest was to figure out the best way to get us alone. Was there really a divine spirit at work trying to connect Clifford and me? Ana believed it. She was anxious to find me a partner, as she felt fortunate to have met her own companion, Rick. She wanted me to experience the joy of companionship; she wanted us to be a foursome once again, sharing our lives together, as it used to be when we were both married. She wanted to get Clifford and me together so badly that she managed to convince me that he would be the right lawyer to help me with the board of nursing issues at the school.

Ana thought up what she believed to be a brilliant idea: a pool party at my house. "Only if he can attend," she said. I agreed to host the pool party. I was elated, my heart beating fast, like a teenager in love. I was grinning softly, even laughing to myself. By then, I truly believed—and even felt—that there was a divine spirit at play. Why else was I constantly encountering this gentleman? He had been in the same city for many years, both of us health care professionals, for about the same length of time. Suddenly, we were continuously bumping into each other. "Why?" I kept asking myself. I reminisced on the request that I had made to God, asking him out loud, in front of hundreds of people at my husband's funeral, not to forget that I was still on this earth. I had asked him to look out for me. Was God putting our two souls together?

The day of the pool party arrived, and my house was filled with friends—some of Ana's, some of mine—and dance music poured out of the speakers buried in the foliage above the pool. The smell of home-cooked Caribbean food infused the air, and the bartender was busy serving both soft drinks and cocktails. I was keeping an eye open for Clifford, although Ana had warned me that his "yes" did not mean that he would show up. He was a busy man. We had decided to have the party anyway, in the hopes he would come, since he had chosen the day that would work best for him.

I was in the pool in a yellow and black polka-dot bikini when he entered the party through the side gate. I noticed him immediately in his gray shirt with small, multi-colored flowers, tucked into a pair of taupe-colored jeans, and simple brown sandals on his feet. He looked very relaxed compared to all the other times I had seen him—always in a suit. Excited that he had come, I quickly dried off my body, threw on a white see-through swimsuit cover, and rushed over to greet him.

He did not know any of our guests, and Ana was inside the house, so he looked relieved to see me. He was quick to kiss me on both cheeks. As he was asking if Ana was there, she walked out the sliding glass door. They chatted for a while, and he was given a drink by Carl, my friend from Canada, who was in town with his wife Sheila. I joined my other guests in the pool, while Ana continued to entertain Clifford. Before long, however, he approached me, bent down close to my ear and said, "I think I would like to get in the pool. Where do I change?"

"I have a powder room on the first floor," I said. "Use this glass door, and then go down the steps. It'll be on your left-hand side."

"I have my swim trunks in the car. I will be right back."

I could not believe what was happening. Not only was he here, but he was getting in the pool with me. My heart was beating faster and faster, in anticipation of his return. His willingness to join me in the water made it clear that he, too, wanted to get to know me. Later, we became so enthralled in our conversation that we did not even notice we were the only two left in the heated pool. We shared personal stories, and I related the events of my husband's passing—and the chaos at the school, especially the action of the Board of Nursing. It was one o'clock in the morning when Clifford and I left the pool. As we entered the house, we were shocked to realize that it was completely emptied of the guests. No one had come outside to say goodbye, following instructions by Ana and Sheila, who had not only gotten everyone out of the pool, but also cleaned up the after-party mess in the kitchen. Ana and my other guests had gone home. Sheila and Carl were upstairs, in the guestroom, sound asleep.

Before he left, Clifford gave me his usual kisses on both cheeks. The next evening, he called—and he continued to call every evening, even if it was late. We discussed the issues at the school, and Clifford was confident that he could help. I, too, was convinced that he was the right lawyer to handle the Board of Nursing and all the drama it brought. Clifford and I soon completed all the formalities for VMT to hire his law firm. The contract was signed, and the retainers delivered. Now, I experienced a real wake-up call: for the first time, I had to defend the company without my husband Keith—my partner, my coach—guiding me along the way.

As a nursing home administrator, I had faced countless lawsuits from families, some involving valid allegations—others, not so much. Those settlements were usually covered by the nursing home's insurance company, which hired its own lawyers to settle out of court, in most cases, for a minuscule amount of money paid by the insurer. The most we had ever had to pay out of VMT's coffers for settlements related to the nursing homes was our insurance deductible.

The school case was different, however, because there was no coverage, since we were initiating legal action. All the expenses had to be absorbed by VMT, and the cost of litigation was unknown, which was unsettling. All I knew was the lawyer's hourly rate, and that number was frightening. Once again, I found myself in a fight-or-flight situation. On the one hand, I was focused on saving the practical nursing program, along with my reputation, which was most important to my career and my pride. On the other hand, I was fighting the legislative body that could decide the fate of the program, and could retaliate by shutting the whole school down. I was afraid of winning the battle, but subsequently losing the war. They say never to show your weakness to your enemy. I did my best not to let them see I was nervous. I had a walk of confidence at every negotiation meeting, and, whenever I attended the Board of Nursing's open monthly meetings, I was in their face at every opportunity.

Clifford convinced me that I had no choice but to first try to negotiate directly with the Board of Nursing. If that failed, he said, we would take full legal action and file a suit against the board. He was determined to win this case and reassured me that the probability of a positive outcome was great. Like a turtle, I stuck my neck out one more time when the Board of Nursing decided to dig their heels in the sand; I got into the sand box with them and decided to file suit to stop the termination of my practical nursing program. To file the suit, we needed a litigation lawyer to defend the case, but defense law was not Clifford's specialty.

Clifford brought in the two litigation lawyers and a host of associates to do research and put binders and other supporting materials together. The new additions came with a high price tag. Because we lived in the District of Columbia, it was inevitable that politics were injected in the mix, and that had to be handled delicately.

Naysayers were adamant that the program should be closed, but we did have some support: Many students wrote to the Board of Nursing, fighting to keep the practical nursing program open, and nursing home administrators wrote affidavits attesting that our graduates were needed to staff their facilities. All the while, bills from the law firm were mounting, and the stress was impacting everyone in the office. We terminated old employees who were not as competent as we needed them to be and hired new employees to deal with the new demands in the office.

To complicate matters, our phones were ringing off the hook with calls from lawyers representing currently enrolled students, trying to figure out the academic status of their clients. Soon, the Maryland Board of Nursing got involved also, since many VMT graduates took their national board examination in Maryland, which shares a border with the District of Columbia. Once licensed, those nurses could work in Maryland's nursing homes as well.

All of that was plenty to keep me challenged, but I had yet another crisis to help manage. One day, out of the blue, Kevin asked me out to dinner. In our house, if a family member said, "We need to go out to dinner," it was a clear indication that something serious required immediate attention. Keith had taught us to have sensitive discussions at a restaurant. This allowed the tone of the conversation to remain civil, and encouraged problem-solving over emotional reactions to sudden and sometimes disturbing news. I wondered if Kevin was worried about how the stress of our business was impacting my health and wellbeing. Was he concerned about me? Did he fear losing his mother, too? Was he going to suggest that I sell the business? *Why in the world is he requesting a restaurant dinner?* I started to imagine the worst. What could it be?

The next evening, after the meal and a couple of drinks, he started. "If Daddy were alive, I would be having this conversation with him," he said.

What is it that this boy would prefer to discuss with his father? Sitting across from him in the booth, I suddenly wondered: how was Kevin doing? Had I been so preoccupied with the business that I had failed to notice his pain? My mind was working overtime, my hands were sweaty, my heartbeat unsteady. The drinks came, which seemed to interrupt his train of thought on a topic, I realize now, was difficult for him to discuss. He appeared in the grip of mixed emotions, and all I wanted to do was to jump over the table and hug him.

He took a sip of his drink. "Kristin is pregnant."

I took a gulp of my alcoholic drink to help steady my pulse. Then, I looked him in the eyes and asked, "So, what is the plan?"

He was quiet for a minute. "You know what they say, Mom. When one person dies, another one is born."

"Yes, son, go on."

"I'm thinking: if Daddy hadn't died, this would have never happened. And, if it had, I would have known what to do about it. But I feel that this child is like Daddy, so I want to keep it."

"Are you going to marry her?" I asked.

"I'm only 25 years old," he said. "I just lost my father, and I'm becoming a father myself. I'm not ready for marriage. We won't be the first couple to get pregnant out of wedlock."

I took his hand. "Kev, do not worry. It is going to be all right. God and Daddy are with us."

We kept silent for a long moment, struggling to find our words, which was unusual for both of us. We ate more food, had a couple of strong drinks, and, finally, I broke the silence. "This child will stop your tears, son, and bring you joy. I am here for you all the way; you can always count on me. Daddy left both of us in a good place in life. We can deal with our issues, because his spirit will always be here with us, guiding us through everything." In that moment, I was the strong one supporting my bewildered son.

We left the restaurant and headed home to bed, only to face our usual hectic work life the next day.

The turmoil in the business continued, and, while I developed a strong professional relationship with Clifford, we were both also aware of a growing affection between us. We were careful, however, not to allow our personal feelings to interfere with the urgency of the matter at hand—until, finally, after several months of negotiations, Clifford called one afternoon to say that the case was amicably settled with the Board of Nursing. We could remain open!

He invited me to dinner to celebrate this big victory. Since his office was in the heart of the city and parking always at a premium, I volunteered to drive. On the way to the restaurant, I had pick him up in my two-seater, a burgundy Lexus with black interior and mahogany wood trim. I arrived with the top of my convertible already down, because it was a beautiful sunny day. I was dressed in an aqua-blue, two-piece suit accentuated with my signature turtle pin on the lapel. He was looking *so fine* in a navy-blue Armani suit. As he walked towards the car, I noticed a square Tiffany box in his hand, and, as I got out of the car to greet him, he kissed me on both cheeks and handed me the teal box. "This is for you, my dear," he said.

"For me?" I was in shock. "Thank you."

He volunteered to drive my car since he knew where he was taking me for dinner.

"Can I open my gift now?" I asked, as I settled in the passenger seat.

"No," he said. "You can do that over dinner."

We dined at Kinkead's and shared a bottle of red wine. For nearly three hours, we talked about the case and its settlement, since I had missed the last few days of negotiations. He was happy to have resolved the dispute in favor of the school, and I expressed my gratitude as I opened the gift. It was a heavy, lead crystal paper weight. The octagonal piece was engraved with the name of the school, and the date of the settlement decision. My eyes moved from the crystal to his eyes. "Oh, my God! It is so beautiful, and so thoughtful of you to get me a gift. You really did not have to do that. I truly appreciate the gesture."

Looking right back at me, he responded, "I just want us to remember this date."

We finished our desserts, and, on the way home, he suggested we stop at the World War II Memorial, since I had mentioned that I had yet to visit it. He held my hand as we walked around the reflecting pool and fountain, and, again, we talked nonstop—except, this time, the conversation was more personal.

"So, what do you do in your spare time?" he asked.

I chuckled. "What spare time? I work, and then I go home to sleep. I used to go out a lot when my husband was alive, but, now, not as much. I do not enjoy going to functions by myself. For the past year, my son has become my escort, and he complains every time I ask him to put on a tuxedo."

"I do not mind wearing a tuxedo," he said with a smile.

"Are you sure that you have the time to be an escort?" I asked. "You seem pretty busy."

"I will make the time," he said, the perfect gentleman. And I knew, then, that I would welcome a more intimate relationship with Clifford. He was gentle, and he treated me like a lady. He was perfect—just as Keith had been. This night reminded me of my first date with Keith at the Playboy club.

Only time will tell, I thought.

As we completed the tour, we noticed that a police officer had ticketed my car. It had been such an exciting night that we had both failed to realize we had illegally parked in a handicap space. Clifford felt terrible for his mistake and offered to pay for the ticket. We stopped by his office to retrieve his own car, and then he kissed me goodbye. This time, however, it was different. In addition to his usual kisses on both cheeks, he gave me a third one: he held me tight and kissed me on the lips.

I drove home on cloud nine, convinced again that I must really have a guardian angel, one who had been following me from birth. Even in the most nail-biting situations, I could rest assured I had come out victorious.

After I won the case against the Board of Nursing, the school turned around, as though nothing had ever happened. I regained my reputation in the city and managed, in the interim, to develop a loving relationship with my lawyer friend. Epictetus said, "It is not what happens to you that matters but how you react to it that matters." I had always made it a point to handle negative events with a conqueror's mindset, well-aware that, like mountains, life is a succession of peaks and valleys. I have had many opportunities to ponder the Caribbean saying, "Behind every mountain is another mountain." I could not be intimidated by the size of my mountains, because, often, it is not the height that is to be feared, but rather, the terrain of the slippery slope that can be dangerous.

I knew full well the Board of Nursing had the power to close my school; yet, I had decided to climb that mountain, and I had made it to the summit unharmed. In the city, two other practical nursing programs, which had been closed during the same period as VMT, never made it to the other side of their mountains. It takes courage and determination to push past fear and insecurity.

Because I had been consumed by the issues with the practical nursing program, I had been unable to pay full attention to another concern that was brewing at the Center for Aging nursing home. The engineering director at that facility, a tall, domineering white man named Ron, managed a staff that was 90 percent black. I was aware that a feud was brewing between the director and his subordinates, but, to my knowledge, these concerns were being handled by the human resources director, who reported to have it all under control. On occasion, HR had asked me to attend specific meetings involving Ron and his cohort.

According to the employees, Ron was demanding they perform certain tasks above their paygrade, based on the Department of Labor's job descriptions included in VMT's management contracts. In response, HR had revised the various position titles and job descriptions, and the revised paperwork had been signed by every employee. I thought the issue was satisfactorily resolved. In reality, Ron ignored the new job descriptions and continued to assign tasks that remained unacceptable. This time, unbeknownst to management, the employees filed a job discrimination violation case. Unexpectedly, in the daily bundle of mail delivered, there was a letter from the Department of Labor indicating the employees' concerns. The letter included a specific date when the Department of Labor would be coming to the facility to investigate.

A visit from a government agency is never good. When the investigator arrived, she ran a thorough, straight-forward, and fair investigation, reviewing both the old and new job descriptions. She met with employees of the engineering department, the facility administrator, the human resources director, and, finally, she conducted an exit meeting with the HR director and me. She indicated that a report on her findings and recommendations would follow, but there was no further communication from the Department of Labor for about two years—until, one day, another letter arrived.

We learned that a new investigation would have to be done, because the first investigator had retired without closing her case. This second investigator was brutal: she not only investigated the concerns at hand, but she also expanded her review beyond job functions and assignment of duties to other matters. After her exit interview, she, too, promised a report. Through it all, the facility managed to operate at a high level of quality, scoring four or five stars from the Centers for Medicare and Medicaid. On occasion, we scored a no-deficiency survey. Money was flowing in, employees were getting raises, and, at times, bonuses were issued, creating the happy-staff, happy-care environment that I strove for.

In general, life was good. I was finally enjoying peace in both my business and personal life. I had become even more social than before, now that I had met my lawyer friend. With him, I attended many black-tie functions. I had my own invitations, and Clifford had his own invitations, and we graciously accompanied each other all over the city, attending galas at the Providence Hospital, the Sibley Hospital, the Hope Connection, the Leadership of Greater Washington, the Choral Art Society, and the Kennedy Center—to name a few. Our picture appeared in *The Washington Life* magazine and on several embassies' websites. We had become known in the high-society scene of the city.

I was scheduled to attend yet another function when a major snow storm engulfed the city. The Metro buses and trains shut down. I was busy assisting management at securing staff to cover two nursing homes, when I received the long-awaited call from Kevin. "Kristin is in labor," he said. Baby Keith was born while I tried to plow my way through snow-covered streets to Washington Hospital Center. When I finally arrived at the hospital, I found Kevin in the large birthing suite he had reserved, so that Kristin, her mother, and Kevin could all be together for the duration of her stay at the hospital.

Baby Keith was the most handsome little human being I had ever seen. I adored him. I had anticipated the birth of my first grandson for so long, and, yet, I had missed the crucial moment because of the snow storm. Although the joy of being a grandmother was pouring out of my soul, and I was almost euphoric, I still could not be completely happy: I felt sad, and even guilty, to know that Keith—the baby's namesake—would never experience being a grandfather. *How happy would he have been?* I wondered. Oh, Lord! How cruel was this? *Why do people have to die?* At this point in my life, I had grown to accept that, as disappointing as it could be, I could never manage to enjoy happiness to its fullest—without *something* to damper my joy. C'est la vie!

In anticipation of my grandson's birth, I had remodeled the lower level of my home to accommodate the baby and his mother, Kristin. We put in a bedroom, dining room/living room combination, kitchen, washer/dryer—a whole apartment downstairs, so they would be comfortable. But it did not work out for Kevin and Kristin. They argued often. She wanted to move out of my house into her own space with Kevin and the baby, and the arguments often grew loud and ugly. None of them seemed happy. My son had never witnessed his parents arguing, so this lifestyle was foreign to him.

Kevin came to me one day and said he was planning to move out into an apartment with Kristin and the baby.

I said, "No. You're not moving to an apartment. If you're moving out, find yourself a house." I would help him purchase a home, so I said, "Go find yourself a house. I don't want you to move into an apartment. You need to have a home for your family. I'm afraid that an apartment will not stop the arguments."

So Kevin went with Kristin and purchased a house of his own for his family. They picked the colors together and filled it with beautiful furniture and household items. I had hoped they would be happy, but they never moved in together in the end. My son realized that even a home would not stop the arguments. It just was not working out for them, and Kevin knew that it would be best for them to split up and go their separate ways.

Kristin moved back to her mother's house; Kevin moved to the new house by himself, and they split custody. Between the two of them, they took care of the baby. Kevin lived alone and took care of the baby by himself during his time with Little Keith. In addition to his work at our company, Kevin became a single parent, raising a baby by himself. It was hard to watch Kevin deal with the extra stress of parenting his son on his own, but he is an amazing father. My grandson was a happy child who was well-loved and well-adjusted.

MAKE IT WORK FOR YOU!

Rule #23: Always Be Aware of Opportunity

Reflection: All Instinct

Little hatchlings are something to behold. Fresh out of the eggs, they follow an amazing biological imperative to merge with the ocean. They do not stop and ask for directions. No time for practice. It is out of the nest and off into the world as fast as their little flippers can carry them. It is all instinct. Follow your instincts. They will lead you where you need to go. Sometimes, we get wrapped in the intrusive warning system built into our brains by past conditioning and miss opportunities. When was the last time you went with your gut impulse? How did it work out?

- Learn how to network. If you are not socially savvy, do not fret. It gets easier. Learn to embrace your discomfort. Get out there and meet people in your field with whom you can bounce ideas around. Join a professional organization or hook up with an alumni network. Find other people with the same interests as you. If you are not in a position where you can meet people in your area, find them online. There is a whole world waiting for you to join it. Get going!

- Part of finding opportunity is just keeping your eyes and ears open and looking for a niche that needs to be filled. Practice paying attention to how things should operate ideally. When you see an area needing improvement, ask yourself, is this an opportunity I should invest my energy in? What are the payoffs?

RULES TO LIVE BY

By this time in my life, I had risen to the top of my field. I ran for election as an officer in a professional organization dominated by white men and had an impressive amount of support for my candidacy. But I also faced some brutally ugly attacks from union organizers that got personal with their smear campaign. And in the middle of all this, one of those phone calls came in with an opportunity I could not pass up.

Rule #24: Short-term Thinking Versus Long-term Success

It is easy to get wrapped up in short-term troubles sometimes and lose sight of long-term success. It is tempting when you are mired in day-to-day struggles to give up and take the easy route. There were dozens of times when my troubles seemed insurmountable, whether it was something simple, like getting my driver's license (see chapter six, "Sweet & Sour") or something more difficult like learning to speak English fluently. As I grew older, my challenges and troubles grew larger, and, looking back, my initial setbacks seemed much less severe in comparison to having my reputation sullied by union campaign (see chapter 10), facing my husband's sudden illness (see chapter 13, "Every Beginning Has Its End"), and facing the possibility that the school I had opened to train nursing assistants might be shut down. Time gives each of us perspective, and, if we cannot always see the long view when we are young, it becomes apparent as we mature. Remember to have faith in your direction, and be certain to keep your long-term goals in mind when you are dealing with short-term crises.

15

Out of My Way

Work continued to be a challenge. The renovation project had now started at the Johnson Nursing Home, and it required that I work closely with the construction company hired by the government. The building, which housed over 200 seniors and young adults, was not designed as a nursing home; thus, it needed to be retrofitted to meet nursing home regulations and standards. I became an octopus, my arms and tentacles reaching all parts of VMT. In addition, I decided to run for office at the American Healthcare Association, the organization that represented all nursing homes in the United States, the Virgin Islands, and Puerto Rico.

The first time I attended the association's convention, it culminated with a black-tie gala, and I was impressed by the grandiosity of the event. On the stage, where the elected officers were to be seated, the dais was skirted with white linen, and a black cloth-covered head table, adorned with beautiful china, and a magnificent centerpiece of roses, orchids, and calla lilies. In addition to the champagne, wine, and water glasses, there were many other types of drinkware whose exact function I could not figure out.

At the beginning of the event, just before the invocation, the elected officers lined up to be introduced and seated. A voice that echoed through the entire ballroom called the name of each officer, followed by his or her official elected title. I was struck by the fact that, every time a name was called, invariably it was a white male who stepped up to the stage, accompanied by a beautiful blonde-haired wife or significant other. The men wore black tuxedos, and the women extravagant designer outfits accented with diamond jewelry. Every year, this same scenario repeated itself. I pledged that, one day, I would be amongst those climbing those steps—my little black Haitian self on the arm of my tall, dark, and handsome husband. I knew that it was going to be an uphill battle, but I was prepared to take on the challenge.

My election would be historic, but I needed enough votes from all the states to win nationally. As I approached election day, I was still running unopposed; my chances looked good. At the convention, however, a challenger was nominated from the floor to run against me. It was a last-ditch effort to maintain an unacceptable status quo.

I was the first black candidate with the audacity to challenge the good old boys club. Many white women before me had tried and failed to reach the president level. While some were determined to stop my momentum, the good old boys of my region decided to fight on my behalf. The state executive for Hawaii whispered in my ear, "Don't worry, Solanges. We are voting for you." As did Tennessee, Texas, and many others. The Coalition of Women in Long-Term Care, of which I was a board member, worked hard on my election campaign. A delegate from New York State volunteered to be in the room to witness the counting of the ballots. Suddenly, it became a nail-biting election—an exciting one. David, the executive director of the District of Columbia Healthcare Association ran to Staples, where he printed VOTE FOR SOLANGES flyers, which he distributed throughout the hall. This was a convention that I will never forget.

On election day, at the 65th convention of the American Healthcare Association, I beat my opponent by 300 votes and became the first African-American woman of Caribbean descent to win election to a vice-president position of this national association. At the time, AHCA represented about 17,000 nursing homes. At the gala, I was sworn in with the other elected officers and claimed my place at the head table. Because this victory happened after Keith's death, I was proudly escorted by my son Kevin, who had learned from me the power of hard work, focus, tenacity, and, above all, the audacity to believe in oneself. Sadly, more than 10 years later, there has not been another African American to break the glass ceiling of this major national association.

As busy as I was with positive achievements, my streak of good luck had not run out yet. I was home on a rainy evening when my phone rang. Ana was at an airport, waiting for a flight. "Solanges," she said, "I just ended a conference call with the owners of the hospital I worked for. They offered to sell me 2 percent of the hospital shares for a million dollars."

Before Ana could utter another word, I screamed, "What? Oh, my God, Ana! That is great! Are you buying?"

"Well, this is why I am calling you," she said. "Of all the people I know, you are the only one I want to discuss this offer with."

"Ana, this is big. I am flattered."

"Just listen," Ana responded. "I cannot come up with a million dollars on my own. Can you come up with half a million? I'll buy 1 percent, and you'll buy 1 percent."

Saying that I was in shock would be an understatement. "Girl—," I started. But then, I remembered. "Didn't they just file for bankruptcy?" I knew all about the problems of that hospital, not only from Ana but also from the evening news and from coverage in the *Washington Post*. Was I willing to stick my neck out for a once-in-a-lifetime opportunity to become part-owner of a hospital? Or would I let fear paralyze me? This unexpected phone call and the opportunity was huge!

"I know, Solanges! I know! They need the money to get the hospital out of bankruptcy. It is a gamble that I am willing to take. Once they are back in the black, it'll be easier and more lucrative to sell the hospital."

I was aware that short-term thinking was the enemy of long-term success. I recognized that a turtle atop a totem pole did not get there alone, and Ana and I were each other's support system. Both of Caribbean descent—she, a white woman from Venezuela, and I, a Black woman from Haiti—we had had parallel lives: We had both immigrated to the United States for a better life. We were both nurses who had graduated from Georgetown University. We had both been directors of nursing in the District of Columbia during the same era, and we had both obtained our licenses as nursing home administrators, and managed nursing homes in the same city. We were both very active on boards and associations in the city as well as nationally. We each gave birth to a male child, and we both became widowed within eight months of each other. After the death of our husbands, we each met a partner (and, after about 10 years in our relationships, we would both end up alone again within no more than two months apart from each other). As Catholics with strong faith in Jesus Christ, we believed that there was a spiritual connection in our lives that brought us together. Ana and I were as close as two sisters, and I trusted her.

Without hesitation, I responded, "Ana, if you're in, I'm in. I can work on coming up with my half a million, but I'll need time."

"There is not much time," Ana said. "You'd have to get the money now. Now, Solanges!" she added with emphasis and pressure. "Hear me out, though. You need to understand that you're taking a gamble: the hospital might not recover from the bankruptcy. There's no guarantee you'll get your money back. You may lose part of it—and even all of it."

"Oh, my God! Ana, I don't know what to say." I was home alone. I started to pace the floor. I could not believe the nature of the call.

Ana's tone was firm. "I need to know. Do you want to do it?"

"I'm game," I said, "Thank you for thinking of me. Let me figure out where to get the money."

"I have to board my plane. Let's talk when I get home," Ana said.

"Great! Have a safe flight."

Bewildered, I called my lifelines—the two most important people alive: Kevin and Clifford. I was advised by both men to come up with the money any way I could and do the deal. And, once I did, I became a shareholder. I was appointed chairman, and Ana vice-chair of the hospital's board of directors. We each received a generous board stipend and, after two years, we doubled our investment by cashing in our shares of the hospital. It turned out not to be such a shabby deal after all.

I was on fire and having a great time in my personal life, but, as it always seemed to be the case, there were challenges that threatened my happiness. The Department of Labor's investigation that had been initiated years before, alleging unfair labor practices, finally reached a determination: the Department sided with the employees and demanded that VMT retroactively pay the affected employees for damages. Once again, I was faced with a situation that I could not handle alone. I was mind-boggled when I tried to figure out how they arrived at such an outlandish decision. VMT was advised to work with both the Federal and District Departments of Labor to find a solution. We needed specialized lawyers with an understanding of labor disputes to help manage this complicated crisis. By now, Clifford had become the official legal counsel for VMT, and, with his firm's partners, he recommended Dan, the right legal counsel to represent VMT in the case. God had given me a new guardian angel, and, like Keith, Clifford was by my side through all my trials and remained very supportive.

This was another very dark period in the history of VMT. I loved working with the elderly. I enjoyed working alongside the staff. I took pride in teaching the students. However, I deeply detested those moments in the business where I felt vulnerable facing situations that were totally out of my control and outside my area of expertise.

From the very beginning of my career, way back to my days as a nursing assistant in the nursery at Misericordia Hospital, I did my best to follow the laws, policies and procedures related to my practice in nursing care. It was a hard blow to have this situation hanging like a cloud over my reputation, which I had fought so hard to build. The legal case dragged on for over a year. Eventually, VMT was able to settle through the Contract Appeals Board with the Department of Labor. We paid out the settlement to eligible employees and bore the high cost of litigation. But my pride was wounded. I hated losing even small battles.

While I was dealing with the Labor Department case, a union had unsuccessfully tried to unionize our home-care agency. Once again, I was faced with the invasion of the outside world into my business, and, again, this came at a cost to the company. On a couple of occasions, several busloads of non-employee union protestors marched outside our Connecticut Avenue office in union T-shirt uniforms, shouting slogans and disrupting our workday with noise.

This group was also unsuccessful in their attempt to unionize the homecare agency, but it was a distraction and a waste of money VMT could have used elsewhere. We learned that it cost a pretty penny to go against one of the most powerful unions in the United States. The soundest advice I received from my labor lawyer was to never allow union activity to become personal, and to just view this experience as part of being a business owner.

As much as my ego was bruised, and my impulse pushed me to respond to their attacks, I managed not to allow any of the protests to affect my psyche. I knew that, in order to succeed, one must not be paralyzed by fear. I grew to understand that adversity often offered up opportunities in disguise. But, just when I thought I was done with the unionizers' attempts to penetrate my business, another group of protesters appeared on the doorsteps of the Center for Aging nursing home.

The government had decided to lease out the two nursing homes under VMT's management. The newly elected mayor had decided that the government should not be in the business of providing nursing home care to its constituents. As a rule, unions capitalize on the weakness of management and infiltrate businesses under the pretense that employees are being treated unfairly. This union felt that our employees would need their representation during the transition from management to lease to protect their interests.

In my working years, I never personally worked as a union employee. However, I had experience working in a unionized environment when I was an assistant head nurse at Mount Sinai Hospital. In that position, I was well-schooled in the best way to work in a union shop environment. This knowledge was key to my being successful in dealing with the unionization attempts on my business. It was important knowledge for me to have, because those union organizers could be brutal in their tactics.

Because the Center for Aging nursing home went on the market for lease first, the union started their campaign efforts there. This meant that, while we were managing a nursing home whose lease was up for bid and under scrutiny from a host of potential leasers, we had to simultaneously cope with a union movement.

I reached out to Littler and Mendelson, the firm that had been so good to me in my dealings with union issues when I began my career in the District of Columbia as a director of nursing. I was heartbroken when I heard that my previous lawyer, who had been excellent to work with, had died. I quickly learned, however, that the whole firm was excellent. I had a new savior to rely on. Tom was not on the heavy side, bald-headed and a pit bull like my first Mendelson lawyer, but he was perfect for the job. Soft-spoken, well-calculated, conscientious, and tall with a full head of hair, Tom was, above anything else, effective; VMT never signed a union contract for that facility. Another crisis averted.

A leader should never be satisfied but should focus on being ahead of the curve, so I continued to pursue my life quest. My ultimate dream as a long-term care professional was not only to manage nursing homes as a contractor but also to someday be the owner of a senior facility that I could operate independently of contract restrictions. It was very disappointing that VMT was not the successful bidder on this long-term lease. It meant that we had to vacate the facility, and we lost the management contract we had held for over 20 years.

The political climate was against the company for many reasons: VMT was in court over the wage dispute with the government, who also provided us with the management contract. The union activity did not help, because unions and politicians tread lightly in shared spaces; they need each other to operate. To make matters worse, a former employee of VMT, who had learned the nursing home business from me, was working for a competitor, and used inside knowledge to bid against VMT. Therefore, we were not surprised when VMT was not awarded the lease. We left the nursing home in much better condition than when we first took over the management contract. There were zero deficiencies in our last survey. But it was a loss that hurt both VMT and me, personally.

Once the leasing bid was decided for the Center for Aging nursing home, it was time for the Johnson nursing home to go up for bids. What a painful period it was! For once, I must admit, I was afraid I would see all that I had worked for vanish. The two nursing homes were the bulk of our business. By then, the school was no longer profitable, as it had been reduced to only two programs. The home care agency was only marginally profitable. Losing the Johnson nursing home could mean the end of VMT. I kept reminding myself that I had been in tight places before and had always managed to squeeze through. As usual, I invoked the support of Mother Mary. I believed that prayer had more power than all the evil that surrounded me. So, I got down on my knees, and I prayed fervently.

Being a long-standing government contractor for over 20 years, I was always on edge, knowing VMT's contract could be cancelled at the whim of a mayor or a city council member pressured by a competitor. Contracts were being snatched away regardless of whether the contractor was in good standing or not, and then awarded to companies with stronger political ties. At a public hearing, I once heard a council member chairman for the health services division recommend that a vendor lose their contract, and, within months, they were out of business. Business owners in the city had to become almost numb to the thought of losing business. I did my best not to let myself get mired in the politics. Keith had always advised me to keep my head low. I focused on quality delivery of care, stayed under the media's radar, and managed the union issues with caution.

VMT prepared and submitted a proposal to lease the Johnson nursing home— the only VMT-managed facility left. The union, angered by the company's failure to sign a contract at the Center for Aging nursing home, vowed to destroy us at any cost. As with the Center for Aging nursing home, we were again under a union infiltration attempt while our contract was up for a long-term lease bid. Having experienced the disaster of the first lease, we knew that our company was on a slippery slope with this lease as well.

This time, the union was vicious. They entered the building in their attempts to launch the union contract. They attacked me personally with a slew of viciously fabricated stories and tore apart the company's policies, salary, and benefits structures. On a couple of occasions, the union organized a gathering in front of my house in the early evenings, right as my neighbors were coming home from work. The police were called immediately by one of the neighbors, who was horrified by this invasion and the violation of their privacy.

Again, I had to face several busloads of people marching in union uniforms, but, instead of limiting their marches to my business address, they staged their protests in front of my private home. The first time this happened, I was inside the house getting a massage. I excused my masseuse and dressed quickly to investigate the commotion in front of my home. When I called my lawyer, he advised me to stay inside, out of sight, and not to engage with the protestors. I did not recognize any of the people marching up and down the street from my vantage point on the other side of the living room window. My lawyer told me they had the right to picket, so long as they stayed off my property.

I was furious. What about my right to peace and quiet? Tom insisted that the best course of action was to ignore the protestors. That was easier said than done. I wanted to defend myself and protect my company. In retrospect, however, it was the best advice I received about the union matter. Since it takes two to tango, we deprived them of a dancing partner and defeated them by becoming a wallflower. Silence was truly golden.

My son and his big, scary-looking dog stationed themselves on the front porch of my house to keep watch over the marchers. They shouted through their bullhorns that I lived in a million-dollar house I could only afford, because I was stealing employee money. I was dying to ask: Where were they when I did not speak a word of English and had to work in factories? Where were they when I had to work as a nanny? Where were they when I had to work during the day and go to school at night to get my degrees, so I could honestly earn a decent salary to afford my lifestyle? Where were they then? Their audacity and ignorance were infuriating.

If the protests in front of my home were not enough, the union plastered an image of me on both sides of a truck that they paraded through the streets of the city. The picture was lifted from a society magazine and was taken at a party I attended. I was dressed in a long, off-the-shoulder, dark-burgundy Valentino dress and held a glass of champagne in my hand. The caption read, "The party is over," implying that VMT was on the verge of losing the contract. The union was determined to do everything they could to make sure my company did not win the lease for the Johnson nursing home. Another caption on the same image read, "This contractor has misappropriated taxpayer money," which, of course, was false. I started to receive calls from people wondering if I was running for political office, for I was being attacked in a manner normally reserved for politicians in heated campaign battles.

But, as many negative forces as there were working against my company, there were equally positive forces working to ensure that VMT came out victorious in our quest to win the lease. In addition to prayer, one major area of support came from the staff at the Office on Aging. I had worked very closely with that team on the Center for Aging nursing home when the facility was threatened with closure by the federal government, and, through my hard work, the facility had been rehabilitated, and closure had been avoided.

I had also assisted the Office of Long-Term Care Administration that had oversight of the Johnson nursing home when it was in jeopardy of closure. Through my efforts, that facility had become a quality nursing home.

Thankfully, we also had support from the District of Columbia Contracting Office that managed negotiation of the lease. They knew of my character, my dedication to the trade, my love for the seniors, and, most importantly, they valued what I had done for the District of Columbia. Together, they decided that it would only be fair to award the Johnson long-term lease to VMT Long-Term Care Management for 20 years.

I had learned from reading the Bible that we should rejoice in our sufferings, knowing that suffering produces endurance, endurance produces character, character produces hope, and hope does not put us to shame. VMT's hope through all these tribulations was that we would not be shamed. I was confident that, through prayer, we would not lose the Johnson facility.

Under District rule, any long-term lease of 30 years or more had to be sent to the council for review and approval prior to being awarded. The lease for the Center for Aging nursing home was for 30 years. It was sent to council, and then awarded to a company that had strong political connections with several of the deciding council members. I understood from the get-go that we were negotiating from a position of weakness, since we did not have the backing of council. There was not really anything we could do to counter the cronyism.

Being a strong believer in Mother Mary, I decided to fight this last battle for the lease on the Johnson nursing home on my knees. I know very well that, at times when the problems are too big to handle on our own, we need to pray for intercession. I started a novena, a ritual of nine days of prayer to any saint with a specific request. I invoked a prayer, asking Mary to untie the knots and erase the challenges facing us in the lease bid. I was confident that my prayer would be answered.

I also attended several meetings with the contracting office staff, and during the negotiations, I learned that VMT would be awarded the lease but for only 20 years. True to form, I argued that it was unfair: the vendor that had taken over management of the Center for Aging nursing home had been offered a 30-year lease. In addition, the terms of our lease required that any maintenance or improvement would come out of VMT's coffers. I fought that too: while VMT was not given a penny to improve its facility, the other vendor had received $2 million to renovate the Center for Aging nursing home. The unfairness in comparison between the two leases was clear. However, when the government negotiating team told me, "Solanges, take the deal and go home," we did just that. What our team did not know was that the most powerful council member was dead-set against VMT being awarded the lease. He wanted it for his own vendor friend.

The team who was responsible for deciding the lease felt strongly that it would have been unfair to strip VMT of both nursing homes after 20-plus years of service to the government, especially considering the clinical and financial turnaround both facilities had seen under our tenure. Given the aggressive councilman whose buddy was competing for the lease, it was a struggle for them to find a way to legally follow contract rules and regulations and configure the lease in a way that it could be awarded to VMT. We did not learn of the political machinations until much later, but it all made sense in hindsight.

While I was grateful we won the 20-year lease, I was also angry that one elected government official could be so evil-minded and greedy. Even after the deal was finalized, the council member called the contracting office, and then the Office on Aging to request that VMT be stripped of the lease. Unfortunately for him, we had an iron-clad contract, and there was nothing he could do to change it.

The union campaign at the Johnson nursing home continued while all this was happening. On election day, only a handful of employees showed up to vote, but the final tally came down in favor of the union, because the result was determined by the number of employees who actually cast a ballot, not on the total number of employees qualified to vote. So, even if only one-third of the employees voted, as long as the majority of the counted ballots were in favor of unionization, the election went to them. However, the bulk of the employees vowed not to recognize the union. They pledged not to pay dues and not to attend union meetings. It was a difficult situation for me as a leader.

As it turned out, with all their gallant efforts, unionization of our facility was a futile exercise. They never collected a penny in dues from the employees. For years after they won over our facility, I believe the union must have spent hundreds of thousands of dollars out of their own funds to represent VMT employees. In a way, it was beneficial to them that VMT was on the list of facilities they represented. It gave them standing in the community, and possibly some bragging rights, but, in the end, it must have been a financial burden, as their representation came without dues from VMT employees.

VMT took pride in treating our employees well. I had worked tirelessly to earn their trust. I cared about my employees, and they knew it. For example, I made sure the nursing homes had an employee cafeteria that opened for breakfast early enough to allow the night staff to have breakfast before they drove home, and the early morning staff to have a meal before they started work. VMT subsidized the cost of the meals for all employees, and our kitchen staff ate free of charge. At the conclusions of each successful survey, of which there were many, our employees were financially rewarded for their efforts and hard work; in addition, they received an annual Christmas bonus that they had come to expect. The union could not match my management style and the types of benefits my employees were enjoying at the VMT facilities. The employees could not fathom any benefits deriving from unionization, since they were already receiving all that a union could negotiate on their behalf.

Since VMT's long-term lease did not include renovation money, the company used its own business funds to add some class to our nursing home. We changed the name of the Johnson nursing home to Unique Residential Care Center and added a front door to the entrance of the building to give it a more home-like feel than the old iron gate at the front. We discarded the lobby's old urine-stained carpet and added beautiful marble to the foyer. With the assistance of an architect, we designed a circular desk to house the security guards and added a receptionist to greet visitors, which gave it the appearance of a five-star hotel. We also remodeled the administrative suites and spruced up the old building.

Everyone who entered the building, from government officials to council members, families, and residents, expressed joy at seeing the changes we made. The staff invited their counterparts from other nursing homes to visit the facility. For six consecutive years after taking over the lease, we enjoyed a five-star rating from the Centers for Medicare and Medicaid, and were on the list of the best nursing homes in *US News and World Report.*

MAKE IT WORK FOR YOU!

Rule #24: Short-term Thinking Versus Long-term Success

Reflection: Be Fearless

Despite their tiny size, baby sea turtles are fearless. They hatch from their shells and head off into great expanses of ocean without doubt or hesitation. They have no worries about how they will defend themselves from predators they will surely encounter—nor do they consider where their next meal will come from. They just go for it! How could you benefit from letting go of your anxiety about the future? Sometimes, you just have to follow the example of the baby turtle—swim with all your might and let the rest take care of itself.

- Practice being spontaneous. Allow yourself to step outside of your routine and do something fun. Give yourself a little freedom from time to time. If you need to do the dishes and have the urge to go for a walk, try it. The dishes will still be there when you get home, but you will have given yourself a walk, and who knows what you will see? You will feel good, and, sometimes, that is more important.

- The next time you are facing a hurdle that seems insurmountable, ask yourself what is holding you back. Are there things in your schedule you could cut out to help give you more time to achieve your goals or master a new skill? Put down your phone, get off social media, and go for it!

RULES TO LIVE BY

When it was time for me to retire, it seemed everything sped up in miraculous and fulfilling ways. I discovered a connection to a woman who lived in France hundreds of years ago and went on a pilgrimage that brought me closer to understanding the force that guided my path all these years. I also started taking time to discover the world. I am not slowing down anytime soon. Good luck keeping up with me now!

Rule #25: Find Time to Give Meaning to Your Life

One thing that kept me grounded and gave me the ability to keep going when odds were stacked against me was my connection to something much larger than myself. My devotion to Mother Mary saw me through numerous tribulations. My connection to God gave me a moral compass to guide my decisions. Discovering my connection to Saint Solange in my later years helped me understand there is a miraculous intelligence at work behind the scenes that we do not always understand as we are progressing towards the twilight of our lives (see chapter 16, "The Good, The Bad, The Ugly"). I have always felt a spiritual connection to that *something* that is bigger and wiser than any of us. Whether it is taking time to notice the miracles right above our heads, such as the arc of a rainbow bending across the sky or traveling to Egypt to see the pyramids, try to link yourself to the eternal.

When you can, do something to leave positive energy in the world. Devote yourself to a cause you believe in. Build a school for children who need an opportunity to learn like I did (see chapter 16, "The Good, The Bad, The Ugly"). Whatever it is, find a way to give meaning to your life so that it is as rich and beautiful a gift as it was intended to be when you entered this glorious world. We all need to tap into the mysterious wonder of how miraculous life is, and how very fortunate we all are to have even a little time to be part of the beauty of life.

16
———

The Good, The Bad, The Ugly

After my husband died, I traveled overseas with friends. One memorable trip was to South Africa, where I visited Nelson Mandela's prison on Robben Island, and then traveled to the townships of Soweto and Johannesburg. I also traveled back to my native Haiti to a province called Jacmel where I built a school for pre-kindergarten to high school-aged children of mostly peasants who could not afford tuition in other schools in the area. I formed a not-for-profit corporation in the United States to assist with the school's construction and to support some of the children once construction was over. I also continued to attend professional meetings throughout America and ran for national office at the American Health Care Association (AHCA).

I dated my friend Clifford for three years. We had remained platonic until, one day, he invited me to an investment trip in the Virgin Islands where we were overcome by temptation and desire. We made passionate love and became a couple. We traveled all over, both locally and internationally. I was living the life of a teenager in love. We double-dated with my son and his wife Felicia in St Lucia, where I went scuba diving and ziplining. We spent one New Year's Eve in the wine country of California. Clifford hired a driver to take us from one winery to another where we ate cheeses and fruits and tasted wines for days on end with famous sommeliers. We spent New Year's Eve dancing the night away in countries like Chile, Australia, Dubai, and Abu Dhabi. With my son and his wife, we attended Super Bowl 50 and partied it up in California. Life was great, and I was on cloud nine most of the time.

* * *

Most of my family had left Haiti for the United States, and, because I had done so well for myself financially, I continued to be a major source of support for them. Our father had died, and I moved our mother permanently to the

United States to be with her children, and, by then, about 30 grandchildren. I took great pride in ensuring my mother experienced a life that was vastly different than the one she had known as a child and young mother in Haiti. I bought her a beautiful five-bedroom house on a lake in a gated community in Florida. I made sure she received the very best care, right up until she departed from this earth at the age of 92.

After she passed, I renovated her home, and it became my sanctuary when I needed to escape the stress of running a business. I was a senior in my late 60s, and very little slowed me down, but it was good to have a quiet place to relax and to contemplate my well-earned retirement, which was approaching.

When he was four years old, Little Keith, Kevin's son, came to me and announced, "Nana, I have a girlfriend." That took me a moment to process. A girlfriend? At four years old?

I asked him, "What do you mean you have a girlfriend?"

As it turned out, his dad, my son, had found someone special, and Little Keith was also in love with her.

I had yet to meet this special woman, until Kevin finally brought her to an event. I was getting an entrepreneurship award from the Institute of Caribbean Studies. Kevin told me, "I'm bringing a date."

I knew right then that something was up. Even as a teenager, he had rarely brought a girl to my house before. When I had asked him why, he had said, "Mom, when you bring a woman to your parents' house, she thinks you're getting married. I don't want to bring nobody until I'm ready."

I did not know most of Kevin's girlfriends when he was young, even as a teenager, aside from Kristin, Little Keith's mother. He never brought girls home.

Felicia, his date for the event, ended up being his wife. She is perfect for him. She looks just like me. Everyone teases him and says he married his mother. We wear the same size clothes, shoes, rings. She likes jewelry like I do. She likes getting dressed up like I do. She fits right in with the rest of our family.

Looking at Kevin and Felicia, I cannot help but notice the similarities between how Keith and I looked together when we were young. And, while Felicia is a lot like me, she also reminds me of my husband Keith in some ways. She pushes Kevin a lot to do things that my son would not do on his own.

My son is very happy, and I am very happy for them. They have two boys together, Kingston and Kevin Jr. But Felicia tells everyone she has three sons, because, when she met Kevin, Keith was only four years old, and they love each other like mother and son.

Most importantly, my son, Kevin, is super happy, and I am happy for him. He has grown up to be a strong man, just like his father, of which I am proud.

I had become disillusioned and frustrated with the changes in nursing education. Nowadays, nurses are trained on computers, and, in many cases, have to find their own preceptors, and their own affiliations for clinical practice. Several nurses had begun work in our facility ill-prepared to deliver quality care to my residents. In response, I developed my own internship to help the new graduates gain some experience before I trusted them to practice without constant supervision. Unfortunately, as soon as they became ready to manage a nursing unit, they often resigned to take a position at the same acute care hospitals that would not hire them as inexperienced graduates.

The core principle of the art of nursing is to provide quality hands-on care to sick human beings. Nursing in the 21st century has become popular only for the salary that can be earned as a nurse—not for the administration of quality care or the love of the practice. It felt to me like the heart had gone out of the profession. I started to express my concerns regarding the level of preparedness to practice nursing as a science and an art by these new "electronic nurses," as I called them. I reflected out loud to my colleagues that, "Many of them are cold. They show a lack of compassion and no bedside manner—both critical skills the computer is unable to demonstrate."

The fast pace of the business was another frustration, as electronic medical records have replaced patient charts and file cabinets. When I had to ask a younger employee for help to use the computer, I vented my frustrations out loud. Yet, as an older person being introduced to computers at a late age in life, I made strides in learning the basics in order to survive in this electronic world.

My son, who had worked in his mother's business since high school, sacrificed his own passion to become the chief executive of the business as I stepped away from the daily operations of all three divisions of VMT.

Throughout my life, I have been blessed with what often felt like something heavenly guiding my path: the divine intervention that brought Ambroise to rescue Lucienne when she was stranded on an isolated road with a flat tire. It has been with me through all my trials and tribulations from learning the English language to my immigration issues and my schooling and my businesses. It is even shown in the strengths that I exhibited when raising my son, becoming a professional, and dealing with the death of my husband. Through all the invocations to Mary that have been answered, and through all the mysteries of my being chosen as a special child from Ambroise's 13 children, I remain thankful.

But there was yet another supernatural revelation about this Haitian woman that was still left for me to discover.

Because of my childhood history of rheumatoid arthritis and fibromyalgia as a young adult, the winters in the northeast region of the country were becoming harder to bear. It was March, and because of the cold weather, I migrated to my house in Florida to join the other snowbirds. A sleepless night turned into a restless early morning as I tossed and turned. My bedroom is on the lake side of the house, and, through the glass doors, my eyes roamed towards the lake. It was a clear night, and the moon created shadows from the trees that were reflected in the lake, giving it an eerie quality.

On an impulse I did not understand, I grabbed my cell phone and Googled "angel of the sun" in search of a title for a book I was writing. I knew that was the meaning of the name "Solange." *Sol* from *soleil,* the French word for *sun,* and *ange* from *angel.* As I read, I became more intrigued by what I learned. I discovered the statue of a beheaded saint named "Saint Solange." What a shock! I never knew that I carried the name of a saint! I continued to read, and, as I delved deeper, I discovered that my life somewhat paralleled that of this saint.

I was certain my parents had no idea there was a saint named Solange, nor could they have known of a place named Bourges in France. I spent the remainder of the night researching her story through my phone. Before I knew it, the sun had come up, and my phone was no longer adequate for me to continue my research. I prepared a cup of tea and sat down in front of my laptop to learn all I could about this saint and her amazing life.

In a whirlwind of research, the similarities between this saint's life and mine grew fantastically apparent to me. I could feel goosebumps on my arms. "Is this real?" I exclaimed. I could not stop reading. I was overwhelmed by curiosity; I wanted more.

I learned that, like me, Saint Solange was brought up by a set of poor, minimally educated but devoted Catholic parents who instilled God's doctrines in her life from birth. Her father was a laborer and her mother a seamstress, just like my parents. At the age of seven, this saint gave her life to Christ to become a servant of the Lord. At 10, I similarly gave my life to Christ when I received my first communion and committed myself to His service.

Saint Solange had dedicated her life to helping the sick and was credited with several miraculous healings; I became a nurse and had dedicated my professional life to caring for sick, elderly, and disabled people. This saint was a shepherdess who loved to care for her sheep. As a child growing up in Haiti, I had dogs, goats, pigeons, and ducks, and, as an adult in the United States, I am always in the company of my dog. As I continued to read, I learned that this saint's passion was to work the land; her death came while tending her crops in a meadow. She worked the land as a means to support her family. Strangely enough, I, too, am passionate about nature and working the land. As a child growing up in Haiti, I also had my own garden. As an adult, I love gardening, so much that my husband used to say that I waited for the long winters to end just so I could go outside and play in the dirt. On my property in Florida, my winter pastime is to till the soil and tend to my bananas, papaya, lemon, lime, bell peppers, beans, and herb garden.

Like me, Saint Solange worked from a young age to help feed her family. I began supporting my family as a child. Each time I visited my godmother, my presence encouraged her generosity. I knew that my visits would end with money or other gifts that would make things more comfortable for my entire family. Once I moved to the United States and began working, I sent money home, even if my paycheck was only a meager factory worker's salary. I purchased houses in a senior community for my aged siblings, because I could afford to help and had done better financially than the rest of my family.

By this time, I started to become frightened by the similarities between my life and that of Saint Solange. The goosebumps had spread from my arms to the back of my neck, and a chill ran down my back. For a moment, it felt as though I was not alone in the house. Something divine and marvelous was happening to me that I could not explain. Who was this saint? Why was I making these discoveries now? Why were our lives so similar? What was it she wanted me to learn from her story? I reflected.

I was switching from one website to another, taking in as much information as I could. I was hungry—not for food but for more knowledge. Little did I know, the best discovery of my research was yet to come.

To my shock and amazement, I discovered there is a feast of Saint Solange. The feast commemorates the anniversary of her martyrdom, which happened when she was 16 years old. History has it that Saint Solange was the most beautiful girl in her village. A young prince, who became mesmerized by both her beauty and her spiritual gifts, asked for her hand in marriage. When he made advances towards her, she refused him on the grounds that she was married to Christ, and her resistance infuriated him.

One evening, he seized the opportunity to kidnap her and take her as his bride by force while she was alone tending to her sheep. He dragged her from her pasture onto his horse and carried her swiftly away. Much to his surprise, Solange put up such a gallant fight that, as they were crossing a river, they both fell in. The prince, an experienced horseman, became so enraged at being unseated from his steed, and with her resistance to him, that he chased after Solange on foot. He charged after her with his sword drawn and extended, and, in a swift slicing motion, he decapitated her. It is said that, as it was falling, the virgin girl caught her own head in her hands, recited the holy name of Jesus three times, and then walked nearly a mile, carrying her severed head the whole way, to the church of Saint Martin, where she later died and was buried.

Saint Solange's death took place in the 9th century in Bourges, France. I was born in Haiti 11 centuries later on the anniversary of her death. This new knowledge was mind-blowing. It felt to me as though her spirit was transferred to my body centuries later.

In what seemed like a trance, I turned off my computer and closed the laptop to collect myself. I thought I might be losing my mind. The coincidences were uncanny. I started to wonder out loud, "Could this girl be somehow living on in me? Had God connected us to one another? Could her ancient spirit still be alive and living once more in me?" These thoughts kept running through my mind as I paced the floors of my house. I walked to the back of my house and looked out over the lake as though I expected nature to have an answer to my questions.

I waited until I recuperated from my shock to extend my research beyond the internet. I contacted my cousin Josiane, whom I had visited with Keith at her home in France. She informed me that there is a village named after the saint and that she has her own chapel and church. Her feast, she told me, has been celebrated annually from the 9th century to the present on the date of her death, my birthday. In addition, Josiane also shared that there is a major procession to honor Saint Solange every year on Pentecostal Monday. The next celebrations in her honor were scheduled to take place in May, exactly two months from the date of my discovery.

The more I talked to Josiane, the more I became convinced I had to travel to Bourges, France, where Saint Solange had lived centuries ago. Saint Solange had taken up residence in all my thoughts. I was convinced that my footsteps were being guided by God. The compulsion to continue my research was quickly changing to a longing for action. Without hesitation, I decided to go on a pilgrimage to get as close to this saint as I could manage.

Passport in hand, I headed to Bourges, France, and attended mass at Saint Solange's Chapel and visited the church named in her honor. I stayed at my cousin's house for two weeks until Pentecostal Monday, when I took my place in the procession to honor her. This trip added deeper meaning to my life. I truly believe there is a bond between Saint Solange and me. Upon my return to the United States, I pledged to introduce this saint to America, since few outside of her native France are familiar with her story. I self-published a book titled *A Revelation: Walking Backwards into the Footsteps of Saint Solange*. I gave the book out widely to my acquaintances. Proceeds from donations for the book, in addition to my personal funds, went towards sorely needed renovations to the Saint Solange Chapel. I continue to visit her village, church, and chapel during the feast of Saint Solange or for the Pentecostal procession.

I have many questions I will likely never have the answers to, but maybe I do not need them. Is there a mysterious correlation between my life and that of the Saint whose name I bear? Many people have questioned my good fortune. It seemed not only to me but often to others that I was being guided along a path throughout my life. I will never forget when my girlfriend Estell asked, "How in the world did you end up with two good men when some of us can't get one?" Of Ambroise's and Francesca's thirteen children, it has been said that I was the chosen one. Was Saint Solange the real guardian angel who entered my life when I was still in utero? Faith carries answers when factual knowledge does not. I know what I believe …

*   *   *

On my 70th birthday, I walked the red carpet into the National Press Club on Clifford's arm. I was wearing a form-fitting, emerald-green Escada evening gown, a solid gold and rhinestone necklace, and matching gold earrings. My hair was cut short in a stylish afro, and I walked as though I was on top of the world. The lights were sparkling from ornate chandeliers above, and the skyline of Washington, D.C., glittered like jewels through the floor-to-ceiling windows. Waiters and waitresses in black and white uniforms were passing hors d'oeuvres and champagne-filled flutes from the trays on their arms.

The tables were draped in white and emerald linen with forested centerpieces perfect for conversation, but they were also filled with lofty branches of small cherry blossoms that lent an air of privacy to the room and allowed my guests to mingle in groups. The music was fun and lively, as I had hired a classic '70s band called "The Right on Band" to commemorate this milestone. It was hard to believe that I had turned 70. My body was flawless; my skin was firm; my breasts were still full, and I looked and felt like a 50-year-old woman. With the theme of my party celebrating "70 is the new 50," life had been good to me. Though it had been hard at times, it was good overall, nonetheless.

As Clifford and I approached the red carpet, I was flooded in flashing lights from the paparazzi who, unbeknownst to me, had been hired by my son. I was the center of attention, with nearly 200 family and friends present for this great occasion; all of them were vying for my attention.

I was overwhelmed, grateful, happy, and at peace inwardly. I was proud of all my accomplishments and the celebration of my life, but not once did I forget the role that my husband, Keith, had played in my growth and development as a professional. My only sadness is that Keith was not present to enjoy the fruits of our labor together. I wish he could have seen me meet my full potential. A copy of my book, *A Revelation,* about Saint Solange, was given to all in attendance as a gift, and I regaled my guests with the story of my discovery of the saint and my trip to Bourges, France.

At 70, I had finally reached my point of saturation with the business. With Kevin turning 40 and no desire to remain the sole owner of VMT, we decided to sell the business. I continue to be, as I have always been, an all or nothing kind of person.

I had accomplished my goals, regardless of the degree of difficulty or the length of time it took to successfully meet them. I have always been decisive and capable of acting when I knew it was time for a change. Once I arrived at that endpoint, I worked hard at effectuating my exit plan. I made it clear to my son that we needed to get out of the healthcare business together, to which he agreed. I knew he had sacrificed his own career path to support my passion. After the death of his father, Kevin committed himself to the company to support me. He even attended law school to prepare himself to be the most capable and dedicated executive he could become. For 15 years, he handled every aspect of the business. He served as my buffer, protecting me, at times, from the pain and mental anguish associated with operating a business.

Most of those painful moments happened during union negotiation meetings, where unpleasant and blatant lies were told. Unfortunately, Kevin was not allowed, on our labor lawyers' advice, to refute any of those allegations. As they say, "silence is golden" or "a silent man is a wise man." Kevin often returned to the office from those union negotiation meetings looking battered, stressed, and angry. He would not allow me to attend union meetings, even when I insisted. He would look me in the eyes and ask, "Why? Why would you want to subject yourself to that?"

Rosalind, vice president for quality who also attended the union negotiation meetings, discouraged me from attending by saying, "I wouldn't wish any of my sons to ever sit at a meeting to hear people talking about me the way they talk about you, Dr. V. You don't understand; those people are vicious. I feel for Kevin. They'll say anything nasty they can, just to get a reaction, using language you don't need to hear." Unfortunately, Kevin had to bear those unpleasant moments on my behalf. One thing he was certain of was that we would leave the business together, as soon as we could get a buyer for all three divisions of the company. It took two years from when we made the decision to reach a closing. I knew I was the owner of a small business. What I did not know, however, was how marketable it was and how many vendors would show interest not only in acquiring VMT's assets but at a higher bid than our asking price.

I was known for never being satisfied. I believe I am still young and that 70 is my new 50. Clifford and I went our separate ways, since we each had a different plan on how we wanted to proceed with the relationship. Without a meeting of the minds, the romance ended. He remained one of the attorneys that provided legal support to VMT until closing. I moved out of the big house and relocated to a luxurious condominium in Maryland. I enjoy gardening at my Florida home, spending quality time with family, and traveling all over the world.

This little Haitian girl has made it from rags to riches. I have grown in my faith, and in my relationship to God. I remain close and supportive in my relationships with a family that has grown from my parents and 13 children to over 30 nieces and nephews and over 20 grand-nieces and grand-nephews. I am proud of having given my very best to my staff, and of meeting my calling to care for the sick and the disabled. I transitioned from being a hard worker to hardly working, from a CEO to a fun-seeker. I remain independent, and I continue to call all the shots.

I take pride in not allowing anyone—nor anything—to spoil my joy of life. I have been all over the world. I took a private helicopter ride in New Zealand and landed on a glacier. I hopped on a helicopter in India and landed on one of the tallest mountains in the world, coming face to face with Mount Everest. I took another helicopter in Kathmandu, Nepal, where I rode an elephant's back touring the safari to see rhinoceros in their habitat. Money is a tool used to accomplish dreams and desires. Remember, happiness is free; having money does not create happiness. Money only gives you access to do some amazing things. Being rich in spirit is the greatest accomplishment in life, and I can say that I am rich in spirit. My revelation of Saint Solange will always be the crown jewel of my spiritual richness, and I will carry it with me the rest of my days.

My pride and greatest joy, however, will always be Kevin, my rock, my last standing lifeline, who grew up to be a super human being—just like his dad, Keith, my forever-loving husband. All I ask of you is to forever remember me as loving you.

MAKE IT WORK FOR YOU!

Rule#25: Find Time to Give Meaning to Your Life

Reflection: Live a Long Life Full of Splendid Adventures

Turtles are symbolic of many things to different cultures all around the world. In the East, their round shells symbolize Heaven, and their rectangular undersides are representative of Earth, so they are seen as a fusion of both Heaven and Earth—the spiritual and the terrestrial. In Hawaiian culture, they represent good luck and wisdom and are seen in representations of guardian protector spirits. In Native American cultures, they symbolize long life and good health. They are representative of Mother Earth, and their hard shell represents triumph over adversity. All around the world, people from different backgrounds find a symbol of strength in an animal whose lifespan is long and filled with splendid adventures. Live long and make your happiness where you can, like the turtle.

- Go be with something bigger than yourself. Find solace in nature, go to the beach, or go relax in the woods. Make time to look at the abundance of stars on a clear night and reflect on how tiny you are. Bask in the glow of a full moon. Remind yourself, from time to time, that you are an integral part of a mysterious universe.

- Build a spiritual practice for yourself, whether it is going to church services or learning yoga or meditation techniques. Find a way to quiet your mind on a regular basis, so, when you go out into the world, you are centered and peaceful.

Once upon a time, there was a beautiful queen named Solanges who lived in a chateau on a hill in Washington, D.C. She was originally from Haiti and had a certain "Jene sais quoi." Sensual, intelligent, stylish, and sold ... She is a true fashionista.

Life has been good to her, so she has an easygoing, no-drama personality. The queen has a wonderful sense of humor and can often be heard laughing and joking with family and friends at the chateau. She loves children and appreciates the time spent with family, so she will always be present at all family events and gatherings, dancing all night to the beat of the beautiful music.

Music plays an intricate part of her life, for she enjoys all different genres. The chateau can always be heard flowing with the likes of
Haitian artists such as Sweet Micky and Fa Wauch, Great Gospel artists including Kirk Franklin, and especially Reggae artist Sean Paul whom she dances to during her workouts ... Queen Solanges believes in being healthy and fit and enjoys sharing her wisdom on living life to the fullest.

She is a wealth of knowledge, for she has worked very hard all her life by being reliable, thorough, and very, very patient. A kind and gentle natured woman, she spends a lot of hours caring for others. Generous to a fault, she is often seen giving her time, her friendship, and even her meals. She is such a nice person. She has many friends, and they will have game nights at the chateau, BBQs, dance parties, or just come over to hang out and hear her read one of her many delightful passages from her novels. Because of her versatility, friends will sometimes see her at an outdoor jazz concert or football game or having dinner in her favorite restaurant, Oceanaire.

During her leisure time, she can be found lounging by the pool writing a novel or traveling to some exotic place around the world. So
touched by the hands of goodness, she has been blessed with many creative abilities. Her culinary skills are often revered by friends who have been invited to dinner.

She and God are best friends, and she calls on Him for everything. Her life has great peace. God revealed to her, one day, that she was a saint who shared a kindred spirit with another saint of lifetimes ago and that her blessings would abound forever ... Queen Solanges is a great blessing to all those God puts in her path, and she is truly loved by us all.

This is not the end, for every day is a new beginning ...